I0799868

POSTCARD HISTORY SERIES

Dearborn County Indiana

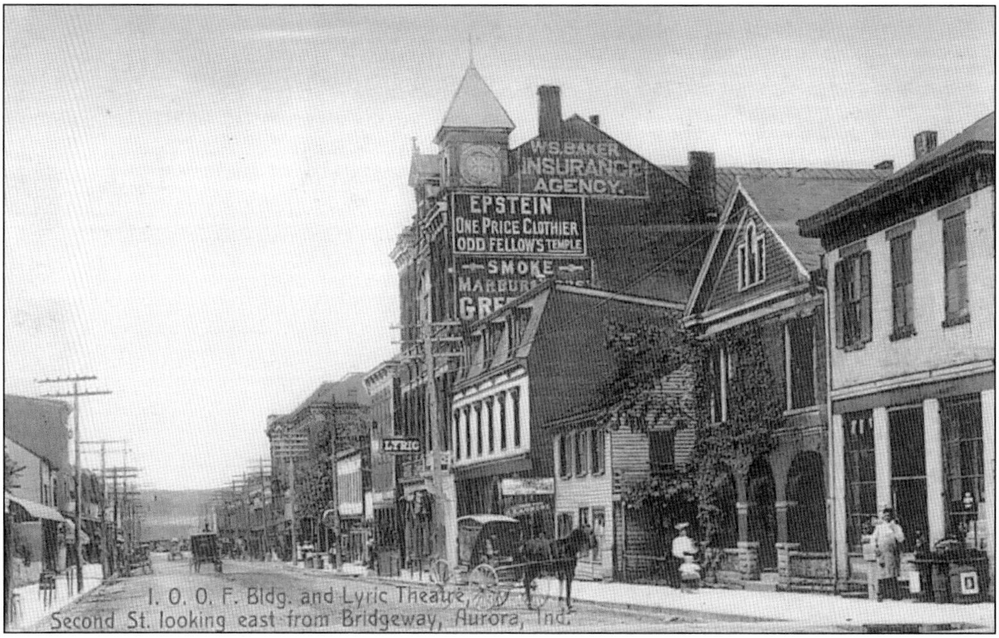

I.O.O.F. BUILDING AND LYRIC THEATRE, SECOND STREET, LOOKING EAST FROM BRIDGEWAY, AURORA, INDIANA. This view of Second Street, looking toward the Ohio River, shows the city back when it had unpaved streets. The horse and buggy was the ordinary mode of transportation at the time. The prominent building in the picture, the I.O.O.F. Hall, which also housed the Lyric Theatre, can be seen on the right side of the street. The building still exists today, but the bottom floors have been "modernized" to accommodate changing commercial needs. (Produced by Kraemer Art Co., for D. Holler.)

Cover Photograph: **AUTO RACES, LAWRENCEBURG, INDIANA.** The grounds of the Dearborn County Fair have long been known for their auto races. This extraordinary view shows cars lined up at the starting line of the dirt track. The card was mailed and marked in 1927, but the actual photograph is probably even older. Racing began at the fairgrounds in 1921. The full grandstand and the large number of people lining the fence of the infield verify the popularity of the sport. Unfortunately, since the fairgrounds were outside of the city levee, they were subjected to frequent flooding. The fairgrounds were particularly hard hit during the floods of 1913 and 1937. (Produced by Indianapolis Post Card Company, for Jackson's Dry Goods Store.)

POSTCARD HISTORY SERIES

Dearborn County Indiana

Milton A. Masing

ARCADIA PUBLISHING

ISBN 978-0-7385-0306-6

Published by Arcadia Publishing
Charleston, South Carolina

Printed in the United States of America

Library of Congress Catalog Card Number applied for.

For all general information contact Arcadia Publishing at:
Telephone 843-853-2070
Fax 843-853-0044
E-mail sales@arcadiapublishing.com
For customer service and orders:
Toll-Free 1-888-313-2665

Visit us on the Internet at www.arcadiapublishing.com

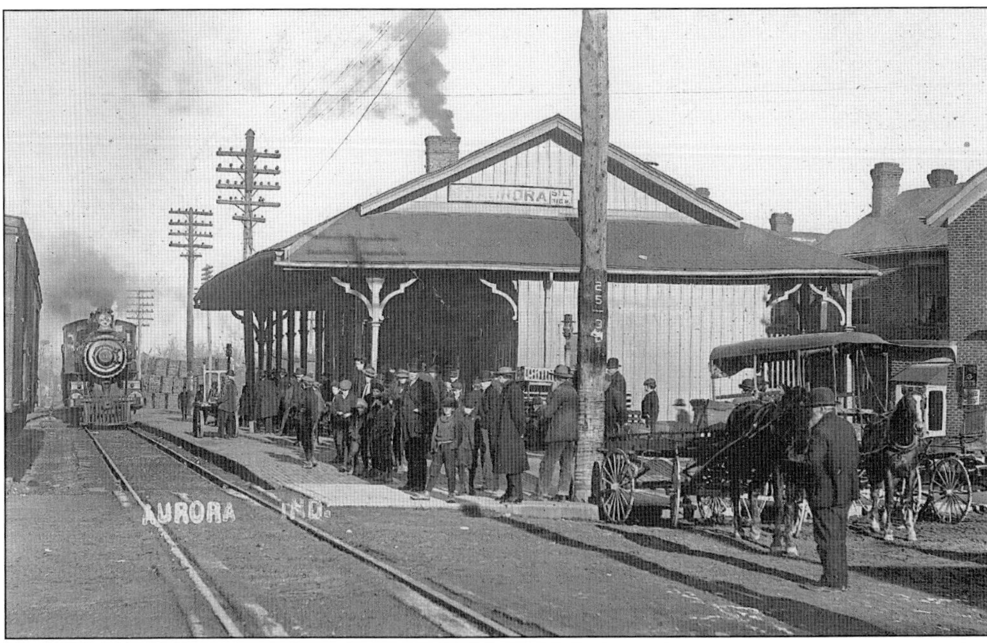

B & O RAILROAD DEPOT, AURORA, INDIANA. The building pictured in this view is no more. It was replaced by a more substantial building in about 1910. In the right corner of the building can be seen a few of the horse-drawn buggies used to transport people to their homes and to other communities not served by the railroad. Careful examination with a magnifying glass reveals that the train approaching from the east, probably Cincinnati, Ohio, is being powered by engine 1120. Also revealed at the top of the building is the fact that St. Louis, Missouri, is 316 miles away. (Real photo postcard from an unidentified photographer.)

Contents

Acknowledgments 6

Introduction 7

1. Aurora 9
2. Dillsboro 41
3. Greendale 55
4. Lawrenceburg 67
5. Moores Hill 95
6. The Small Villages 105

Index 125

Acknowledgments

Numerous individuals have assisted the author of this volume by providing suggestions and information important to the formulation of the final result. Some of these individuals are knowledgeable about Dearborn County and provided assistance in areas where the author lacked background. Others provided postcards used for the production of the book.

People that contributed information about various subjects relating to Dearborn County are: Sandra Brown, Mark Drury, Shirley Drury, Eddie Gordon, Bill Hartwell, Bill Kerr, Susie Kittle, Clifford Kuhlmeier, Frank Martin, Sharon Masing, Susan L. Maxwell, Chris McHenry, Reverend David Patterson, Dellas Ross, Marlow Smethurst, Adeline Smith, Alan Smith, David L. Steigerwald, Mary Ann Steigerwald, Carroll Sutton, Mildred Webster, and Robert Webster

People that furnished postcards used in the book include: Jerome M. Currin, Alan Smith, David L. Steigerwald, and Carroll Sutton.

INTRODUCTION

This book is a collection of Dearborn County, Indiana postcards, starting from the "golden age" (about 1904–1930), up through the era of standard chrome cards that were manufactured for two of the communities in the county in the 1950s. It continues with the continental card and four-by-six-inch card eras up to the present time. The book has been illustrated with postcards from the personal collection of the author, as well as a few individuals that have loaned cards specifically for use in this book.

To a large degree, this book is also about Dearborn County history. Most of the cards that have been produced of Dearborn County depict prominent landmarks, historic events, or people who have had a great influence on the development and enrichment of the county.

Historical text and informational data has been used to supplement each card. The task of assembling pictures and data, composing texts, and planning each page and space in a book involves making decisions that are likely to be contestable. Additionally, fitting these pictures and their text into a format that fits in the series means that entries must be somewhat standardized in size. The author hopes that such considerations will be taken into account by the reader, and that the amount of space given the various topics and cards will not be assumed to reflect the considered status and importance of the subjects selected for inclusion in this project.

In the collection of pictures and related facts, the judgment of the author was essential to the selection process. Any errors in historic data, authorship, or dates and names, are sincerely regretted, and it is hoped that such mistakes will not affect the pleasurable use of this book.

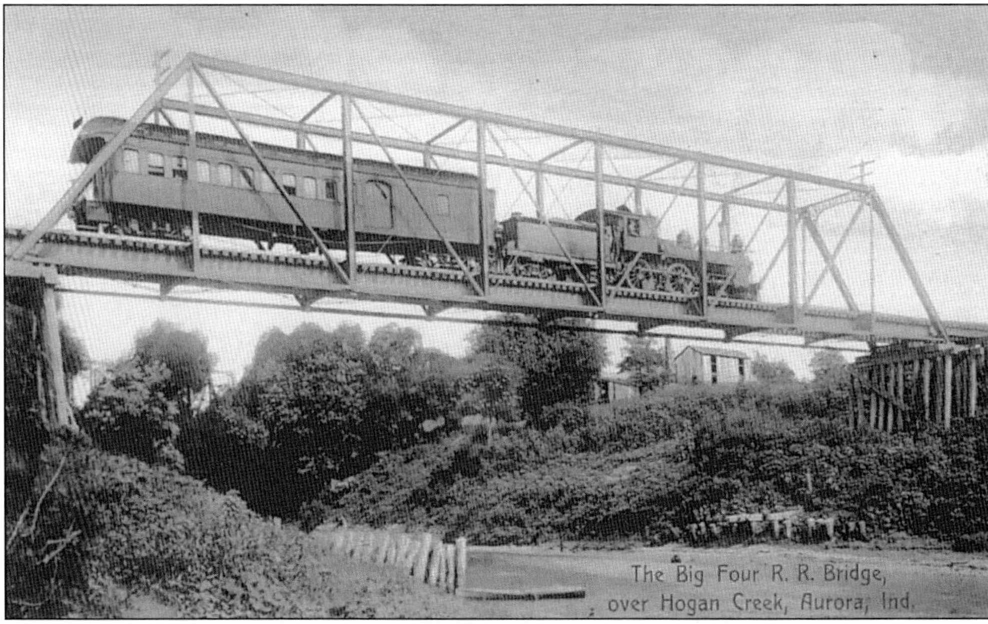

The Big Four Railroad Bridge, Over Hogan Creek, Aurora, Indiana. The Big Four Railroad Bridge crossed over Hogan Creek just a few feet from the place where the creek empties into the Ohio River. During the many floods that inundated the bridge, loaded railroad cars were parked on the bridge to weight it down and keep it from floating away. This *c.* 1909 view shows a passenger train crossing the bridge, probably headed east towards Cincinnati. The bridge has now been torn down. (Produced by Kraemer Art Co., for D. Holler.)

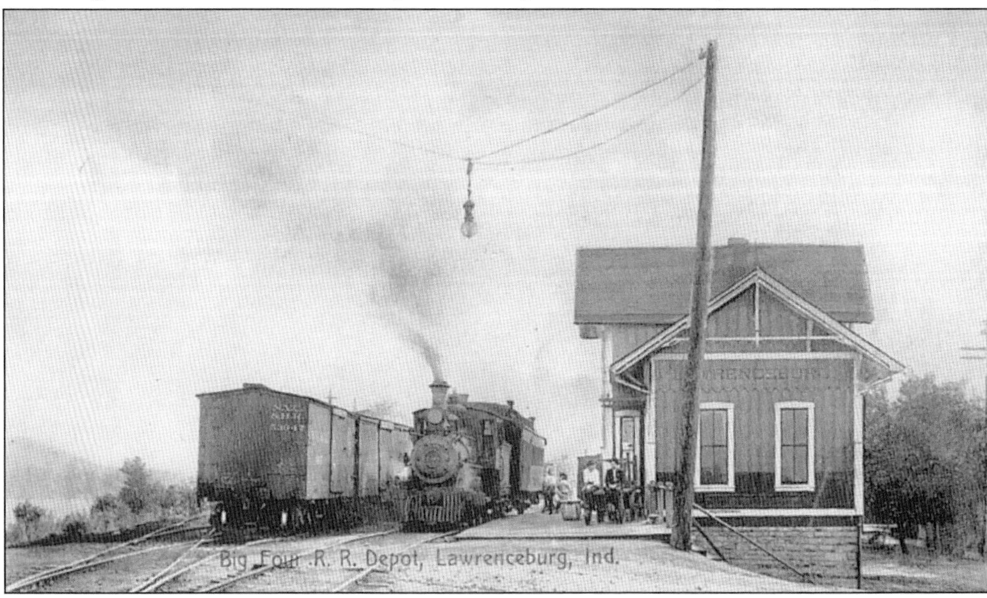

Big Four Railroad Depot, Lawrenceburg, Indiana. This view, *c.* 1909, looks almost as if the train shown above proceeded on to Lawrenceburg and posed for this picture in front of the Lawrenceburg Depot. The depot was located on New Street at the end of Short Street, near the Ohio River. It was later owned by the New York Central System. (Produced by Kraemer Art Co.)

One

AURORA

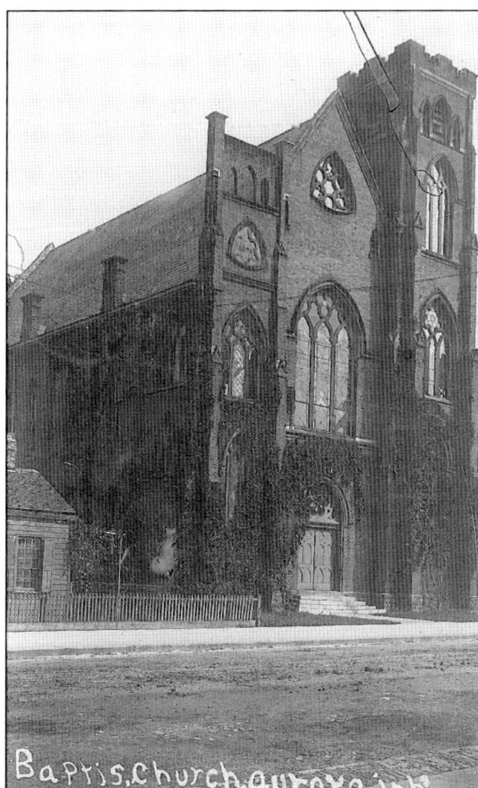

BAPTIST CHURCH, AURORA, INDIANA. At a cost of $25,000, the Baptists of Aurora built this imposing 1874 structure in the 200 block of Main Street. It was the second structure used for worship by the Baptists [see page 27 for the first building]. During the flood of 1937, it is believed that the building's electrical system was damaged in the high water, and on June 4, 1937, the building was destroyed by fire. After the fire, the Baptists relocated to a new building on higher ground at 304 Fourth Street [see page 27 for information on this building]. (Real photo postcard from an unidentified photographer.)

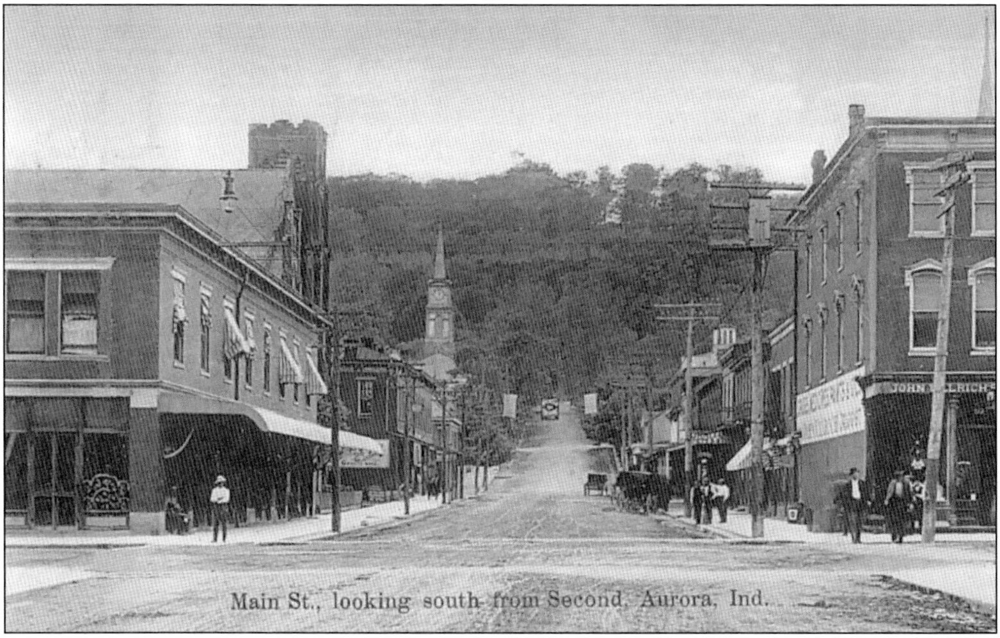

Main Street, Looking South from Second Street, Aurora, Indiana. This view, taken c. 1910, looks remarkably similar to the way it looks today. The Baptist church is gone, the dirt roads are gone, the horses and buggies are gone, but most of the buildings remain, and few new buildings have been added. Business signs and the addition of automobiles would be the most noticeable differences. (Produced by Kraemer Art Co., Cincinnati, Ohio, for D. Holler.)

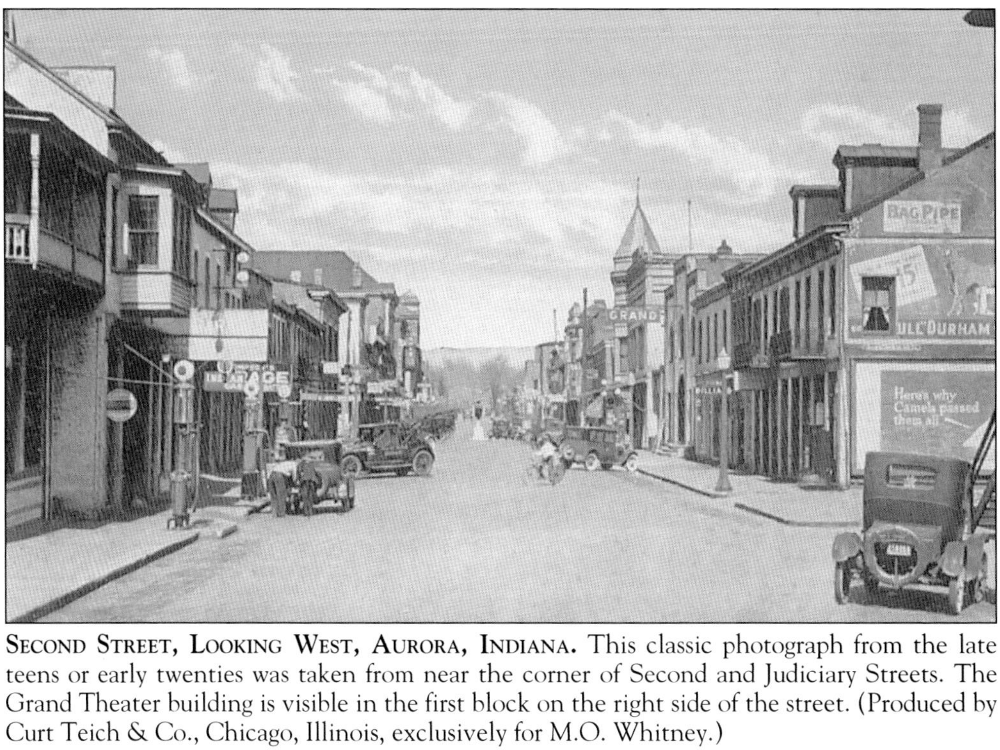

Second Street, Looking West, Aurora, Indiana. This classic photograph from the late teens or early twenties was taken from near the corner of Second and Judiciary Streets. The Grand Theater building is visible in the first block on the right side of the street. (Produced by Curt Teich & Co., Chicago, Illinois, exclusively for M.O. Whitney.)

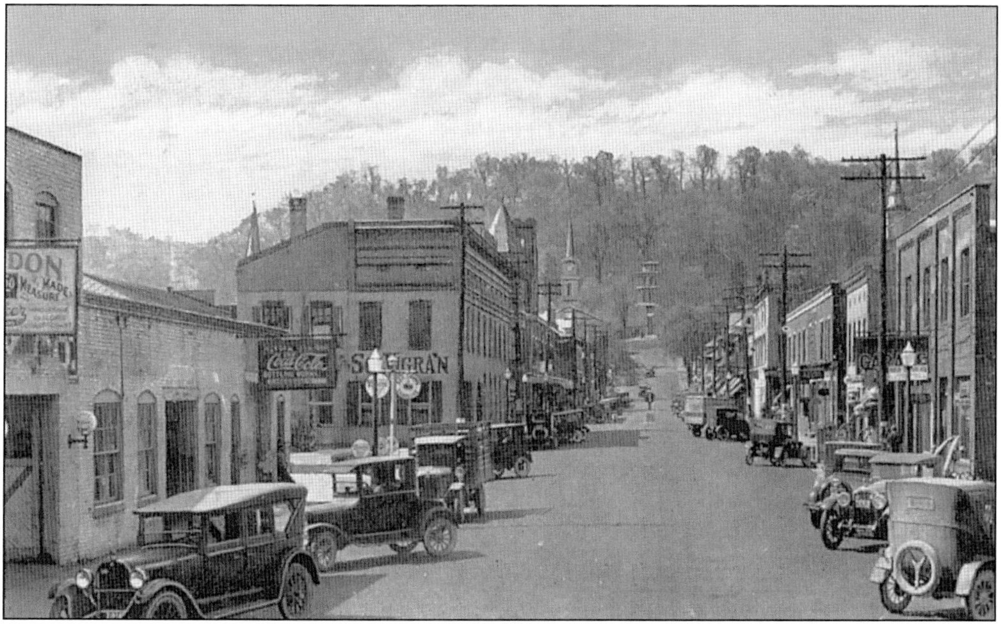

Main Street, Looking South, Aurora, Indiana. Automobiles in this photograph indicate that the picture was probably taken in the late teens or early twenties. The view is looking south towards the end of the street at Hillforest. Visible on the left side of the picture is the Chambers-Stevens building. Ullrich's drug store can be seen on the right side of the picture. (Produced by Curt Teich & Co., Chicago, Illinois.)

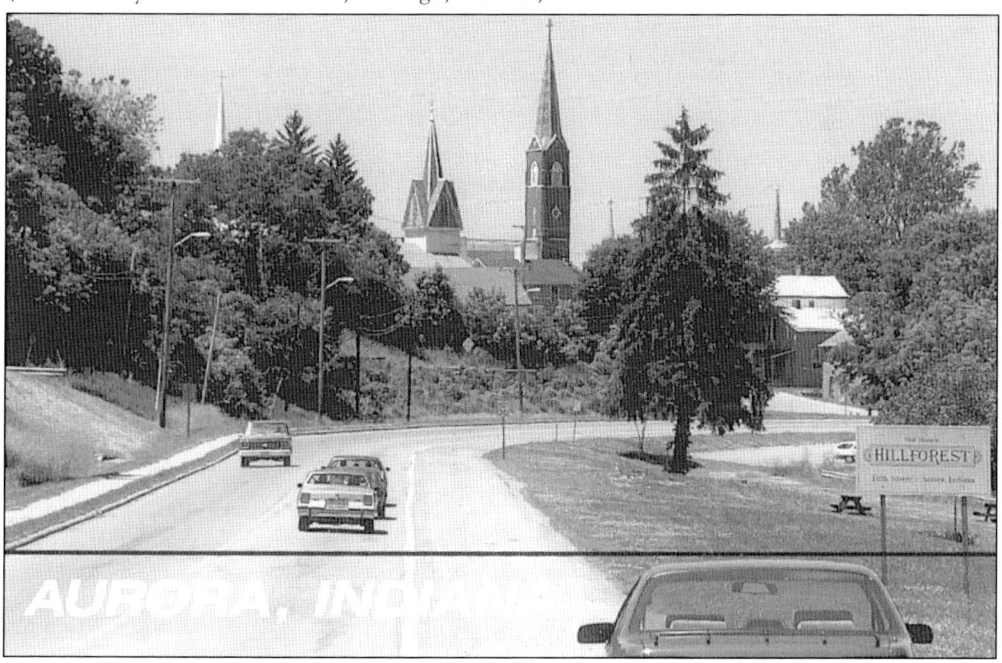

View from Riverside Drive, Aurora, Indiana. Actually a view of DeCatur Street, this 1990 view is looking toward Aurora from Lesko Park. Church spires, a narrow roadway, and historic homes add a feel of quaintness to the community in this continental-size chrome card. (Photograph by Milt Masing, published by Tri-State Visuals.)

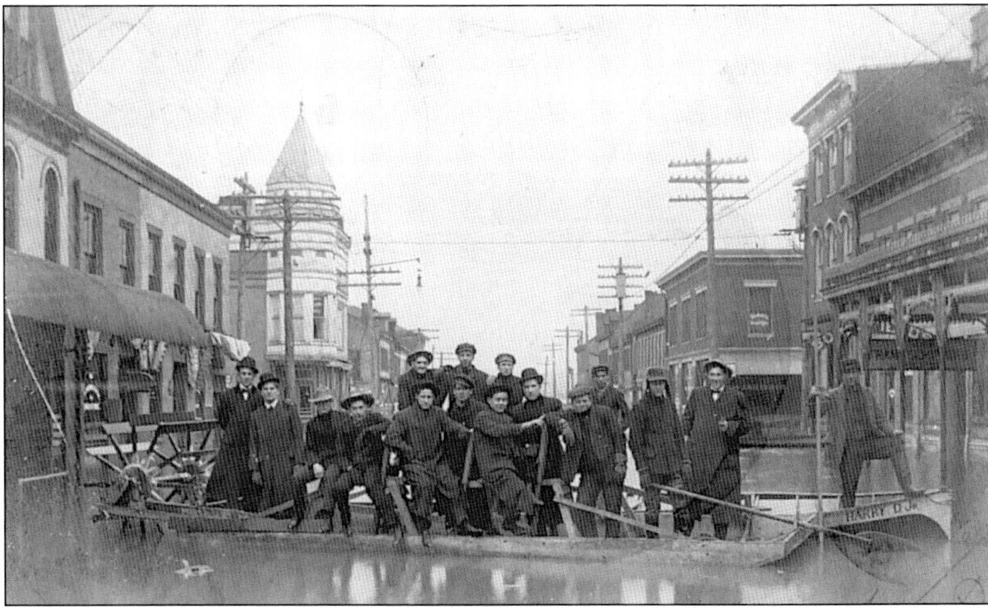

SECOND STREET, 1907 FLOOD. Compared to some later floods, the flood of 1907 was relatively minor. This view, looking to the east on Second Street, shows a group of men posing for the camera in front of the Coulter building in a boat identified as *Harry D. Jr.* The water level during the 1907 flood crested at 66 feet, the highest since 1884. (Real photo postcard by an unidentified photographer.)

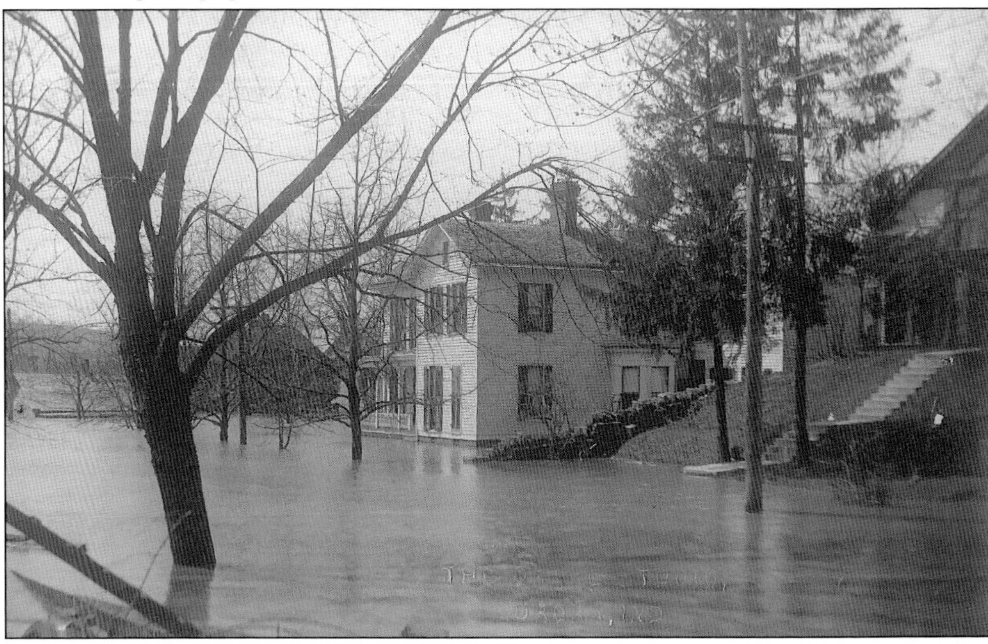

MANCHESTER STREET, 1913 FLOOD. The flood of March and April of 1913 was heralded on postcards mailed to locations around the world as the greatest disaster of modern times. In Aurora, however, because the residents took precautions to safeguard property, damages were kept to a minimum. After the flood receded, normal activity was quick to resume. (Real photo postcard, published by the Drake Studio.)

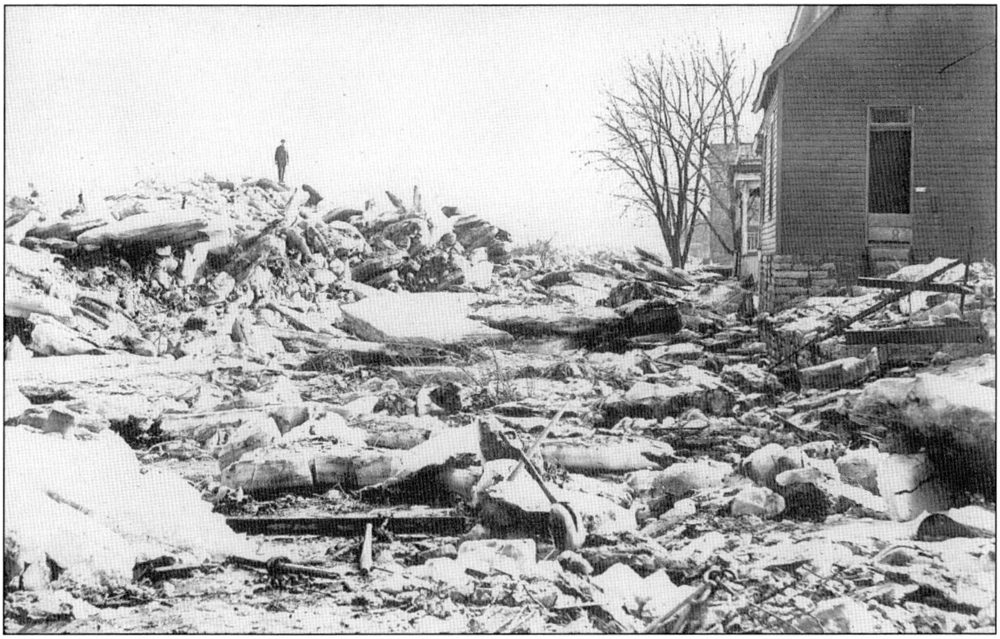

Ice Gorge, 1917–1918. Most of the damage caused by the great ice gorge of 1917–1918 in Aurora was limited to those areas and structures near the Ohio River. One postcard in the collection of the author describes the damage along Judiciary Street as, "looking like scrambled eggs." (Real photo postcard by an unidentified photographer.)

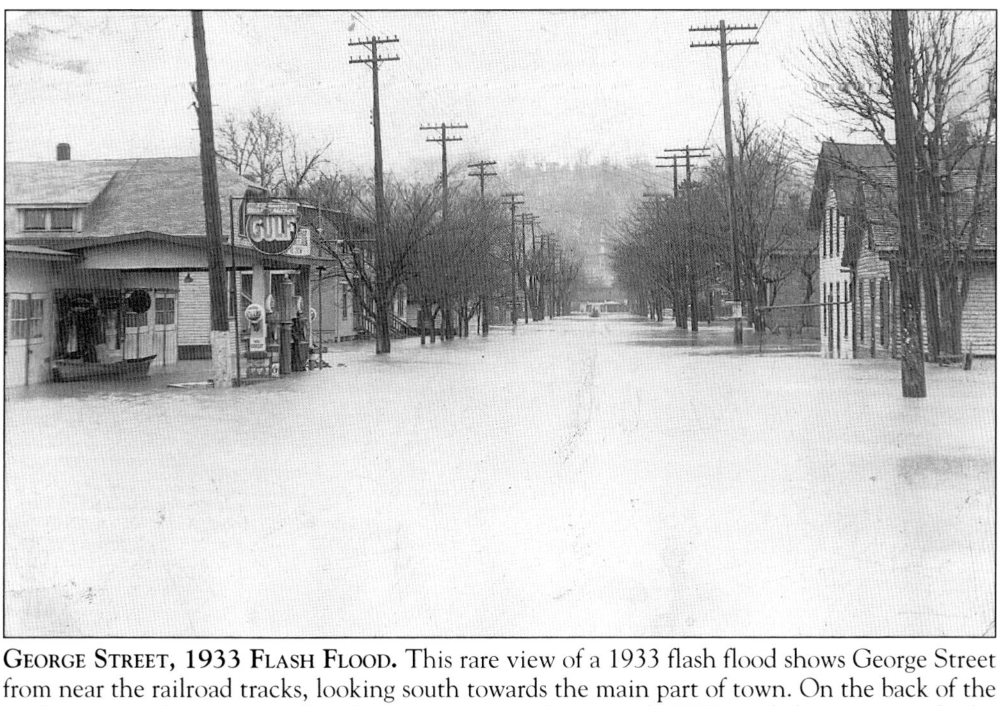

George Street, 1933 Flash Flood. This rare view of a 1933 flash flood shows George Street from near the railroad tracks, looking south towards the main part of town. On the back of the card, someone has written that the event occurred in March 1933, and the water reached a depth of a little over 64 feet. (Real photo postcard from an unidentified photographer.)

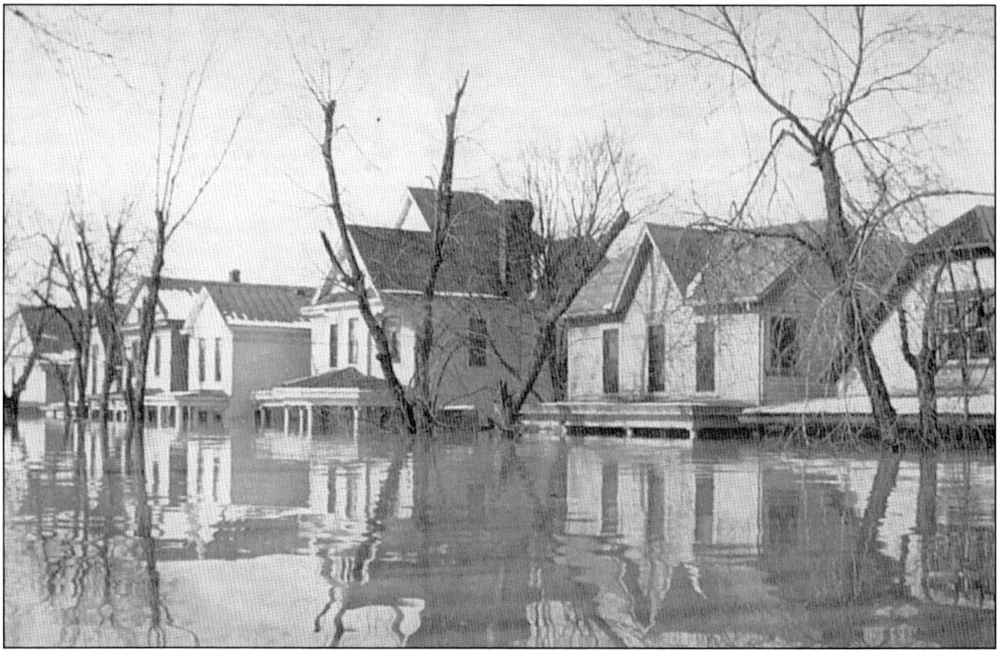

BROADWAY STREET, 1937 FLOOD. The most serious flood ever to occur in the Ohio River Valley took place in January of 1937. The water came up so rapidly that many people did not have time to prepare. Damage in Aurora was extensive, and virtually the entire city was inundated. Homes on Broadway Street in Aurora had water nearly to the second floor when this picture was taken. (Unidentified printer and publisher.)

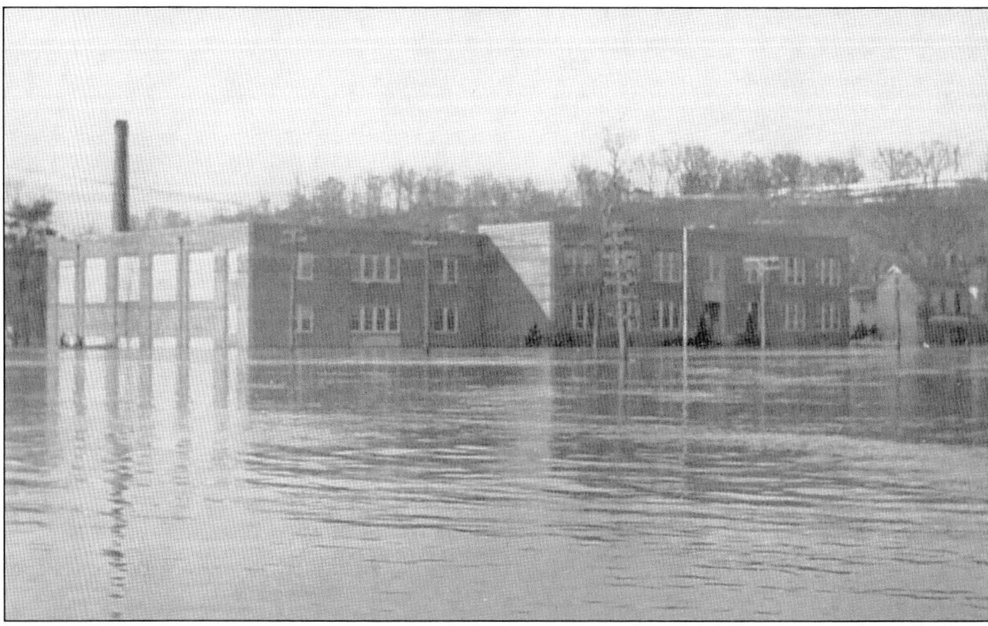

SENIOR HIGH SCHOOL, 1937 FLOOD. The back of this card reads: "This $160,000.00 Senior High School was placed where it was thought to be immune from the highest water possible, but Look! Aurora, Indiana, 1937." Actually, in Aurora, little was immune to the effects of the high water in the 1937 flood. (Unidentified printer and publisher.)

CITY BUILDING AND FIRE ENGINE HOUSE, AURORA, INDIANA. Constructed 1887–88, the Aurora City Building and Firehouse was designed by the McDonald Brothers architectural firm of Louisville, Kentucky. It was contracted to Louis Kriete of Aurora for $8,499. The style of architecture is known as Romanesque Revival. Although somewhat altered in appearance, the building is still being used today as a city hall and fire engine house. (Produced by Curt Teich & Co., Chicago, Illinois.)

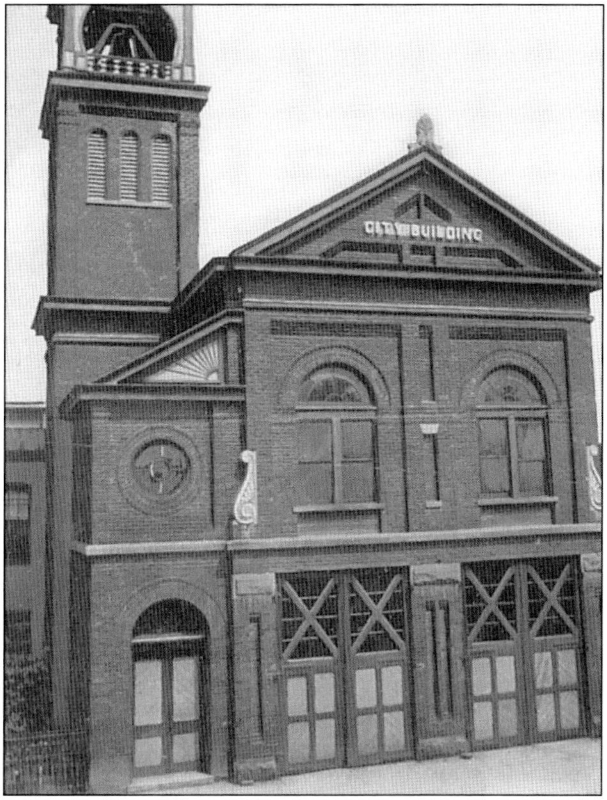

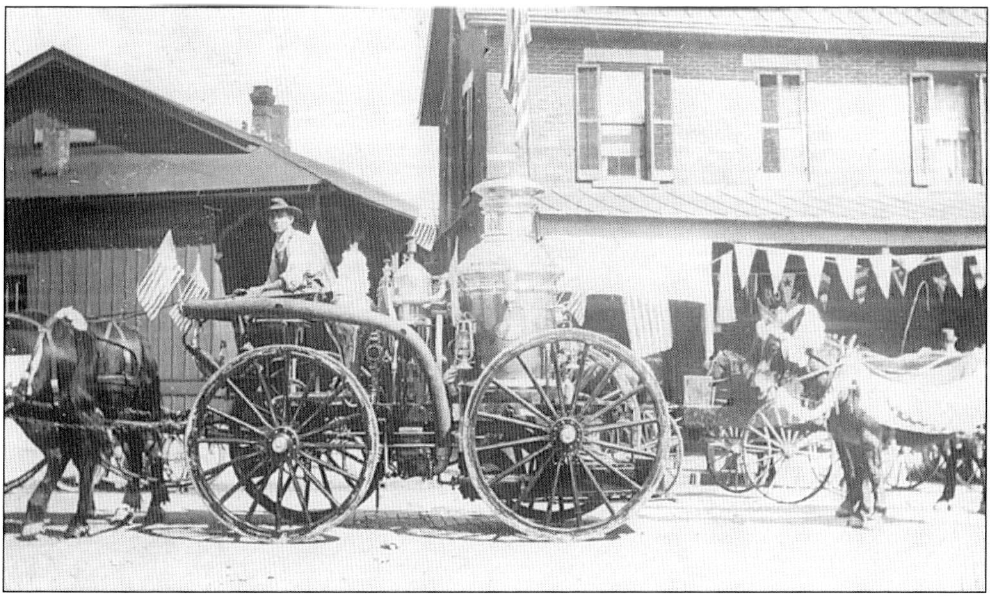

EARLY FARMERS FAIR PARADE. This view shows a turn-of-the-century, horse-drawn fire wagon in one of the first Farmer's Fair parades. Today the fire wagon is the feature display in the Cincinnati Fire Museum. (Real photo postcard by an unidentified photographer.)

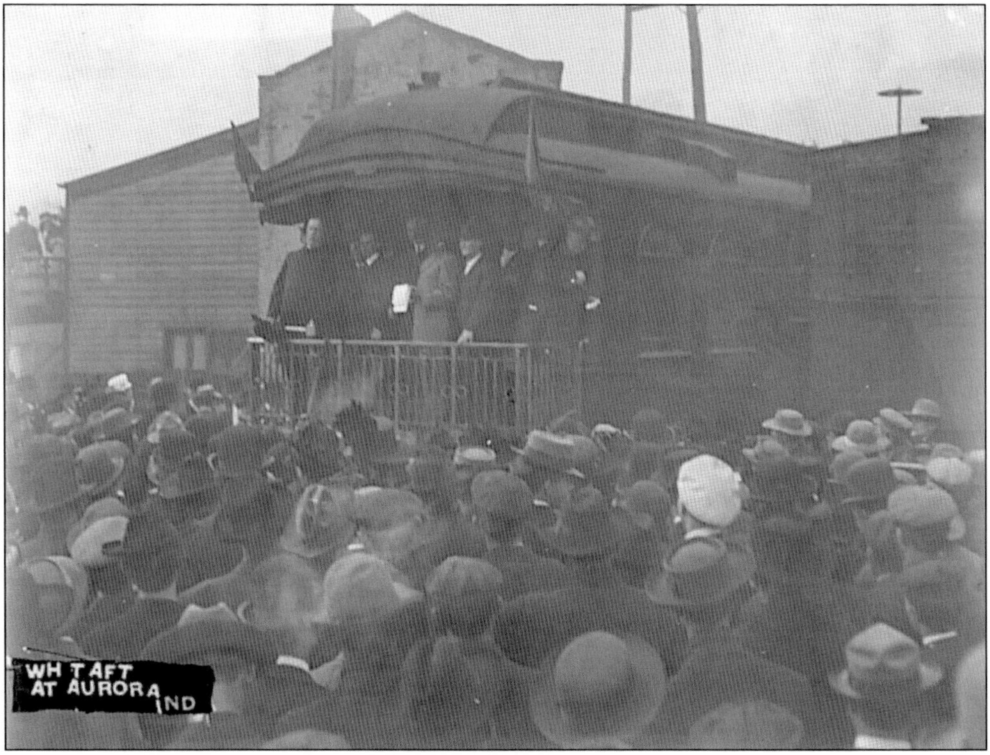

W.H. Taft at Aurora, Indiana. While campaigning by train in the fall of 1908, William Howard Taft made a brief stop in Aurora at the top of Second Street to speak. His speech, given from the rear platform of the last train car, was short, and the mostly partisan, Democratic crowd did not respond enthusiastically. (Real photo postcard by an unidentified photographer.)

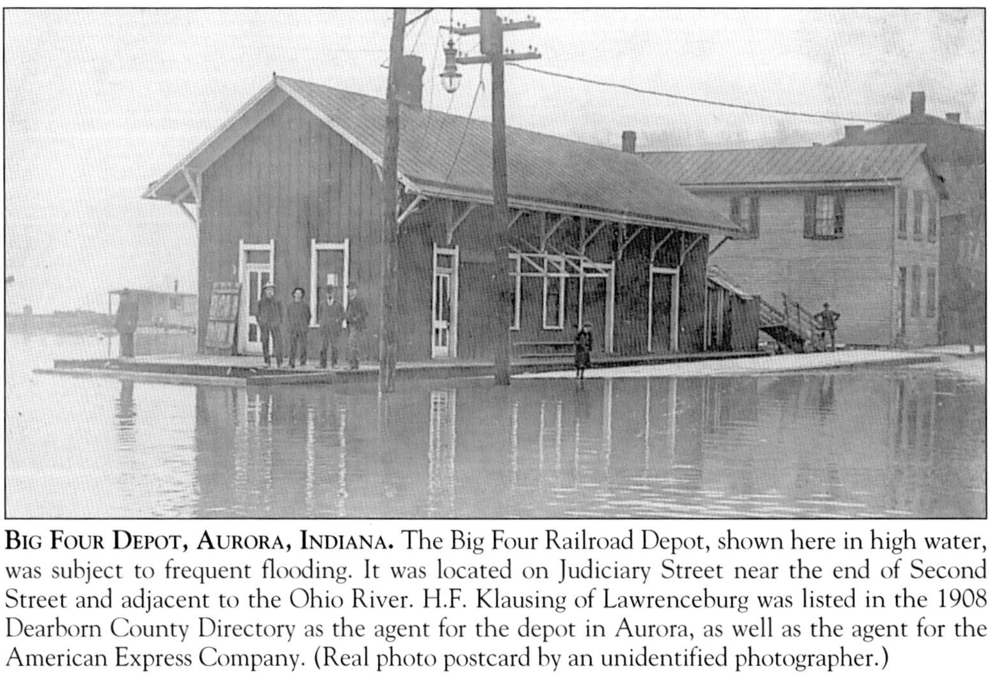

Big Four Depot, Aurora, Indiana. The Big Four Railroad Depot, shown here in high water, was subject to frequent flooding. It was located on Judiciary Street near the end of Second Street and adjacent to the Ohio River. H.F. Klausing of Lawrenceburg was listed in the 1908 Dearborn County Directory as the agent for the depot in Aurora, as well as the agent for the American Express Company. (Real photo postcard by an unidentified photographer.)

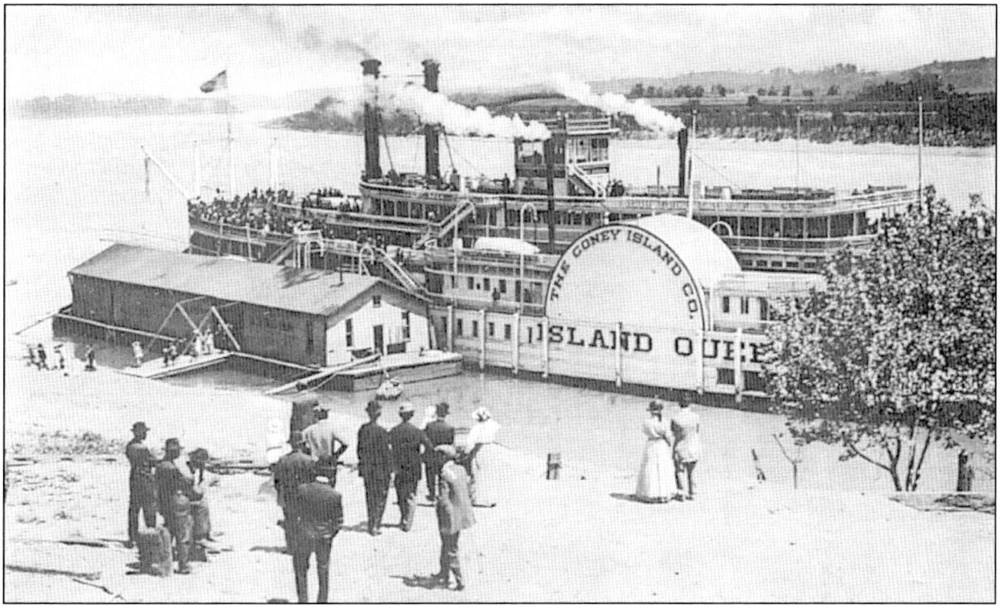

OHIO RIVERFRONT, AURORA, INDIANA. The steamer Island Queen was a riverboat that transported passengers from various Ohio River communities to the Coney Island Amusement Park on the east side of Cincinnati, Ohio. During the winter months, the boat was kept in the mouth of the Licking River or Kentucky River. (Produced by Kraemer Art Co., Cincinnati, Ohio.)

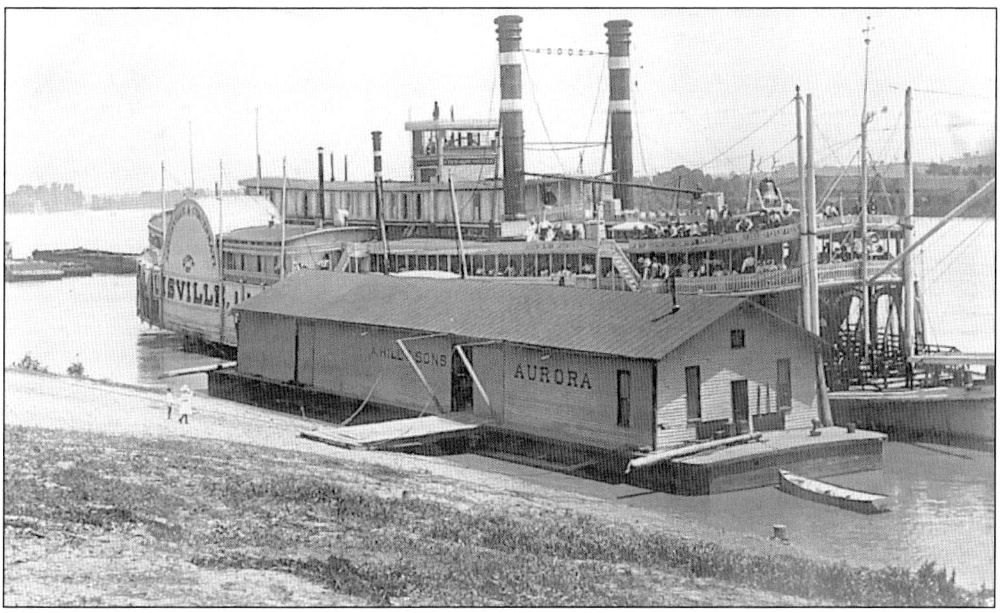

STEAMER CITY OF LOUISVILLE, AURORA, INDIANA. During the last half of the eighteen hundreds and the early years of the nineteen hundreds, the Aurora dock of A. Hill & Sons played host to many steamboats. This view shows the 1894 steamer *City of Louisville* docked in Aurora. The vessel shown was well known for its record speed trips between Louisville and Cincinnati. It sank in Cincinnati on January 30, 1918, during the ice jam. (Real photo postcard by an unidentified photographer.)

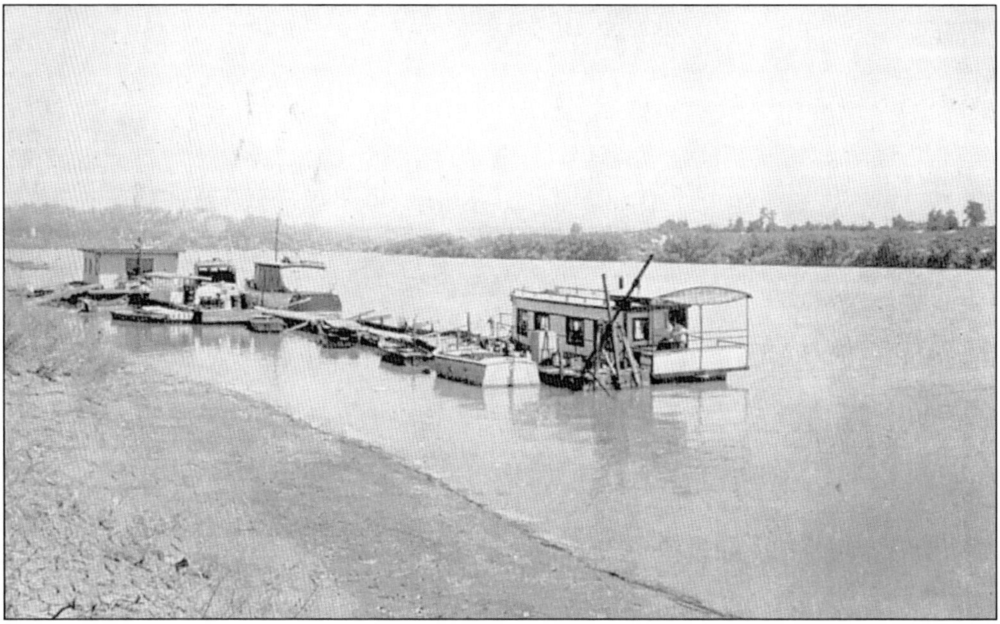

MONKS BOAT CLUB ON THE RIVER, AURORA, INDIANA. This silver-bordered card was postmarked in 1937. The business shown was probably located near the mouth of Hogan Creek, in the area later known as Lischkge's Boat Harbor. (Produced by Wayne Paper Box & Printing Corp., Fort Wayne, Indiana.)

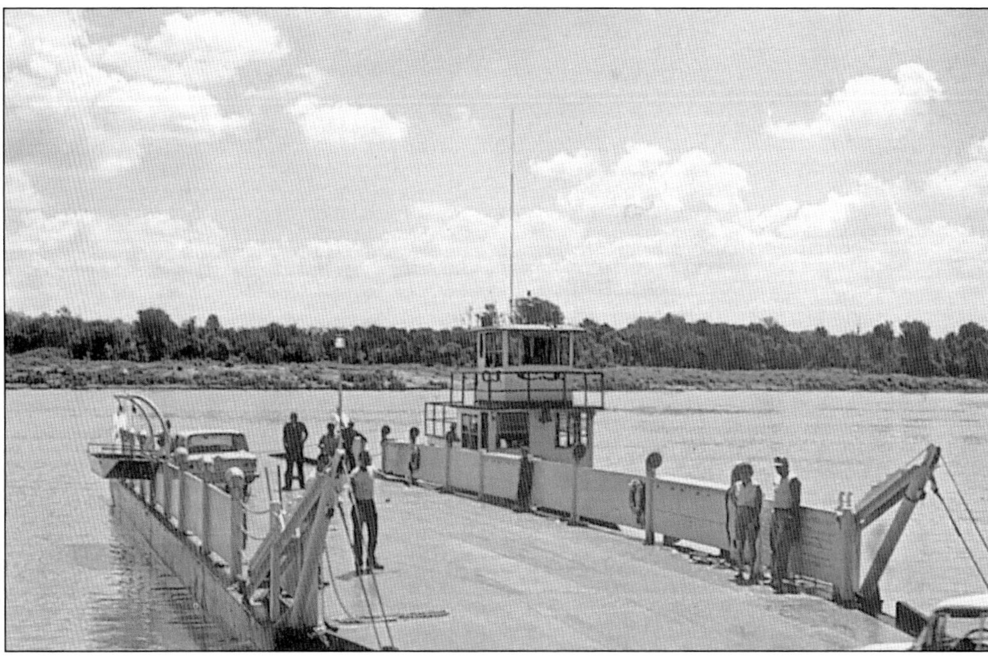

FERRY AT AURORA, INDIANA. The ferry boat *C.J.* connected Aurora with Northern Kentucky and the Greater Cincinnati Airport for many years. *C.J.* was owned by Charles and Jessie M. Farrar and named for their two daughters, Carol and Jane. Chrome postcards such as this one were first produced from a halftone printing process in 1939, by the Union Oil Company. (Produced by W.M. Cline Co., Chattanooga, Tennessee.)

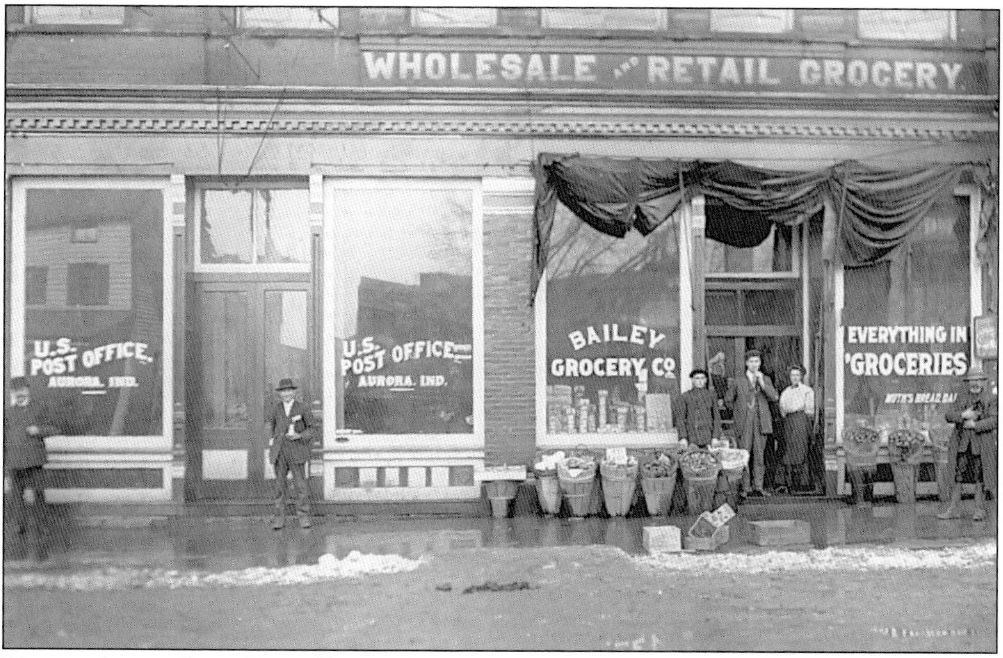

United States Post Office/Bailey Grocery Co., Aurora, Indiana. Just after the turn of the century, when this photograph was produced, the United States post office was located in the left half of the I.O.O.F. building on Second Street. It shared the first floor with the Bailey Grocery Company. (Real photo postcard by an unidentified photographer.)

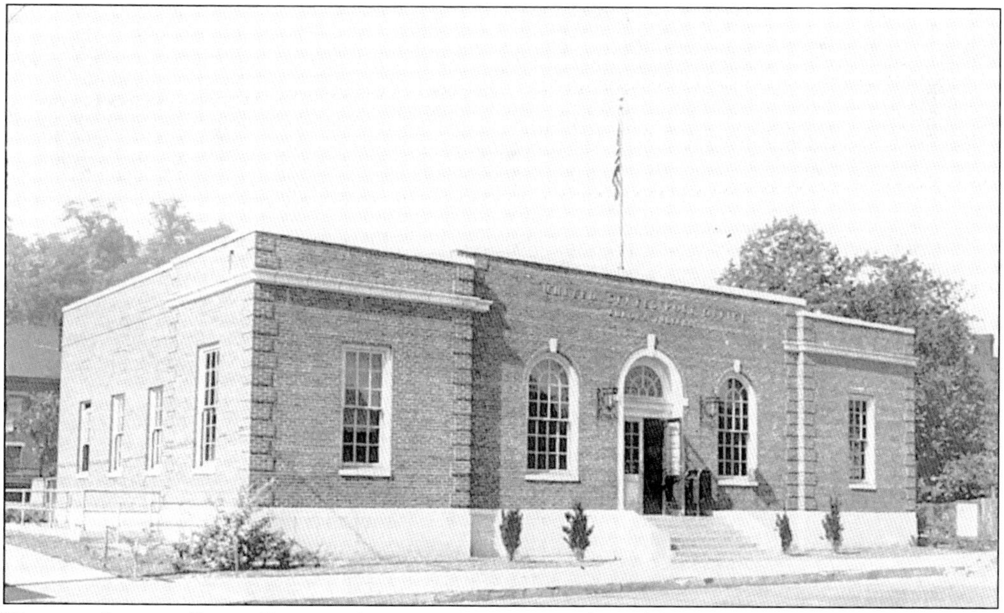

United States Post Office, Aurora, Indiana. The address of the Aurora Post Office building, depicted in this white-bordered, black-and-white picture, is 511 Third Street. The building was designed by Louis A. Simon, government architect, and completed in 1935. It was designed in the Neo-Georgian style of architecture. (Produced by Wayne Paper Box & Printing Corp., Fort Wayne, Indiana.)

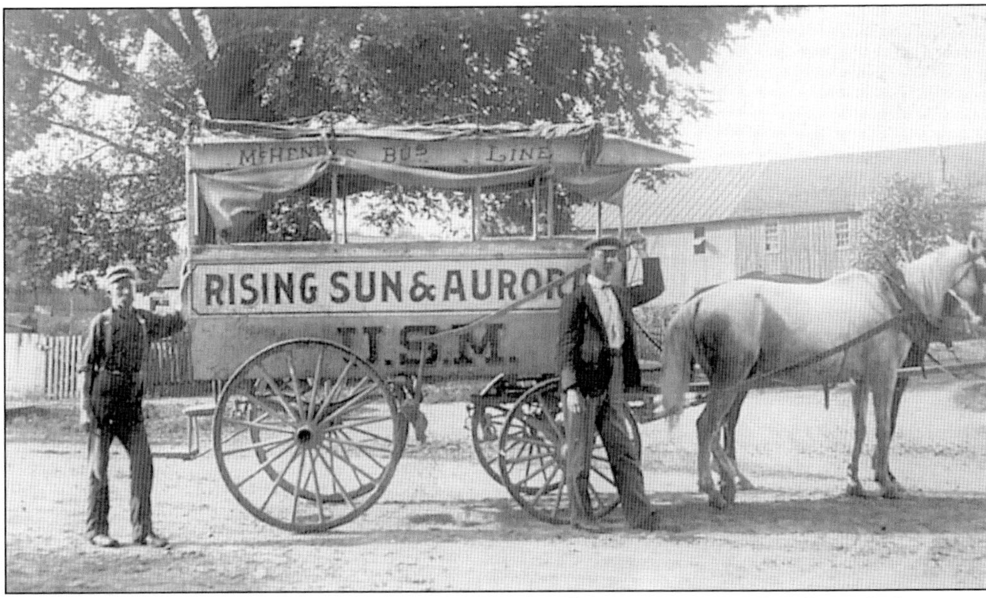

McHenry Bus Line. Rising Sun, and many other small communities in Southeast Indiana, was not, and is not, served by any railroad. In the past, people in such communities that wanted to travel long distances needed to have transportation to a town that was served by a railroad. The Timothy McHenry bus line provided this service. In 1879, McHenry purchased half of the interest in the Anderson bus line. The bus line also provided service for the United States mail. (Real photo postcard by an unidentified photographer.)

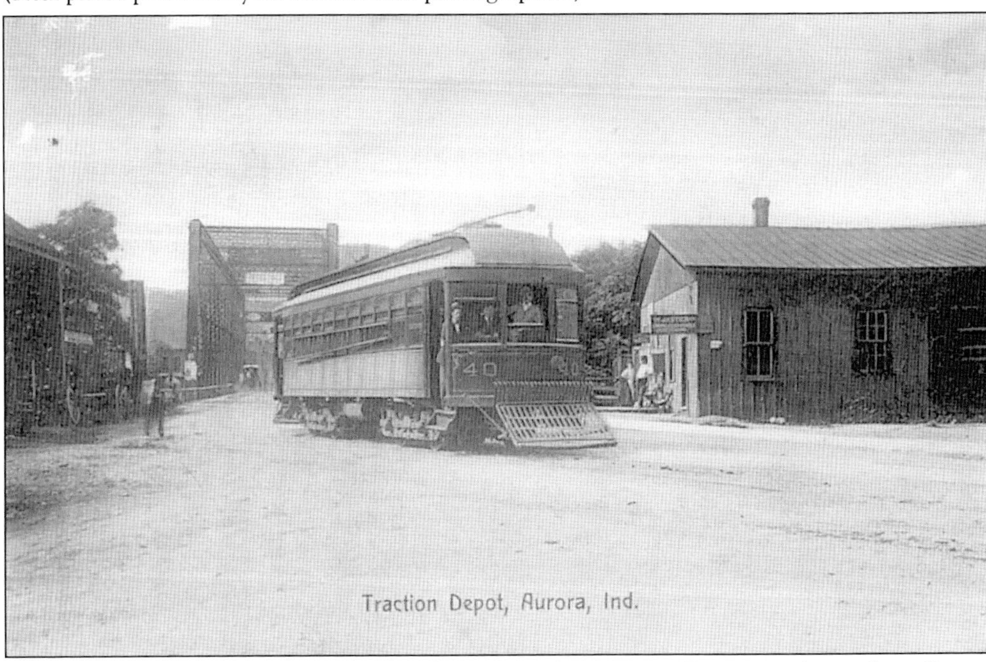

Traction Depot, Aurora, Indiana. The C.L. & A. Traction Depot was located on George Street, just to the east of the Hogan Creek bridge. It served the Cincinnati, Lawrenceburg, and Aurora Traction Company. The last car stopped running the route in November of 1930. (Produced by Kraemer Art Co., Cincinnati, Ohio.)

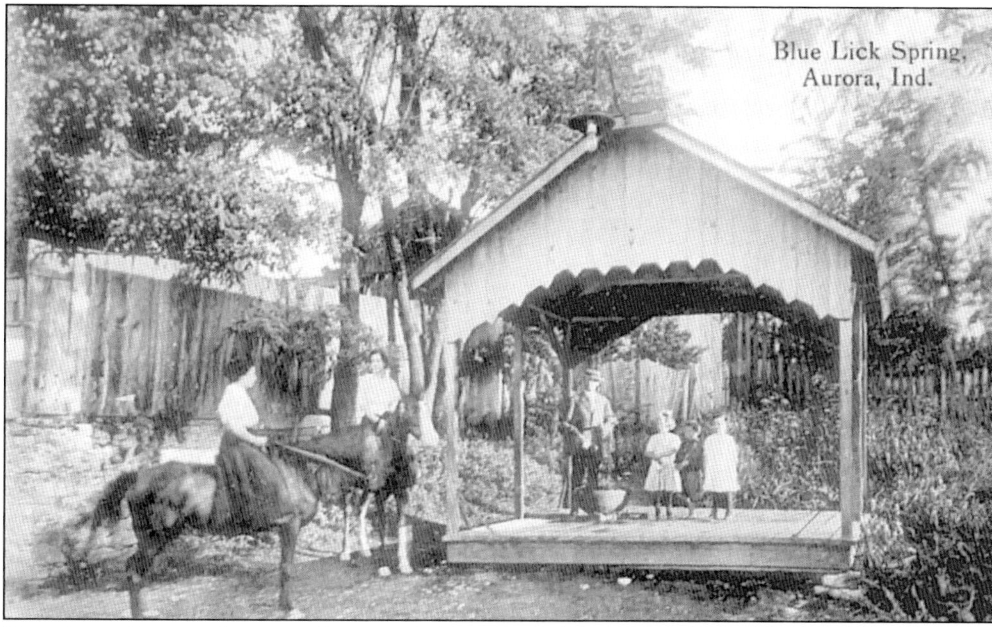

Blue Lick Spring, Aurora, Indiana. This postcard shows the first enclosure for the old Blue Lick Spring Well that was discovered in 1888. The well produced a stream of so-called health-giving water that filled the air with a strong odor. During the 1937 flood, the pavilion and well were both lost. In 1966, a gazebo-like structure and picnic facilities were constructed and still remain today. (Produced by Kraemer Art Co., Cincinnati and Berlin, Germany.)

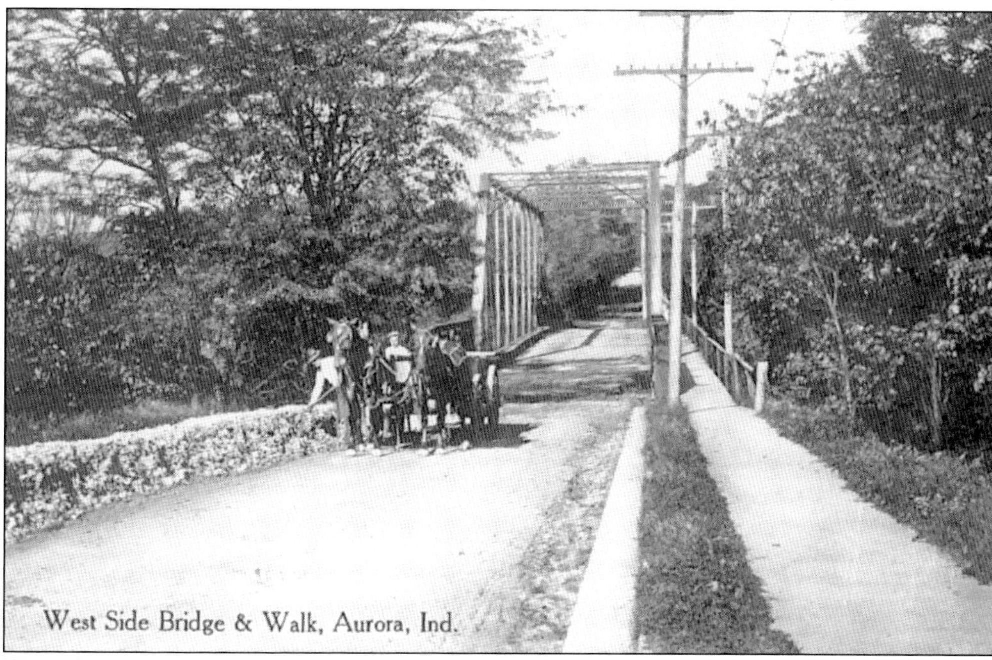

West-Side Bridge & Walk, Aurora, Indiana. This old, iron bridge connected the West-Side neighborhood and communities to the west part of downtown Aurora via the Wilmington Road. The well shown above would be to the left of the person that took this picture. (Produced by Hoover-Watson Printing Co., Indianapolis, Indiana.)

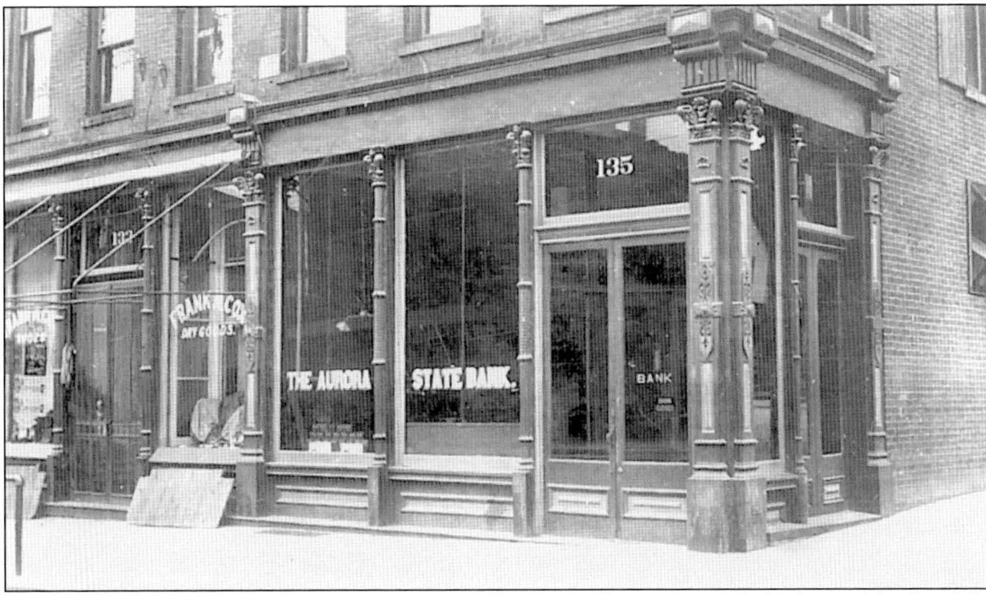

THE AURORA STATE BANK, AURORA, INDIANA. At the time of this photograph, the Aurora State Bank was located at 135 Second Street, on the southeast corner connecting with Mechanic Street. In the 1908 County Directory, the bank advertised capital stock of $50,000. Its officers are listed as: H.P. Spaeth, president; Philip Horr, vice-president; Clarence B. Wilson, cashier; and Frank B. Shutts, attorney. (Real photo postcard by an unidentified photographer.)

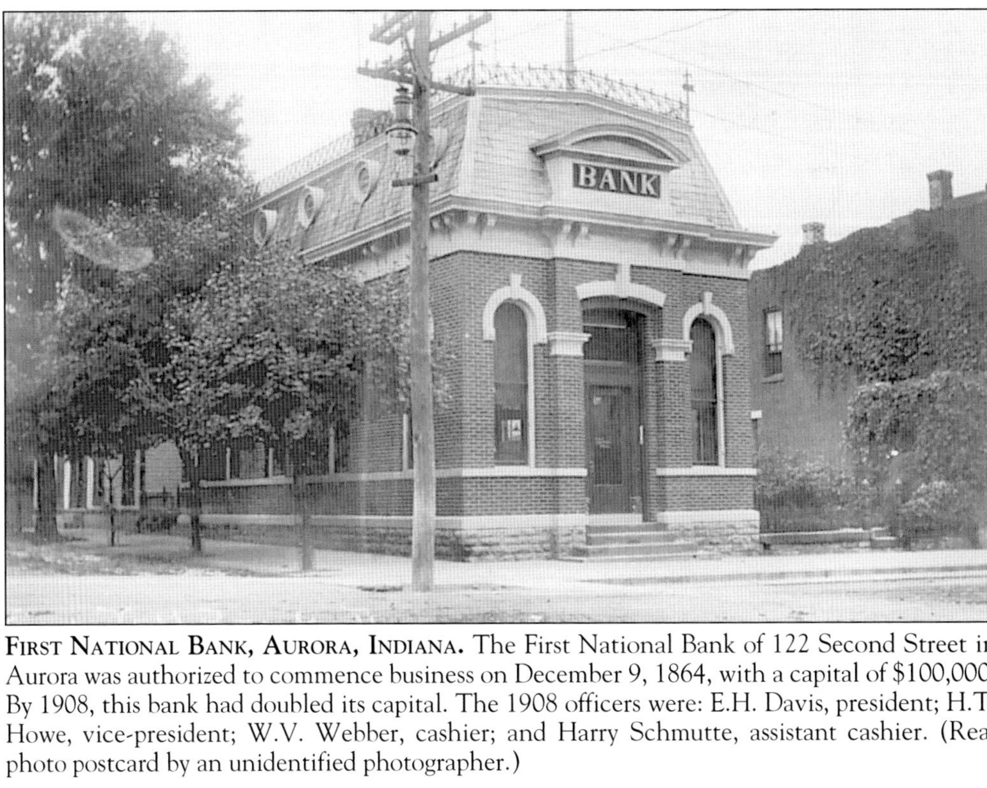

FIRST NATIONAL BANK, AURORA, INDIANA. The First National Bank of 122 Second Street in Aurora was authorized to commence business on December 9, 1864, with a capital of $100,000. By 1908, this bank had doubled its capital. The 1908 officers were: E.H. Davis, president; H.T. Howe, vice-president; W.V. Webber, cashier; and Harry Schmutte, assistant cashier. (Real photo postcard by an unidentified photographer.)

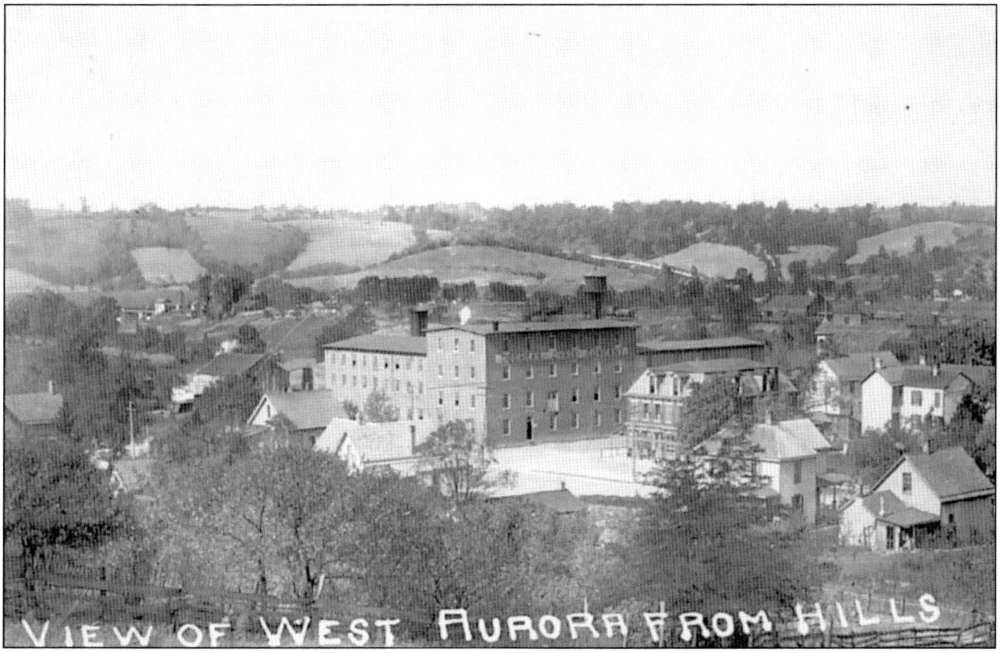

VIEW OF WEST AURORA FROM HILLS. The Cochran Chair Company dominates this view, looking east from the hills. The factory was started in 1879 by John Franz, Frederich Schmutte, and Herman Leive. The factory buildings were demolished in 1984. They are now replaced by self-storage garages. (Real photo postcard by an unidentified photographer.)

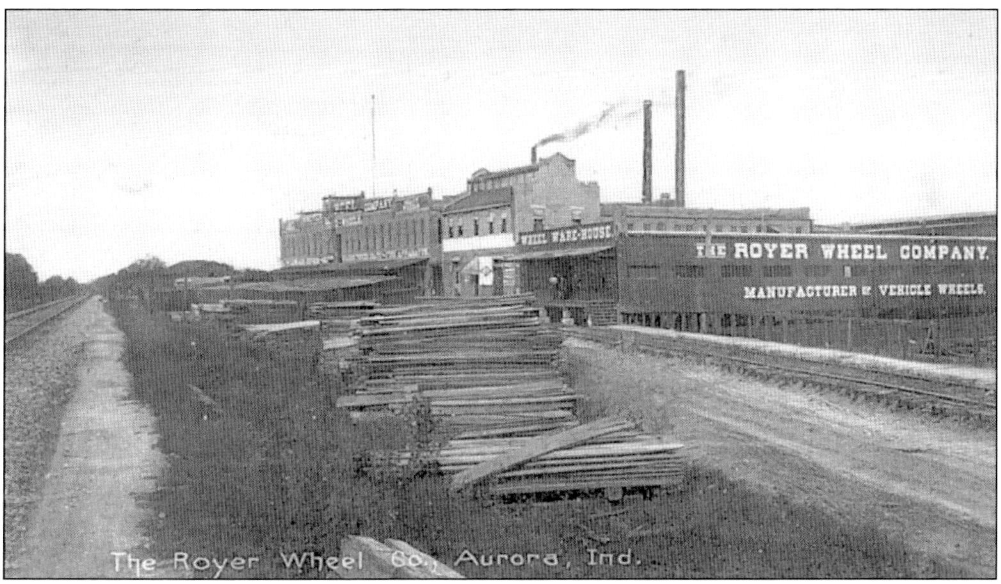

THE ROYER WHEEL CO., AURORA, INDIANA. The buildings used by this factory still remain in Aurora today, at 610 George Street. Their future, however, is undetermined. After being used as a wheel factory, the building was converted to a box factory and used in that capacity by different corporations for several decades. While used as a wheel factory, the company was promoted as the largest wheel works in the United States. The plant was constructed in 1901. (Produced by Kraemer Art Co., Cincinnati and Berlin, Germany, for D. Holler.)

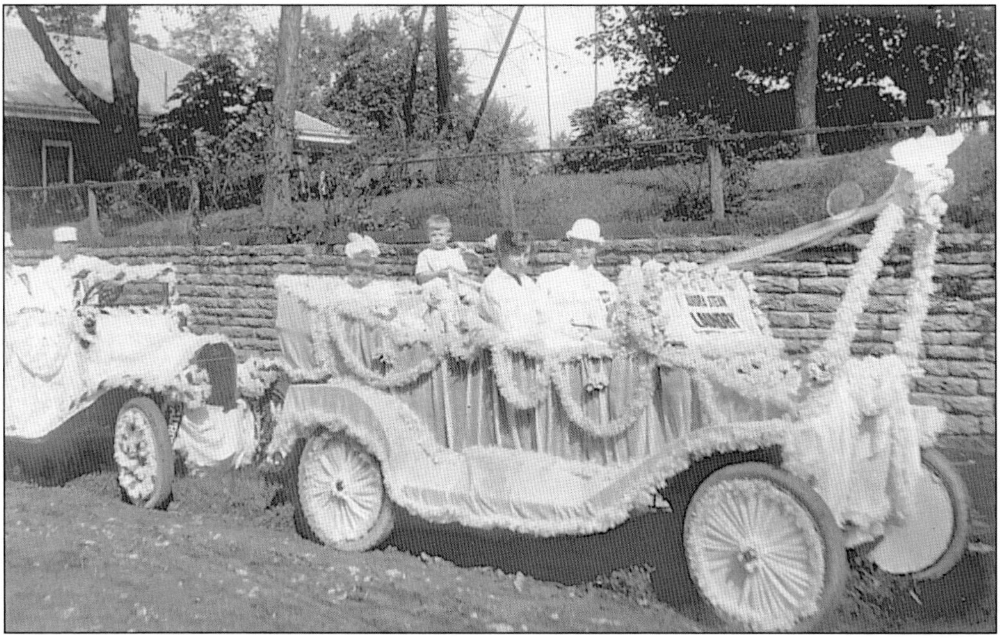

EARLY FARMER'S FAIR PARADE ENTRY, AURORA, INDIANA. This is a parade entry decorated by the Aurora Steam Laundry. The Aurora Steam Laundry was located at 79 Second Street. W.W. Walker was the proprietor. (Real photo postcard, published by Drake Studio, Aurora, Indiana.)

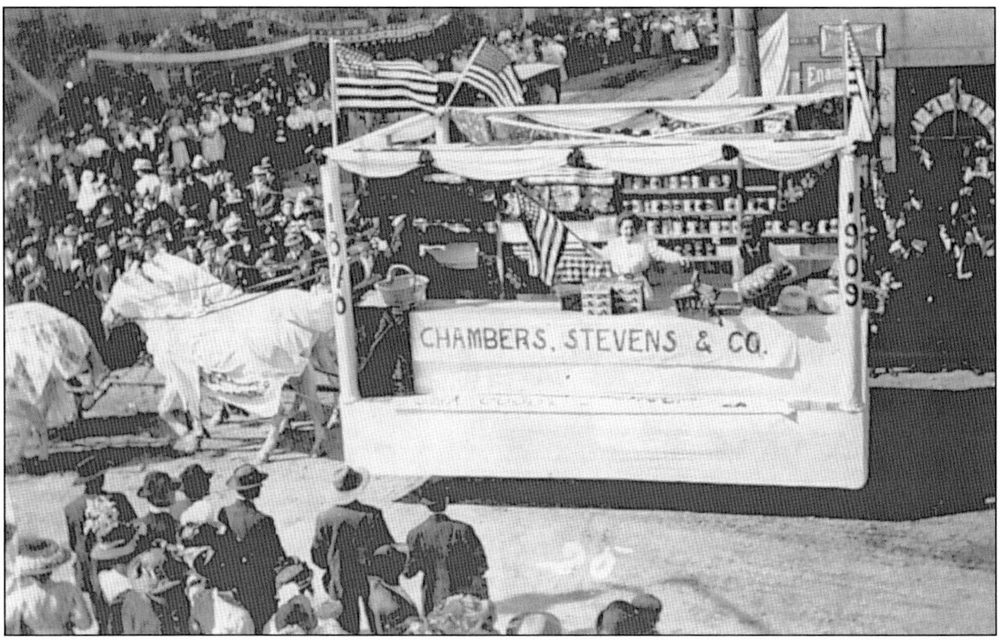

EARLY FARMER'S FAIR PARADE ENTRY, AURORA, INDIANA. The postmark on the back of this card indicates that this scene is from the second Farmer's Fair, on October 9, 1909. The parade entry was sponsored by the Chambers-Stevens & Company. The company was located on the northeast corner of Second and Main Streets. Their building was constructed in 1900, and was destroyed by fire in 1997. (Real photo postcard by an unidentified photographer.)

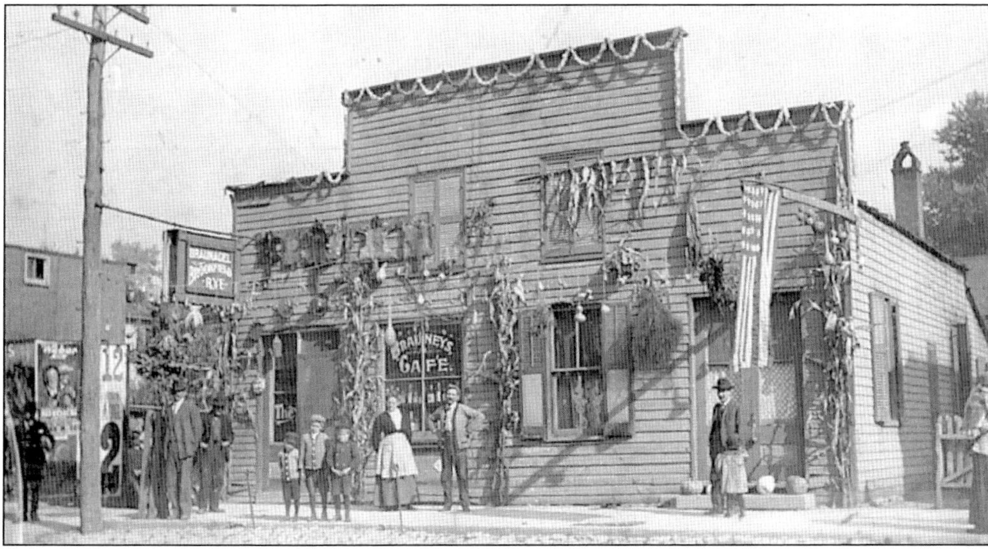

Brauney's Cafe, Aurora, Indiana. In 1908, many of the businesses in Aurora decorated their establishments in celebration of the first annual street fair. This view shows the 126 Third Street cafe of G. Michael and Maggie Braunagel. (Real photo postcard by an unidentified photographer.)

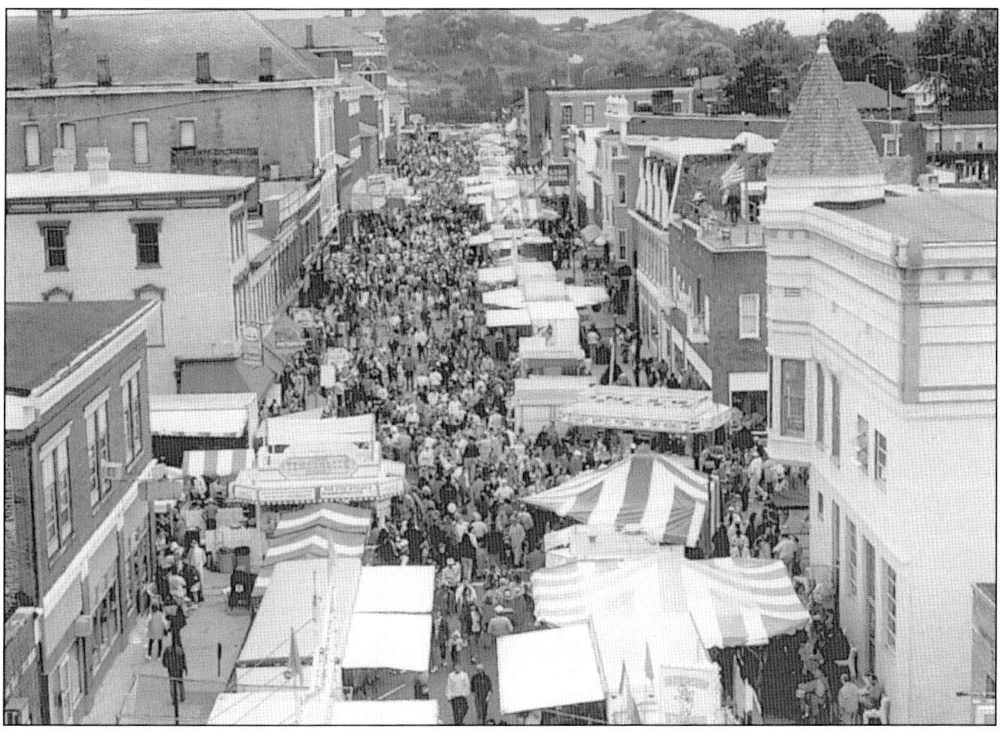

Farmer's Fair Crowd of 1995, Aurora, Indiana. Originally started by the Aurora Business Men's Association as an agricultural show in the streets of Aurora in 1908, the annual Farmer's Fair now boasts of being Indiana's oldest festival. This 1995 view shows the crowd of fair patrons filling Second Street immediately after the parade. (Photograph by Milt Masing, published by Tri-State Visuals.)

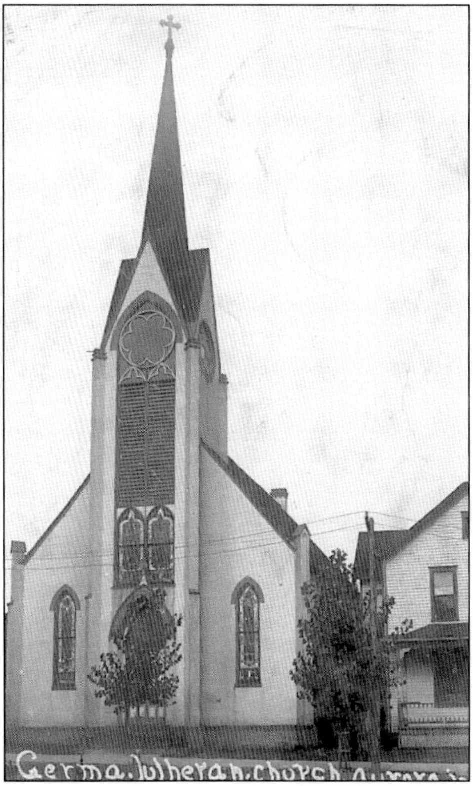

German Lutheran Church, Aurora, Indiana. Built in 1873–74, this church was planned by Reverend Stephens. The church was dedicated on February 8, 1874, in a memorable service that included the congregation marching from the old church building to the new one in solemn procession. The Gothic Revival-style building cost $13,000. Today the church is known as St. John's Lutheran Church. It is located at 220 Mechanic Street. (Real photo postcard by an unidentified photographer.)

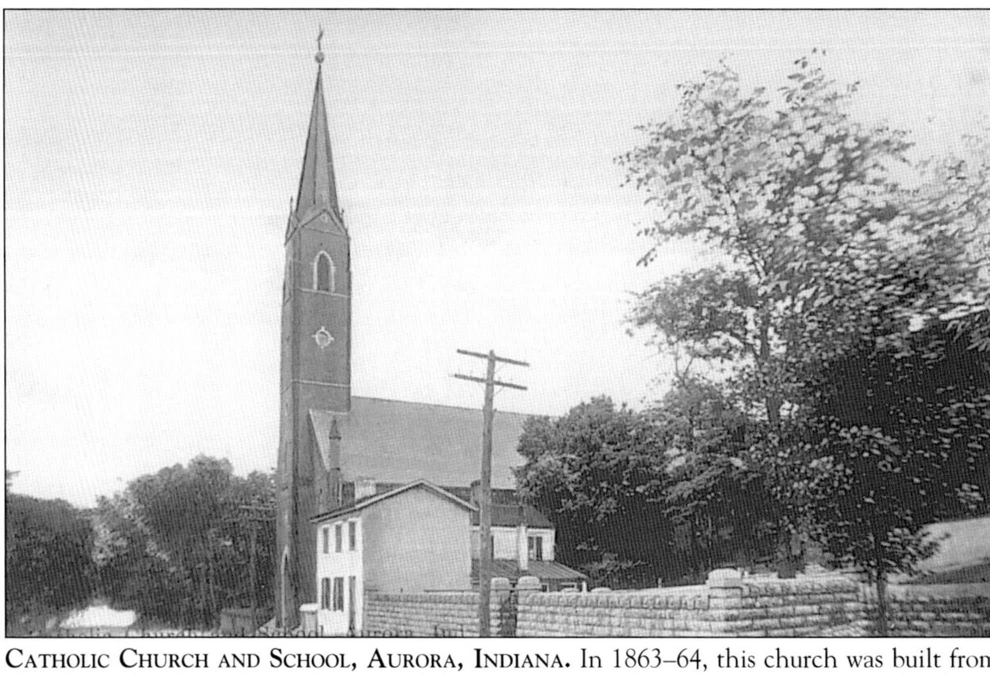

Catholic Church and School, Aurora, Indiana. In 1863–64, this church was built from the plans of Father Klein. The cost of the structure was $24,000. In 1866, the school was constructed, and in 1876 the steeple was added. (Produced by Kraemer Art Co., Cincinnati and Berlin, Germany, for D. Holler.)

FIFTH STREET GERMAN PROTESTANT CHURCH, AURORA, INDIANA. This church building was constructed in 1848 as a Baptist church. In 1874 it was sold to the German Reformed Church, which later became the German Protestant Church and, later yet, the United Church of Christ. When the building was sold in 1874, the Baptists were in their new building on Main Street (see page 9 for information on this building). The architecture of the building is a blend of Classical and Gothic styles. (Produced by Kraemer Art Co., Cincinnati and Berlin, Germany, for D. Holler.)

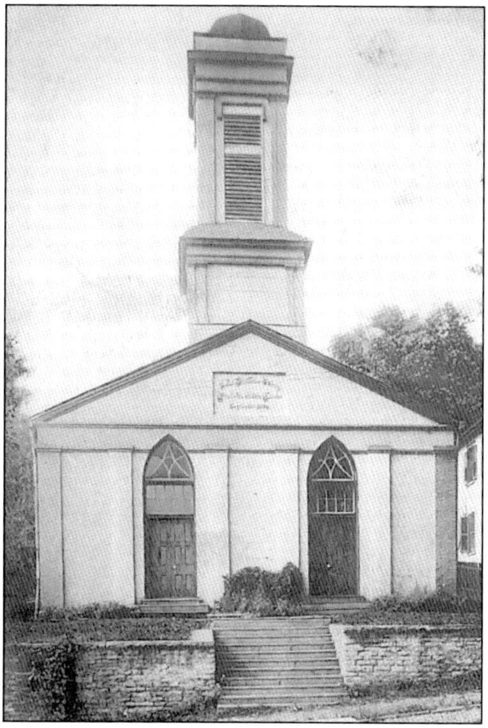

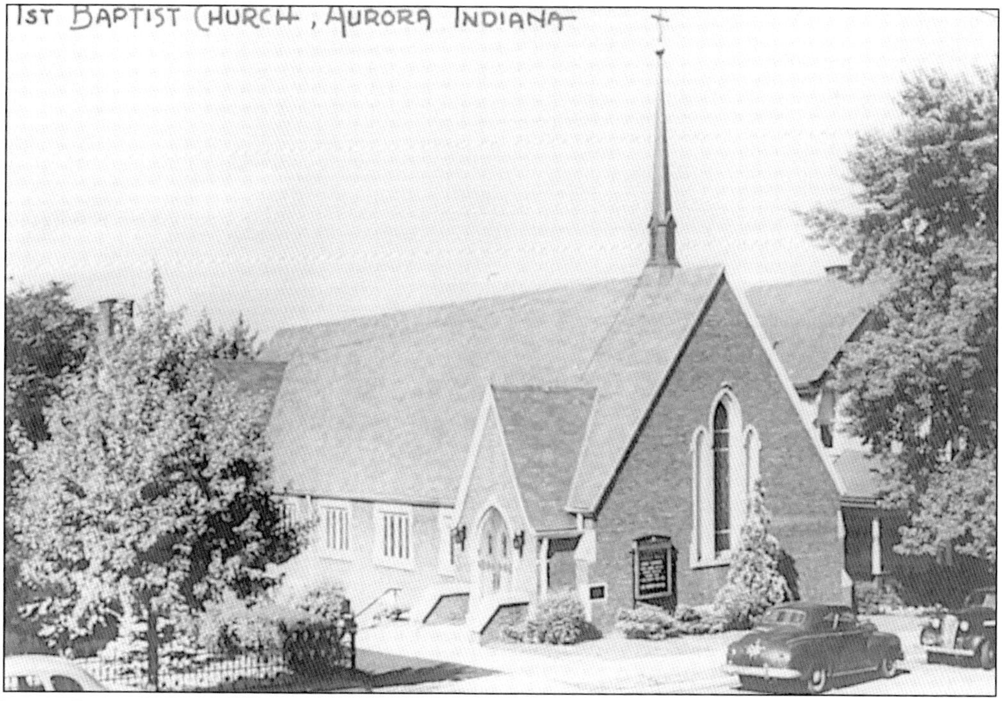

FIRST BAPTIST CHURCH, AURORA, INDIANA. Ground-breaking ceremonies for this building, the third edifice constructed by the Baptists of Aurora, was May 1, 1938. It was dedicated on November 16, 1938. H.M. King, of Louisville, Kentucky, was the architect. The building is located at 304 Fourth Street. (Real photo postcard by an unidentified photographer.)

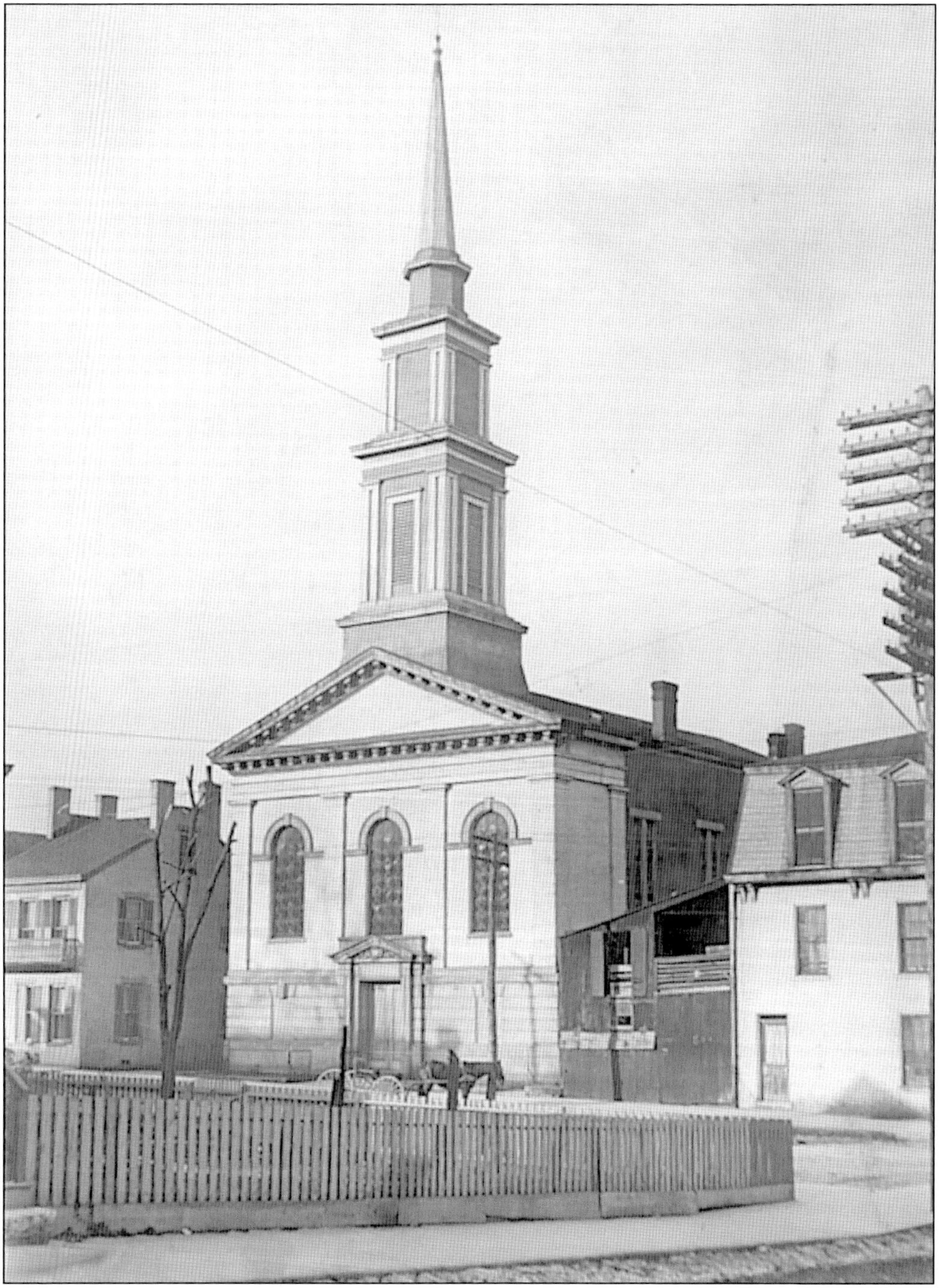

First Methodist Church, Aurora, Indiana. This is the third church building constructed in Aurora as a Methodist Church. It was constructed in 1862. In 1830–1838, the first structure was built near the site of the B & O Depot. In 1842 it was sold, and the second church was built in 1845 near the corner of Third and Bridgeway Streets. The present church is a mix of Classic and Gothic Revival styles of architecture. (Real photo postcard by an unidentified photographer.)

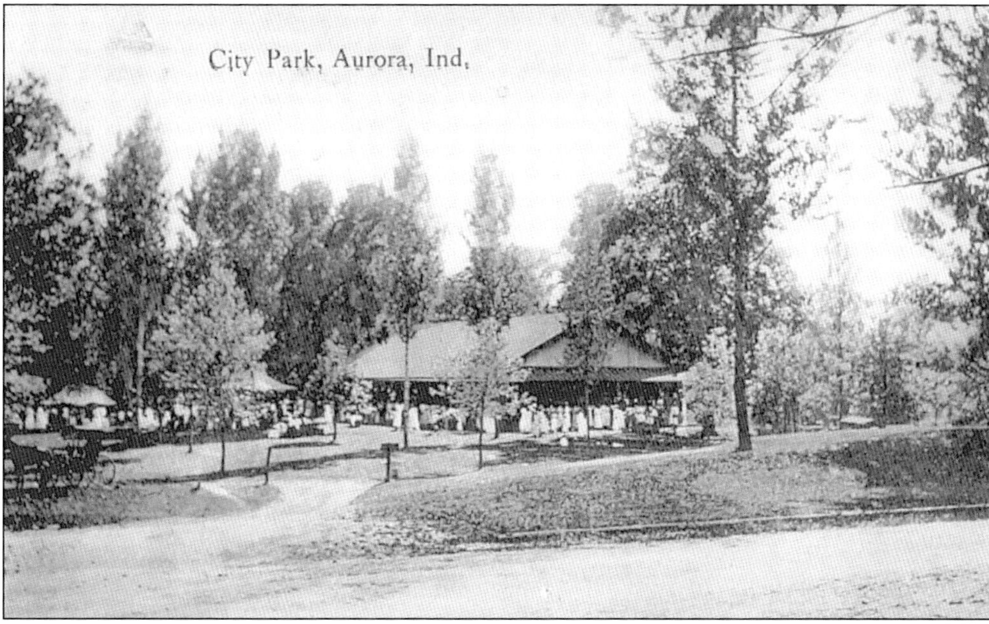

CITY PARK, AURORA, INDIANA. This view of the Aurora City Park shows the shelter houses that have dominated the park's activities for many decades. In 1860, the land that comprises the park was deeded to the City of Aurora for the use of the Dearborn County Agricultural Society for use as a fairgrounds and city park. The card is postmarked 1912. (Produced by Kraemer Art Co., Cincinnati and Berlin, Germany.)

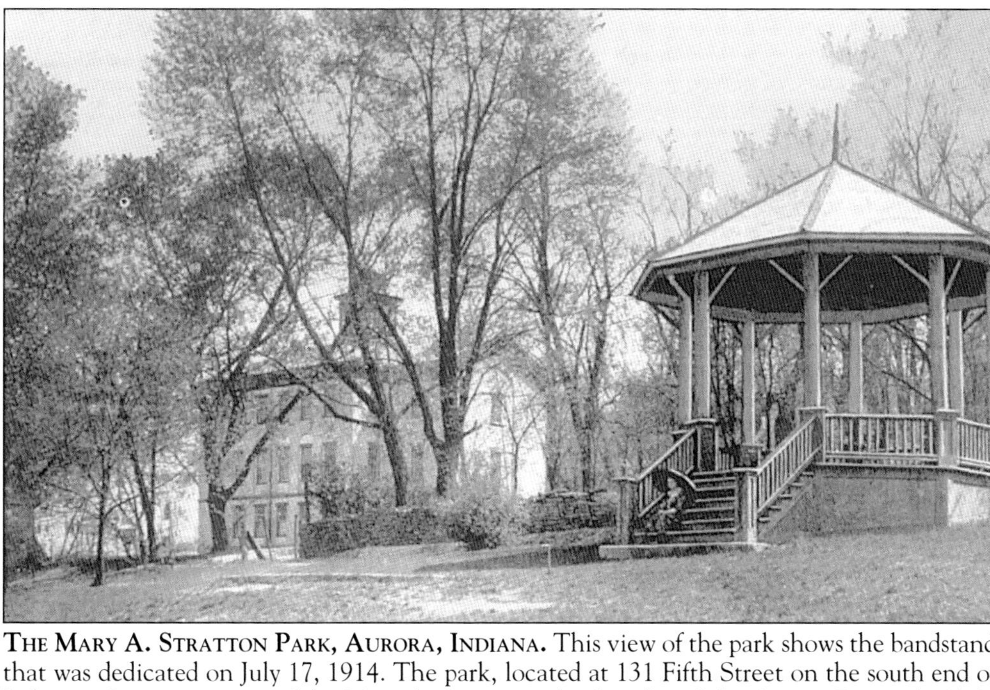

THE MARY A. STRATTON PARK, AURORA, INDIANA. This view of the park shows the bandstand that was dedicated on July 17, 1914. The park, located at 131 Fifth Street on the south end of Judiciary Street, was named for Mary A. Stratton, the founder of the Aurora Research Club. Mary was the daughter of Jesse L. Holman, the founder of Aurora in 1819. (Produced by Curt Teich & Co., Chicago, for M.O. Whitney.)

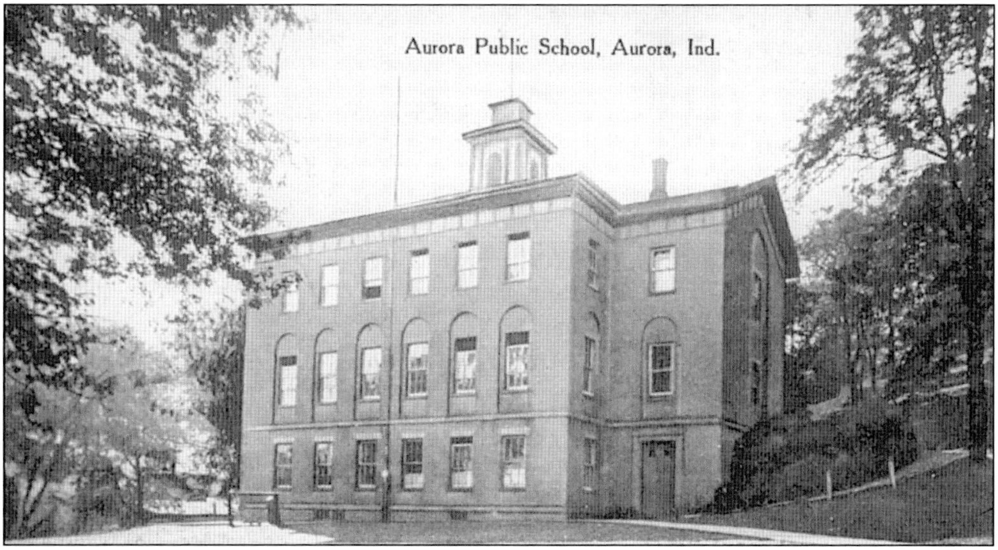

Aurora Public School, Aurora, Indiana. The first schoolhouse built in Aurora, later known as Southside School, was completed in 1863. It took nearly four years to build. In the mid–1970s it was demolished to make way for a multi-unit apartment complex. (Produced by Hoover-Watson Printing Co., Indianapolis, Indiana.)

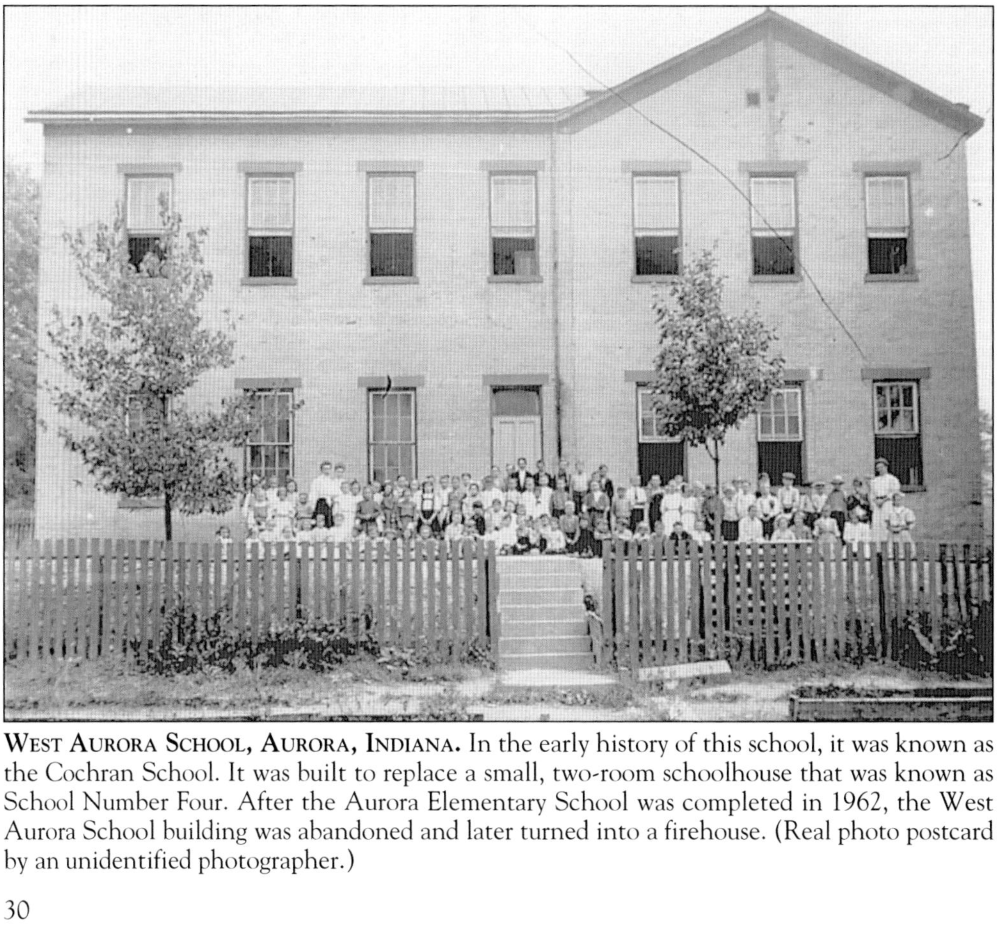

West Aurora School, Aurora, Indiana. In the early history of this school, it was known as the Cochran School. It was built to replace a small, two-room schoolhouse that was known as School Number Four. After the Aurora Elementary School was completed in 1962, the West Aurora School building was abandoned and later turned into a firehouse. (Real photo postcard by an unidentified photographer.)

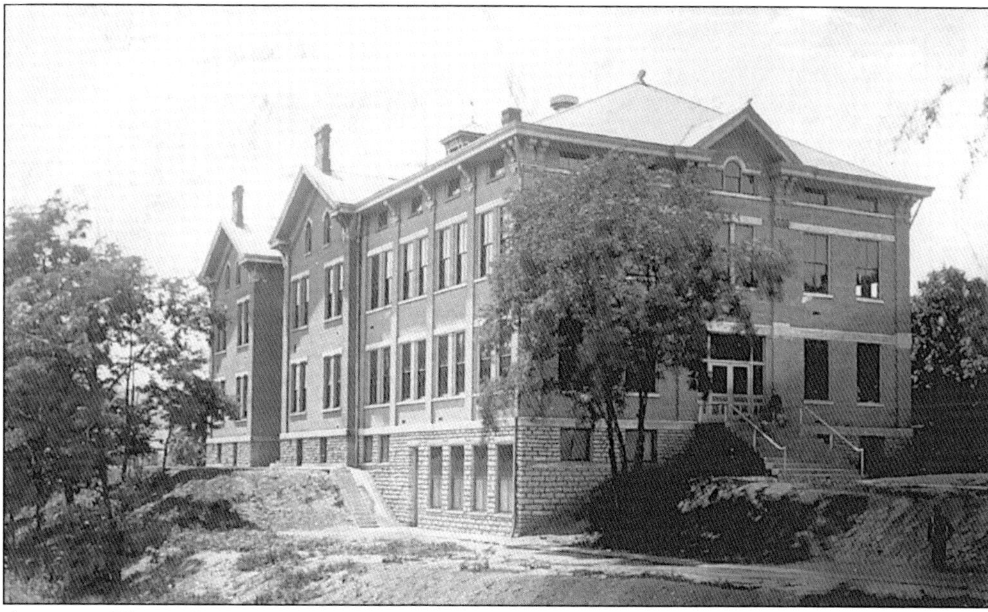

AURORA HIGH SCHOOL, AURORA, INDIANA. After a new high school building was constructed on Green Boulevard in 1934, this school became known as Northside School. The first section of this building was completed in 1867; the second in 1881; a third in 1881; and the final section, seen in the front of this view just after completion, in 1908. The building was razed c. 1979. (Real photo postcard by an unidentified photographer.)

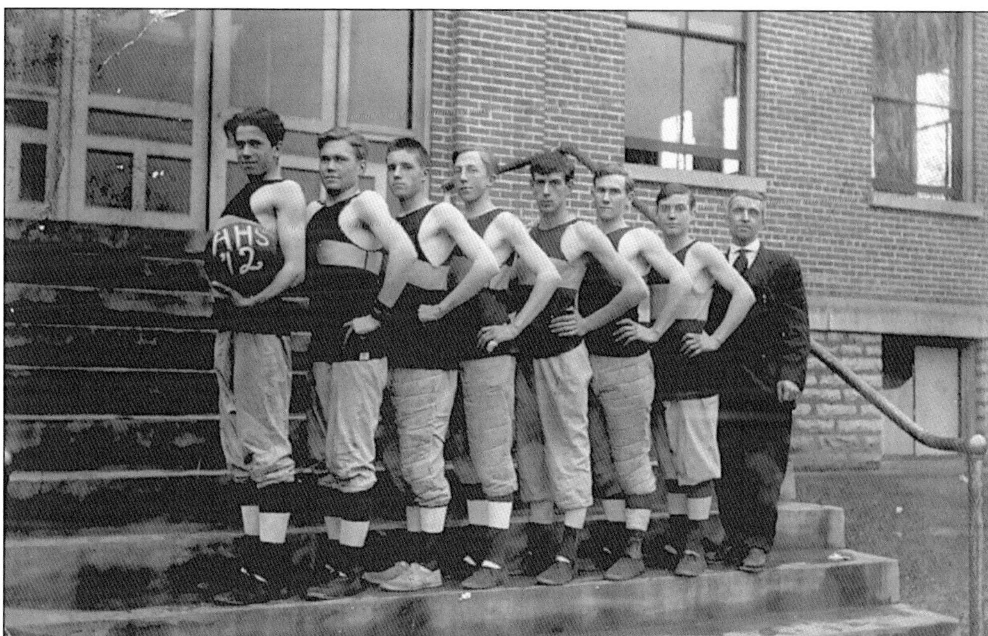

AURORA HIGH SCHOOL BASKETBALL TEAM, AURORA, INDIANA. This card was sent by Hal Driver, AHS basketball coach at the time, in December of 1911. In the message on the card, Mr. Driver reports, "we beat Madison H.S. 25-11." Mr. Driver was later the superintendent of Aurora Public Schools. (Real photo postcard by an unidentified photographer.)

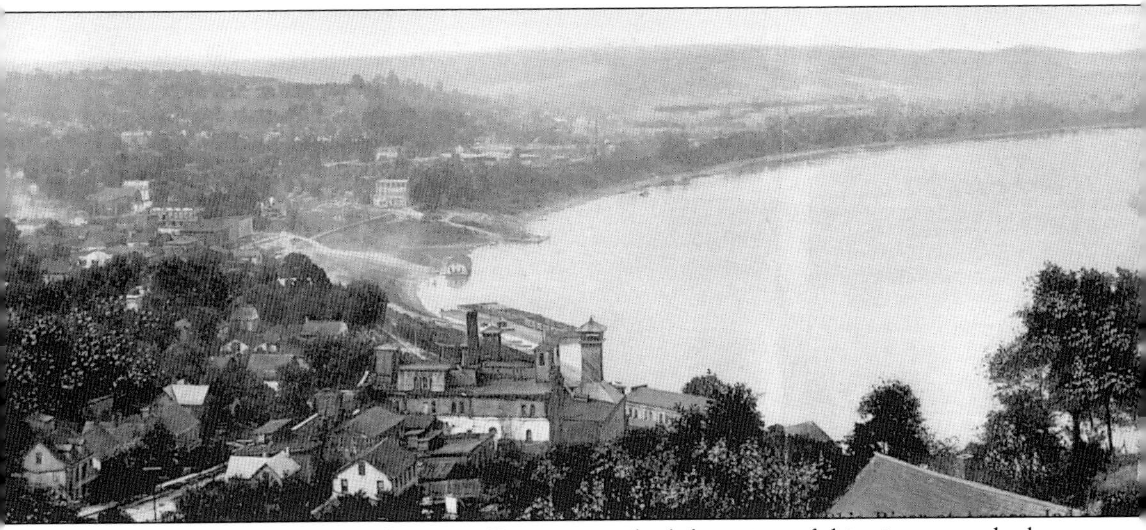

OHIO RIVER AT AURORA, INDIANA. Dominating the left portion of this picture, at the bottom of the hill, is the Crescent Brewing Company. The brewery was started in 1874 as the Thomas W. Gaff & Co. Brewery. In 1877, it became the Crescent Brewery. During the years of 1913 and 1914, the buildings of the brewery were dismantled.

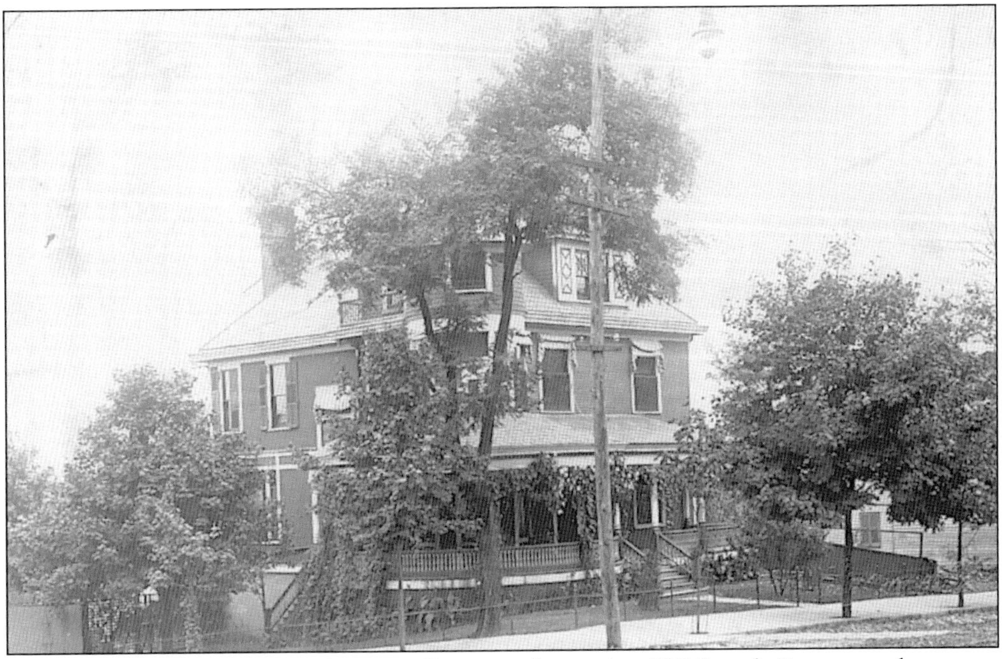

FOURTH AND MAIN STREETS, AURORA, INDIANA. Located at 220 Fourth Street, on the corner connecting with Main Street, this Queen Anne-style house was built in 1890. Today the house is used as a bed & breakfast. (Real photo postcard, published by Wilson & Son Photography.)

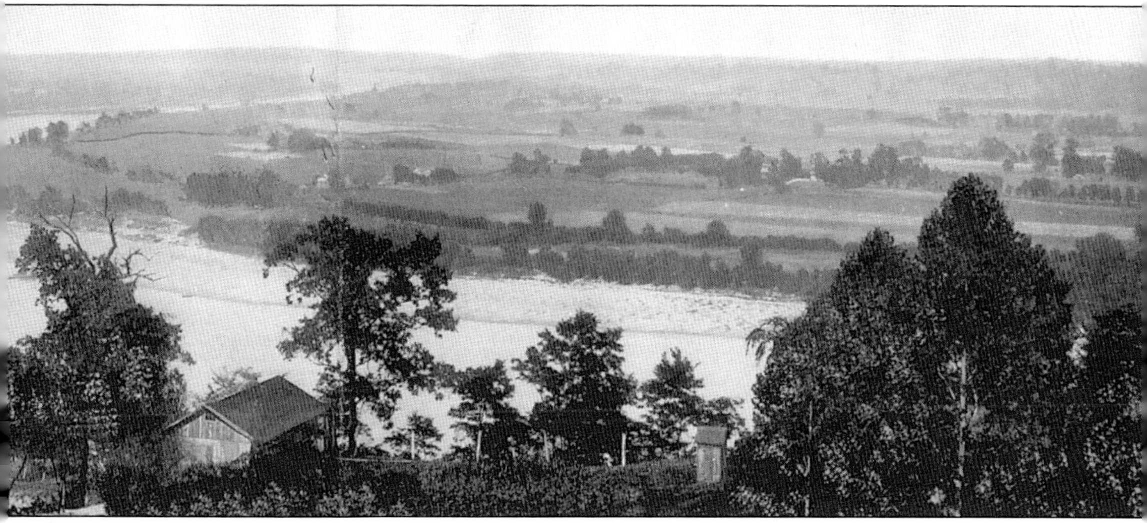

Ohio River, Aurora, Indiana. The right portion of this rare scene shows only rooftops, the Ohio River, and the hills of the three states—Indiana, Kentucky, and Ohio. The card was produced in both a black and white and a hand-colored version. (Produced by Kraemer Art Co., Cincinnati and Berlin, for D. Holler.)

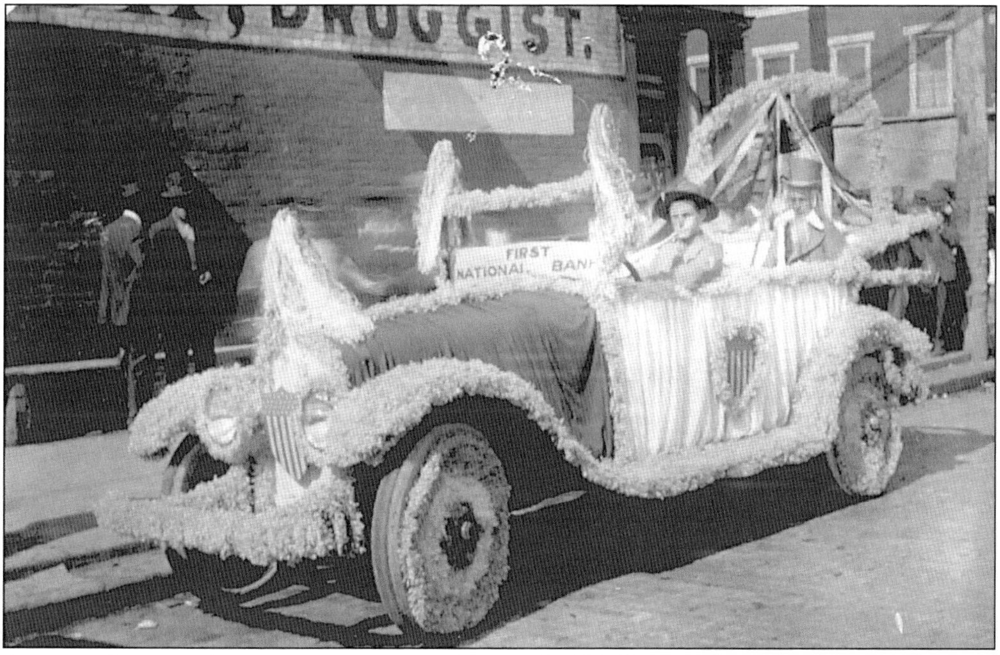

Aurora, Indiana. Longtime newspaper columnist Earl Huffman is posing for this picture, taken on Main Street. He is dressed in his soldier suit, sitting behind the wheel in a prize-winning, decorated automobile of the First National Bank. An unidentified boy dressed as Uncle Sam sits in the back seat. It was entered in the Farmer's Fair in 1919. (Real photo postcard, published by the Drake Studio.)

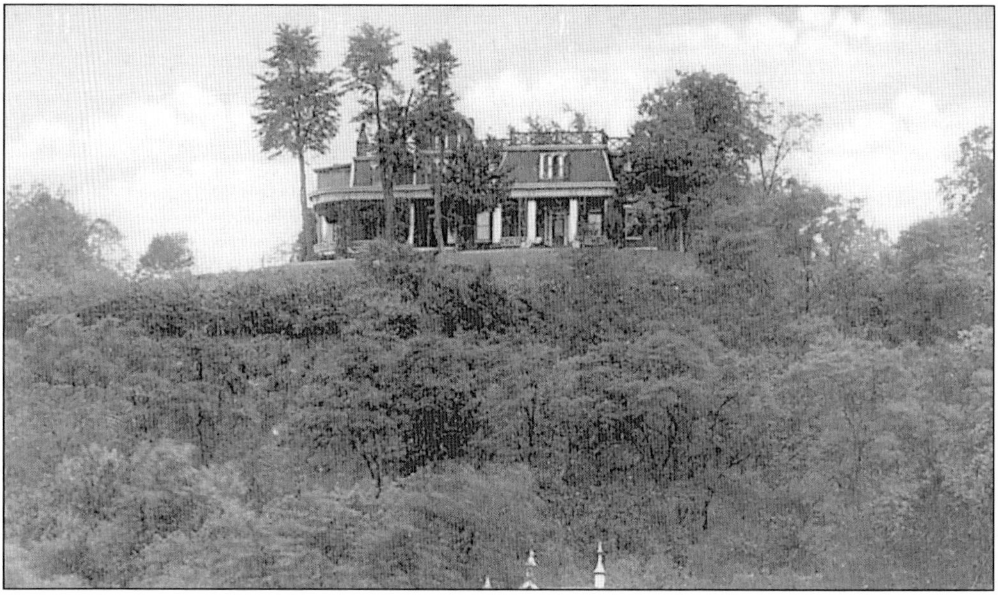

SUTTON'S HILL, AURORA, INDIANA. The house of Doctor Harley H. Sutton is featured in this view. Dr. Sutton was born in 1852, the son of Dr. George and Sarah Folbre Sutton. The actual house is a mix of several different architectural styles, including classic porch columns and Italianate detailing around the roof line. Dr. Sutton had the house torn down in 1937 and replaced by a "modern" house. (Produced by Kraemer Art Co., Cincinnati, Ohio.)

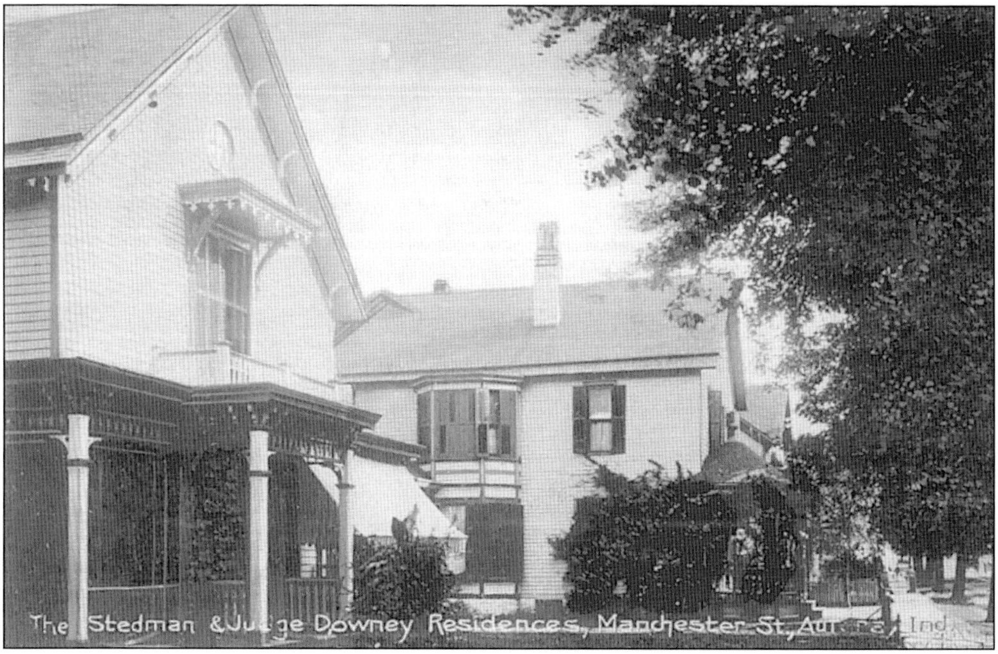

THE STEDMAN & JUDGE DOWNEY RESIDENCES, MANCHESTER STREET, AURORA, INDIANA. Featured in this picture are the homes of District Judge George E. Downey, at 139 Manchester Street, and Nathan Stedman, at 130 Manchester Street. Mr. Stedman was the president of Stedman Foundry & Machine Works. (Produced by Kraemer Art Co., Cincinnati and Berlin, Germany, for D. Holler.)

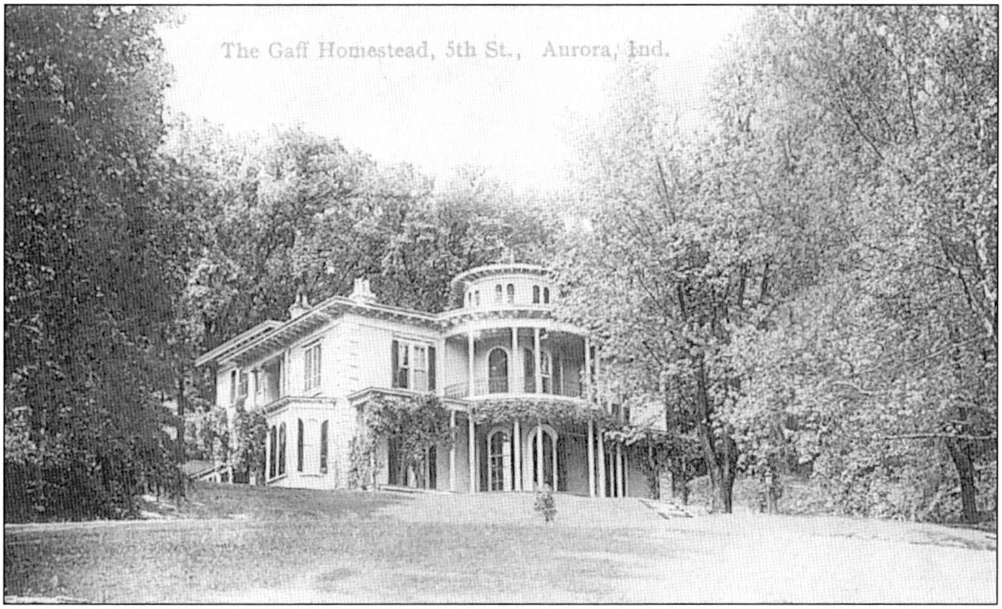

THE GAFF HOMESTEAD, FIFTH STREET, AURORA, INDIANA. The Thomas W. Gaff residence, commonly known as Hillforest, was built in 1852–54 from plans drawn by prominent architect Isaiah Rogers. The house was designed with Italianate details and structural parts used to make the house resemble a steamboat. (Produced by Kraemer Art Co., Cincinnati, Ohio.)

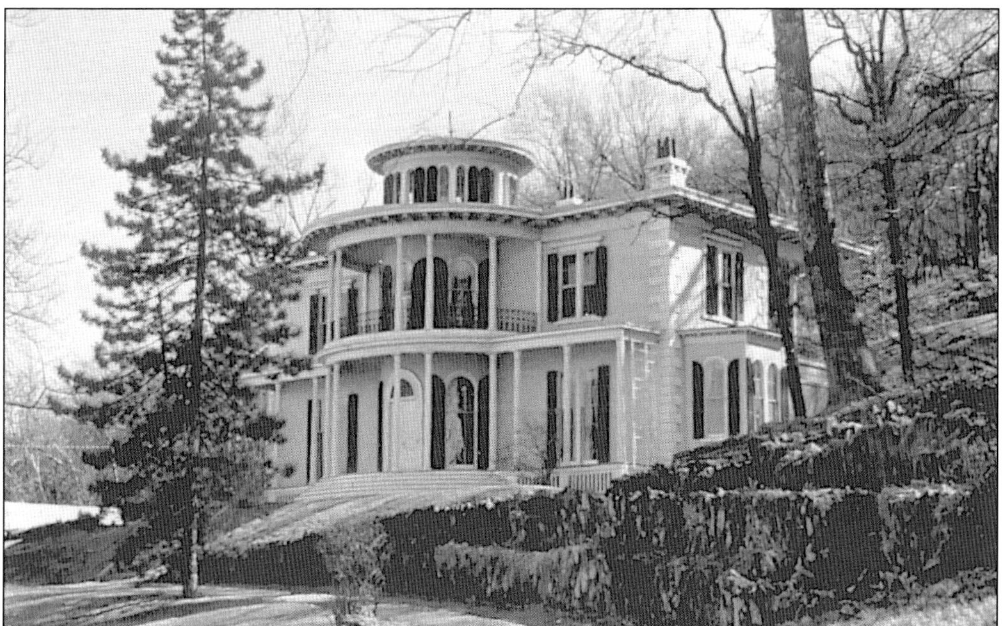

HILLFOREST, HISTORIC RIVER VALLEY MANSION, AURORA, INDIANA. This is a 1980s view of the same structure in almost identical condition. In 1993 the house was designated a National Historical Landmark. Today the house is operated by Hillforest Historical Foundation and is open to the public during the warm season. (Photograph by Tom Detmer, published by Brown & Bigelow, Division of Standard Packaging Corp.)

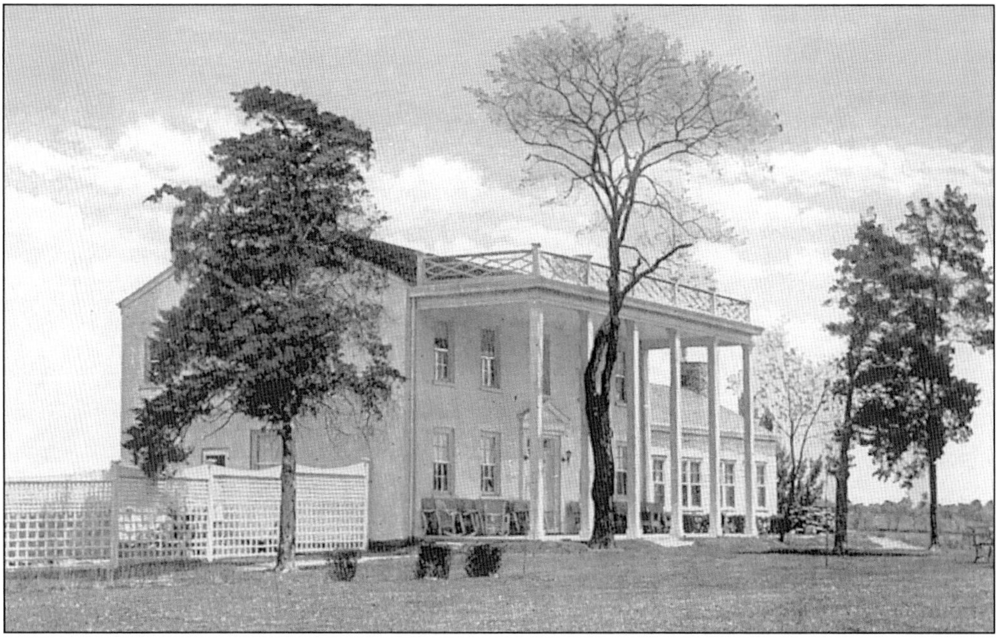

THE DEARBORN COUNTY GOLF CLUB, NEAR AURORA, INDIANA. In 1925, a group of Lawrenceburg citizens purchased the old Wymond residence and incorporated it as the Dearborn Country Club. The main building, used by the Wymond family as a residence, was probably built sometime before 1850. (Produced by Curt Teich & Co., Chicago, Illinois.)

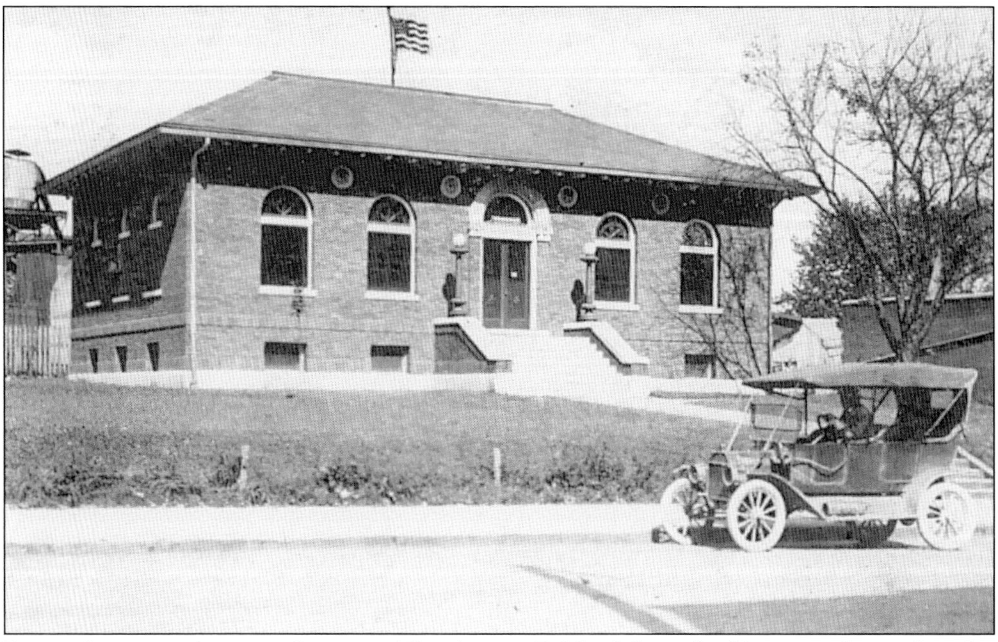

PUBLIC LIBRARY, AURORA, INDIANA. The Aurora Public Library building was donated to the City of Aurora by Miss Georgiana E. Sutton. It was designed by the Cincinnati architectural firm of Garber & Woodward. The building was completed in 1914, and dedicated on October 13, 1914. J.C. Wright & Son was the contractor. A restoration of, and addition to, the building was started in 1996. (Produced by Kraemer Art Co., Cincinnati, Ohio.)

I.O.O.F. HALL AND POST OFFICE, AURORA, INDIANA. The Oddfellows Hall in Aurora was completed in 1887. It was planned in the Romanesque style of architecture. In addition to the Oddfellows Hall, the building also included the Lyric Theater and commercial space. In 1974, the building, along with 423 Second Street, was incorporated into the R.L. Johnston Company Store. The name of this store was later changed to Gambles, and this store still remains a fixture in the Aurora business community. (Produced by an unidentified printer, taken by an unidentified photographer.)

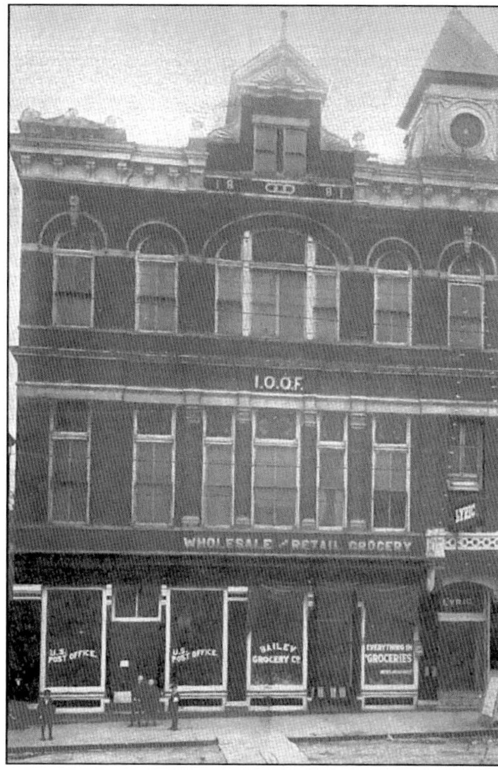

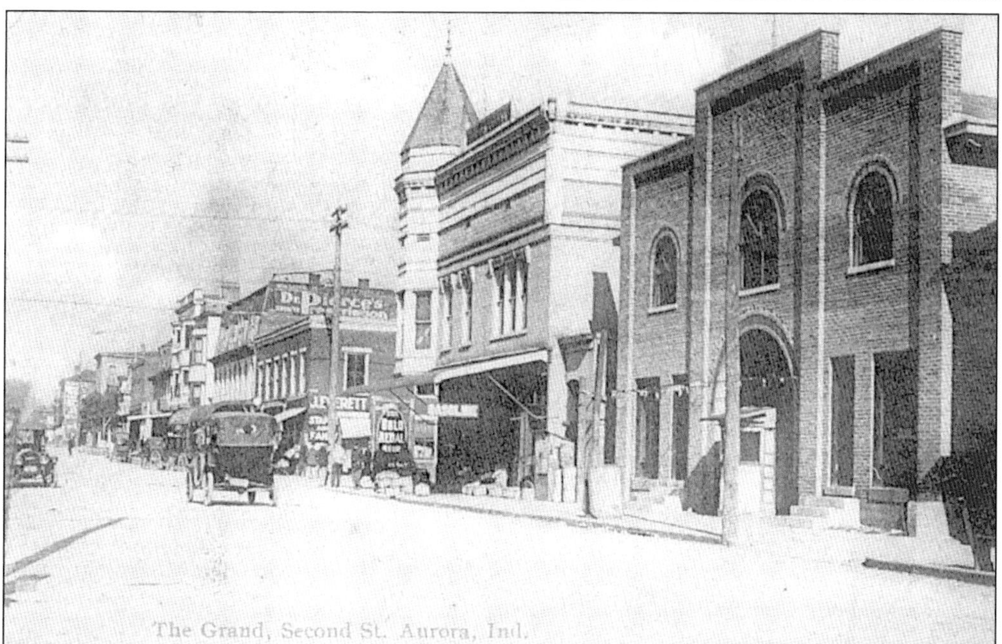

THE GRAND, SECOND STREET, AURORA, INDIANA. Three lost, but well-known buildings dominate this early Aurora street scene. The Cobb Building, destroyed by fire in 1930; the Grand, a theater building destroyed around 1949; and the Chambers-Stevens Company building, destroyed by fire in 1997. (Produced by Kraemer Art Co., Cincinnati, Ohio.)

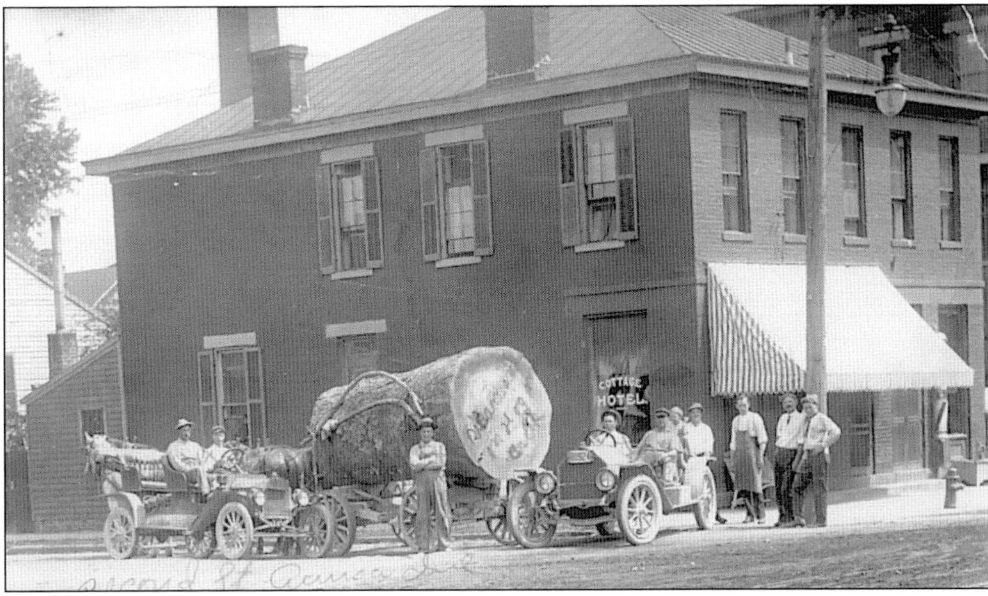

FALLEN TREE BESIDE THE COTTAGE HOTEL, AURORA, INDIANA. Bridgeway Street, near the corner adjoining Second Street, is the scene of this 1913 photograph. The *c.* 1850 building, behind the featured large log, is at 438–450 Second Street. At the time of the picture it housed the Cottage Hotel and the Cosby Barbershop. (Real photo postcard, published by the Drake Studio.)

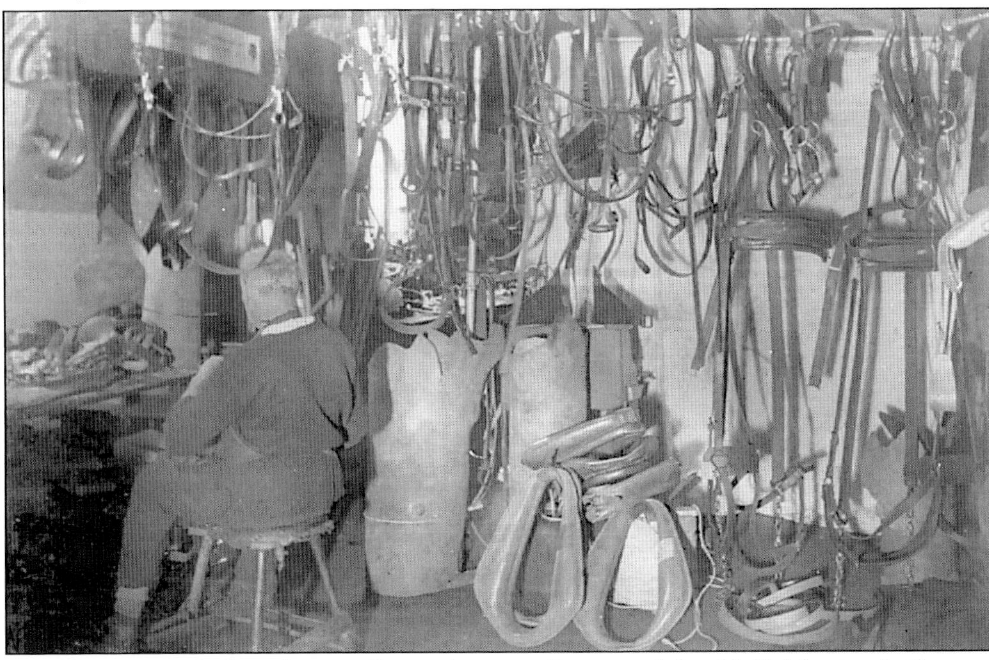

J.H. KUHLMEIER & SON SADDLE SHOP, AURORA, INDIANA. John H. Kuhlmeier & Son was located on Second Street on the site of the former Palace Theater. Early advertisements for the store read: "Dealers in Hardware, Buggies, Harness, Farm Wagons, Bicycles, Gasoline Engines, Seeds, Stock, Etc." John was an immigrant from Germany. The son's name was Frank. In about 1932, the business closed. (Real photo postcard by an unidentified photographer.)

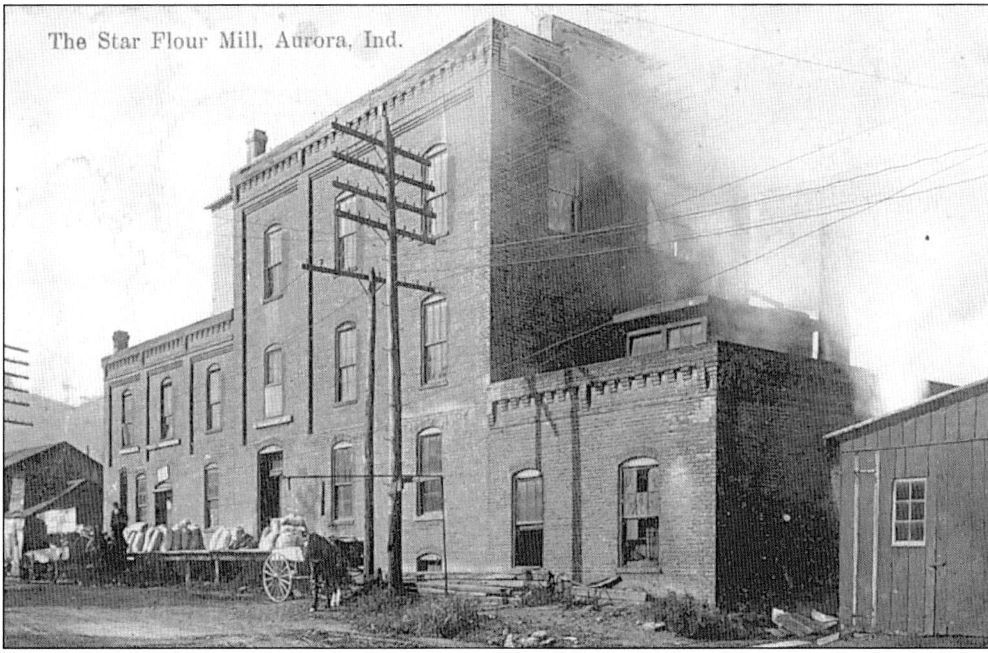

STAR FLOUR MILL, AURORA, INDIANA. In 1891, Henry H. Rullman of Dillsboro started this business on Bridgeway Street. In later years the business was known as Dearborn Mills Company. When it burned on February 15, 1994, it was virtually the same as when first constructed. (Produced by Kraemer Art Co., Cincinnati, for D. Holler.)

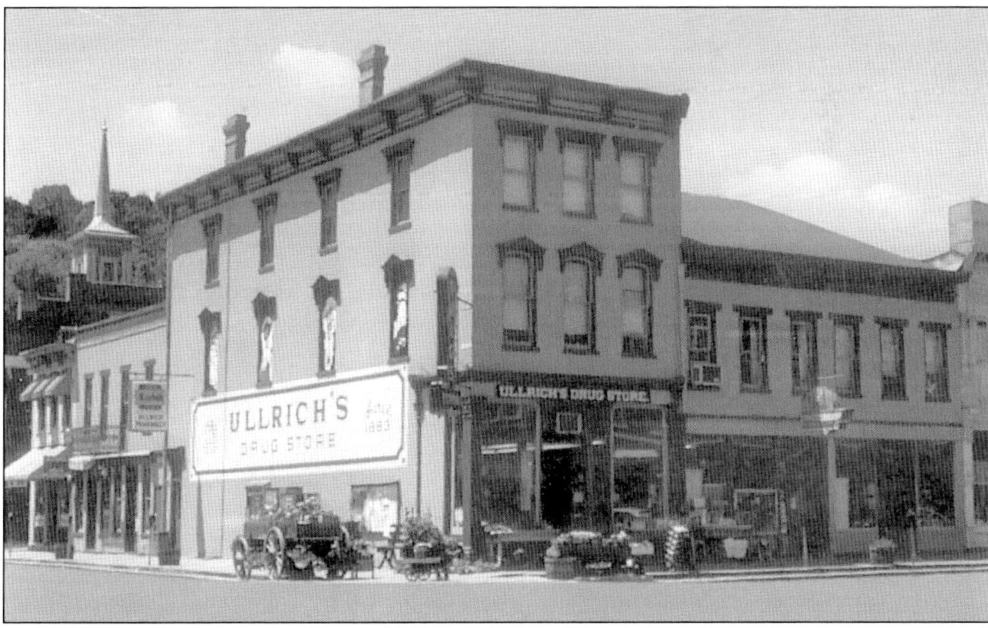

ULLRICH'S DRUG STORE, AURORA, INDIANA. The southwest corner of Second and Main Streets has been known as Ullrich's corner since 1883, when John Ullrich purchased the c. 1860 building shown in this view for use as a drug store. The family-owned business thrived for over one hundred years, closing in 1987. This view dates to just after 1983. (Photograph by Robert J. Mattingly, published by the Ketterer Company, Cincinnati, Ohio.)

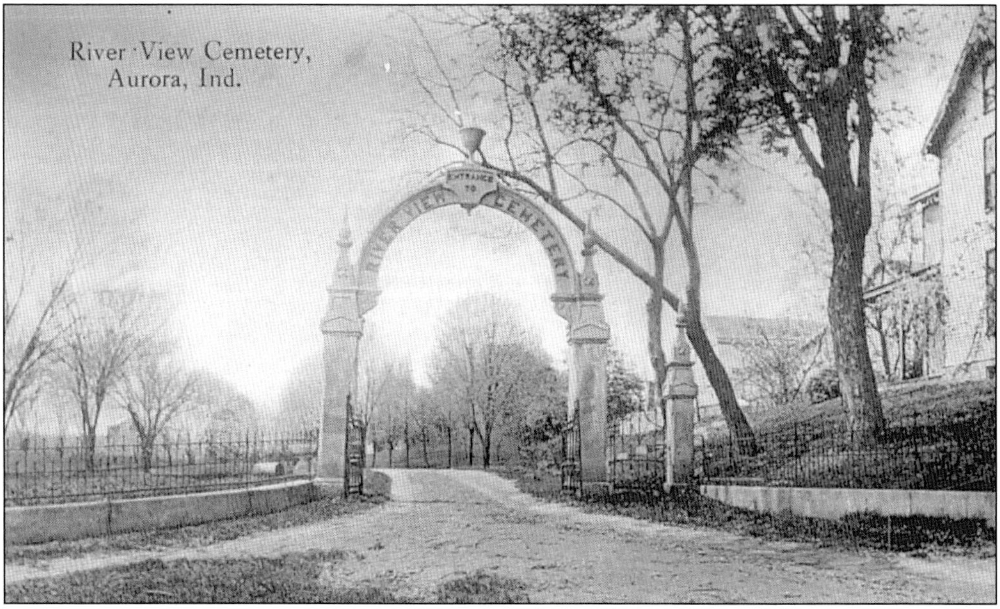

Riverview Cemetery, Aurora, Indiana. Plans for Riverview Cemetery were drawn by the architect William Tinsley, at the time a resident of Cincinnati. The first burial in the cemetery was Jesse Jones in 1869. The grounds contain a wide variety of trees, two archaeological sites, a soldiers' monument and circle, and over 12,000 burials. (Produced by Kraemer Art Co., Cincinnati and Berlin, Germany.)

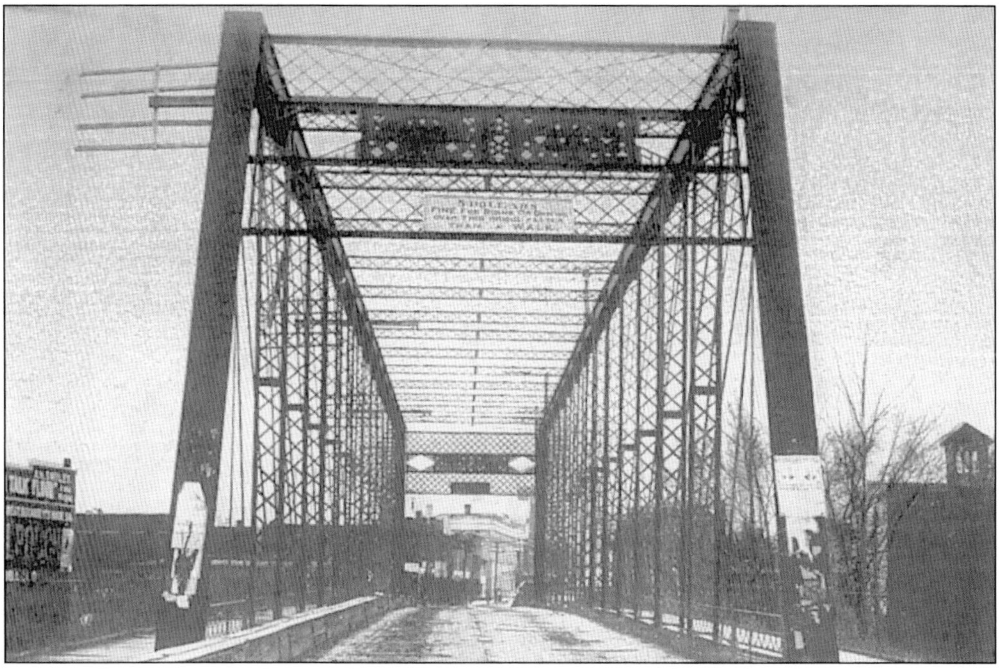

Wagon Bridge over Hogan Creek, Aurora, Indiana. Often referred to as the George Street Bridge, this bridge connects George Street on the north and Main Street on the south. It was constructed in 1887. From 1983 to 1989, the bridge was closed for a million-dollar renovation. It is now back in use once again. (Unidentified publisher.)

Two

DILLSBORO

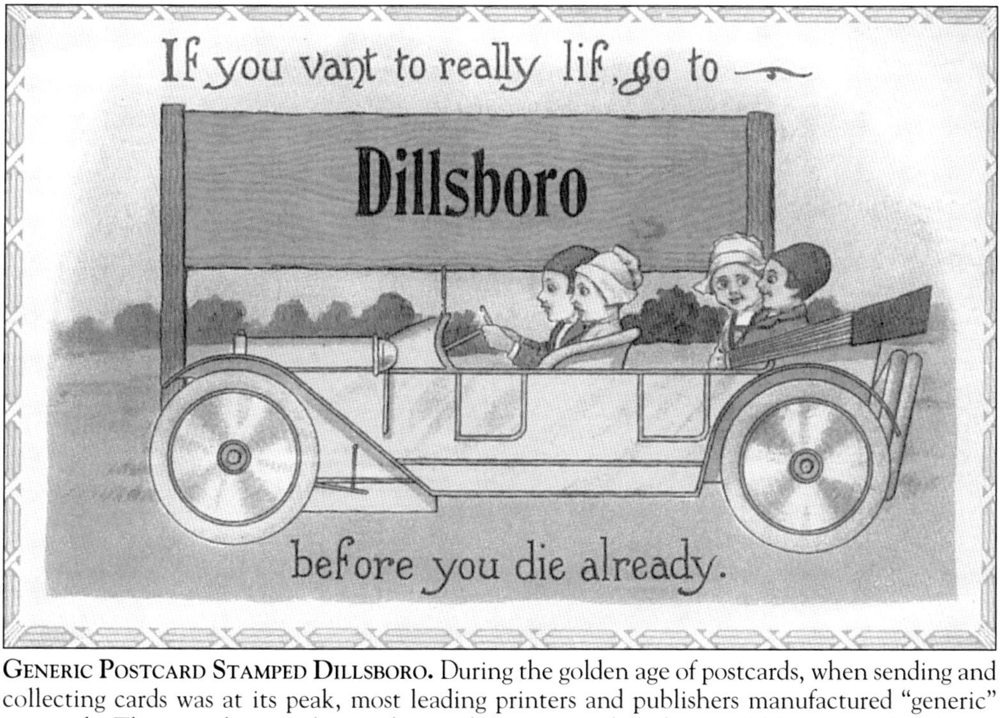

GENERIC POSTCARD STAMPED DILLSBORO. During the golden age of postcards, when sending and collecting cards was at its peak, most leading printers and publishers manufactured "generic" postcards. These cards were designed in such a manner that they could be stamped with any local name and sold from any locality. Many of these cards had comical or humorous themes that would also be appropriate in any locality. The card shown above was post marked in 1913. Because the cost of producing cards has increased faster than the cost of living has increased, this marketing technique is not as common as before, although it is still in use in smaller towns today. (Unidentified printer and publisher.)

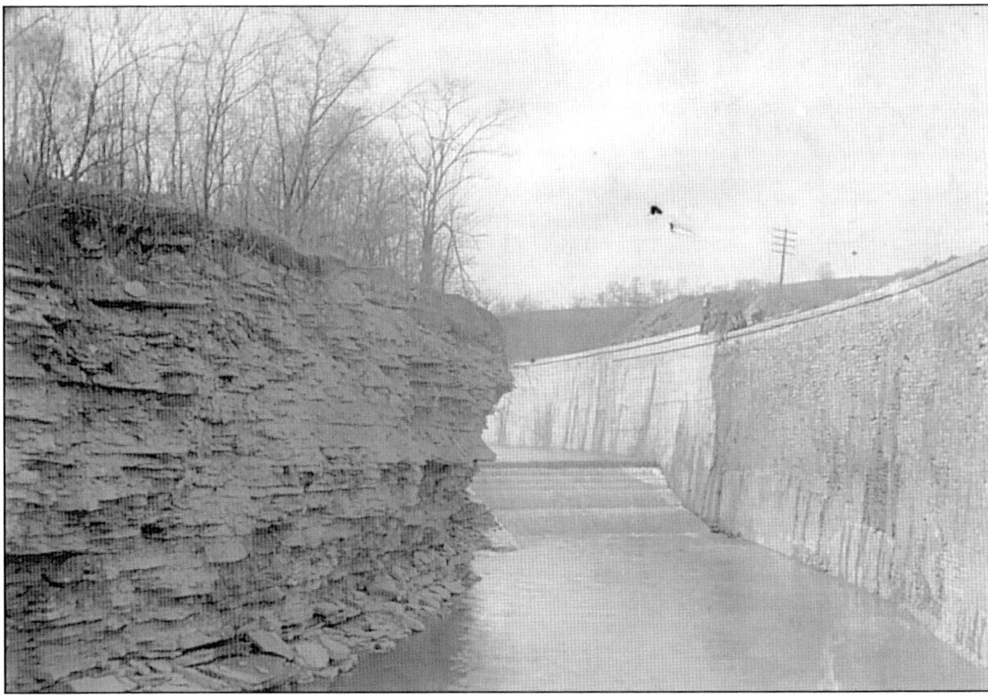

B & O Canal. Completed in 1903, this canal was constructed to keep the flood waters away from the tracks of the Baltimore & Ohio Southwest Railroad. The Canal, sometimes referred to as Millers Cut, carries the water of Hogan Creek between Dillsboro and Cold Springs. (Real photo postcard by an unidentified photographer.)

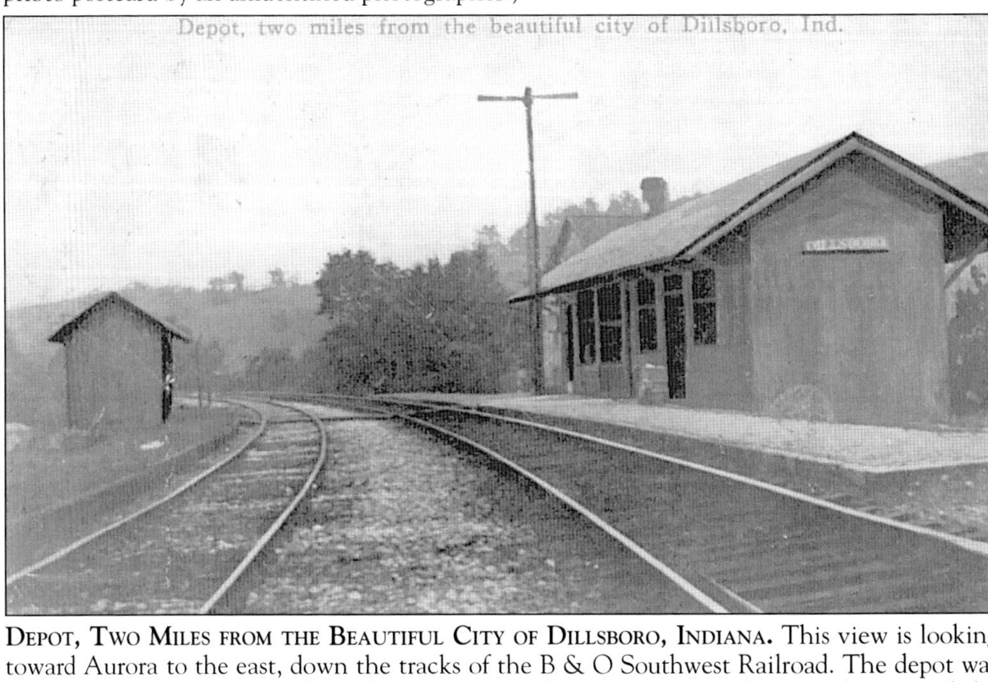

Depot, Two Miles from the Beautiful City of Dillsboro, Indiana. This view is looking toward Aurora to the east, down the tracks of the B & O Southwest Railroad. The depot was used as both a passenger and freight station. The B & O Southwest Railroad has served the State of Indiana since its completion in 1857. (Unidentified printer and publisher.)

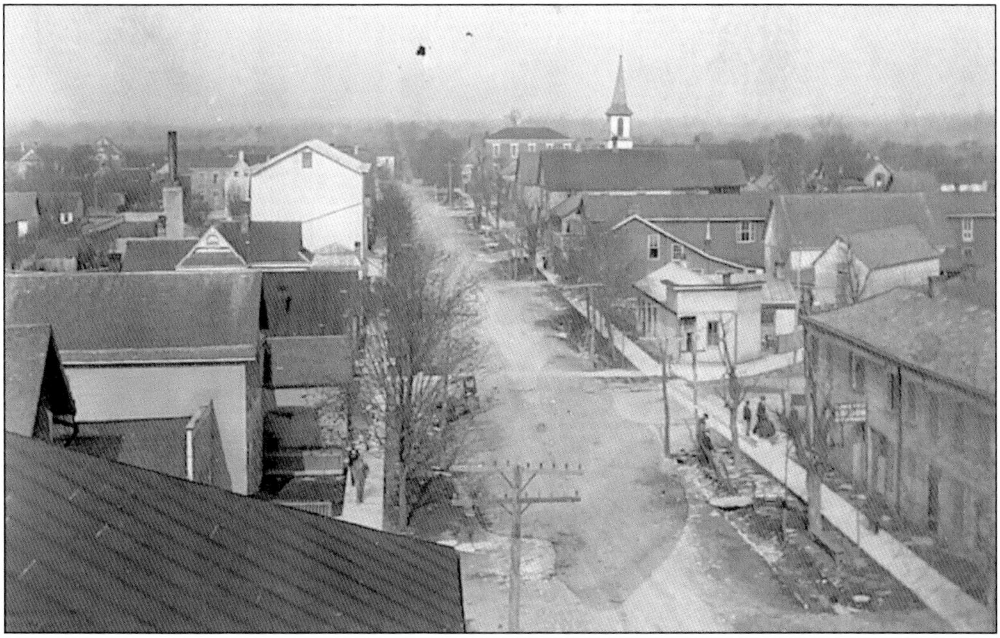

VIEW OF DILLSBORO, TAKEN FROM THE TOP OF THE MASONIC TEMPLE. The steeple of the Lutheran Church dominates this view down North Street to the west. Also visible on the right side of the street is the Viet Hotel, in the foreground, and the I.O.O.F. building in the distance. Note the dirt road still in use when the picture was taken. The card is postmarked 1907. (Real photo postcard by an unidentified photographer.)

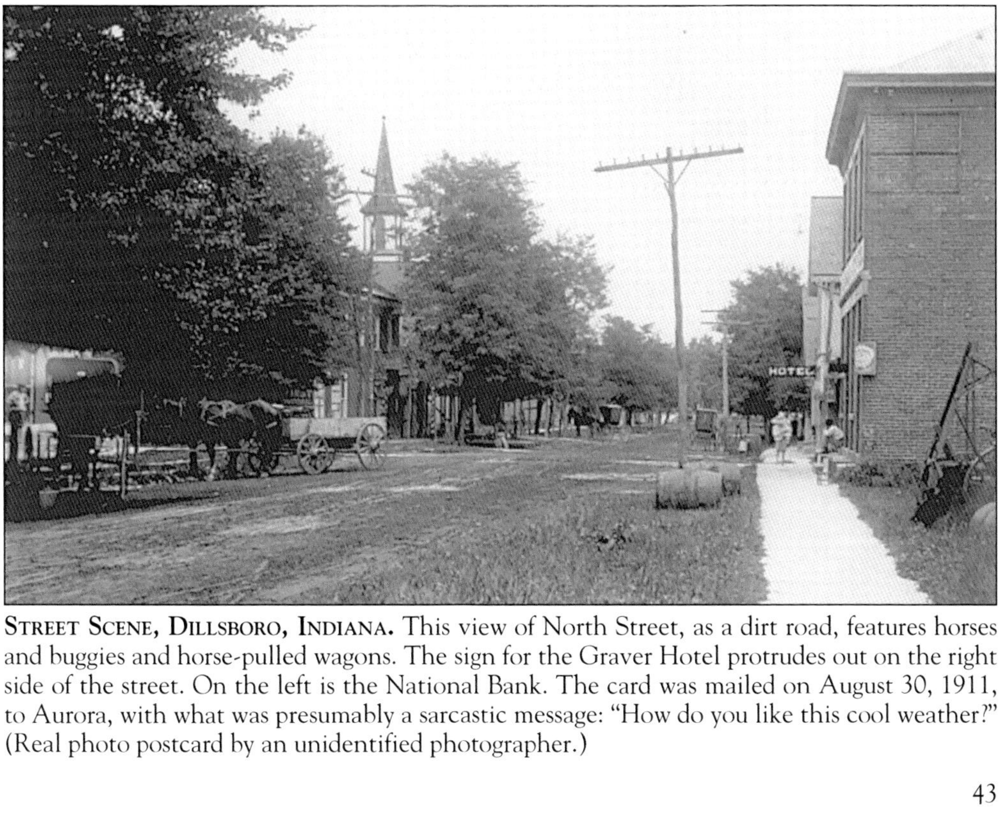

STREET SCENE, DILLSBORO, INDIANA. This view of North Street, as a dirt road, features horses and buggies and horse-pulled wagons. The sign for the Graver Hotel protrudes out on the right side of the street. On the left is the National Bank. The card was mailed on August 30, 1911, to Aurora, with what was presumably a sarcastic message: "How do you like this cool weather?" (Real photo postcard by an unidentified photographer.)

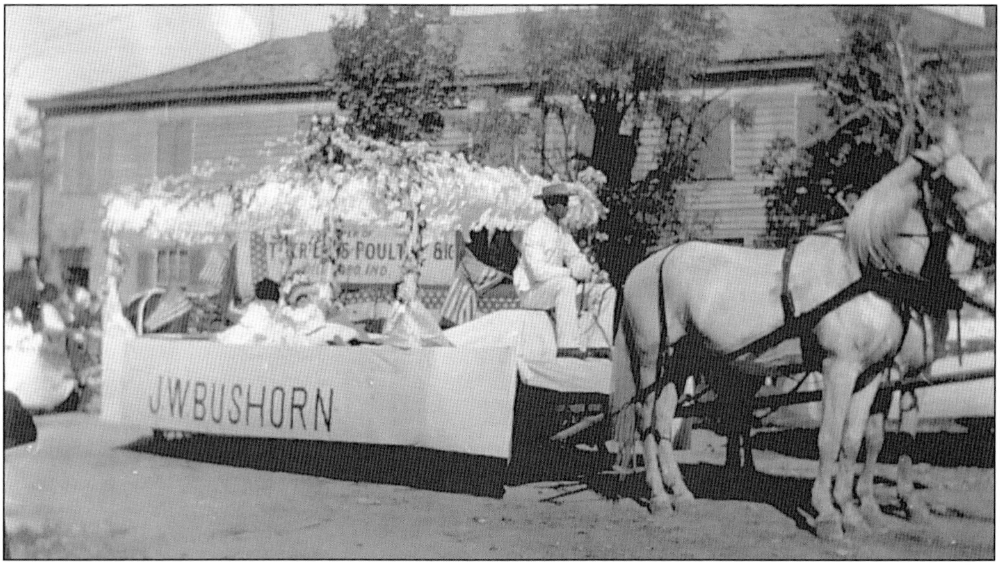

J.W. Bushorn Parade Entry, Dillsboro, Indiana. J.W. Bushorn operated a hotel, restaurant, and confectionery business. He also sold ice cream, sodas, fruits, cigars, and tobacco. His wife Gertrude also helped operate the business. (Real photo postcard by an unidentified photographer.)

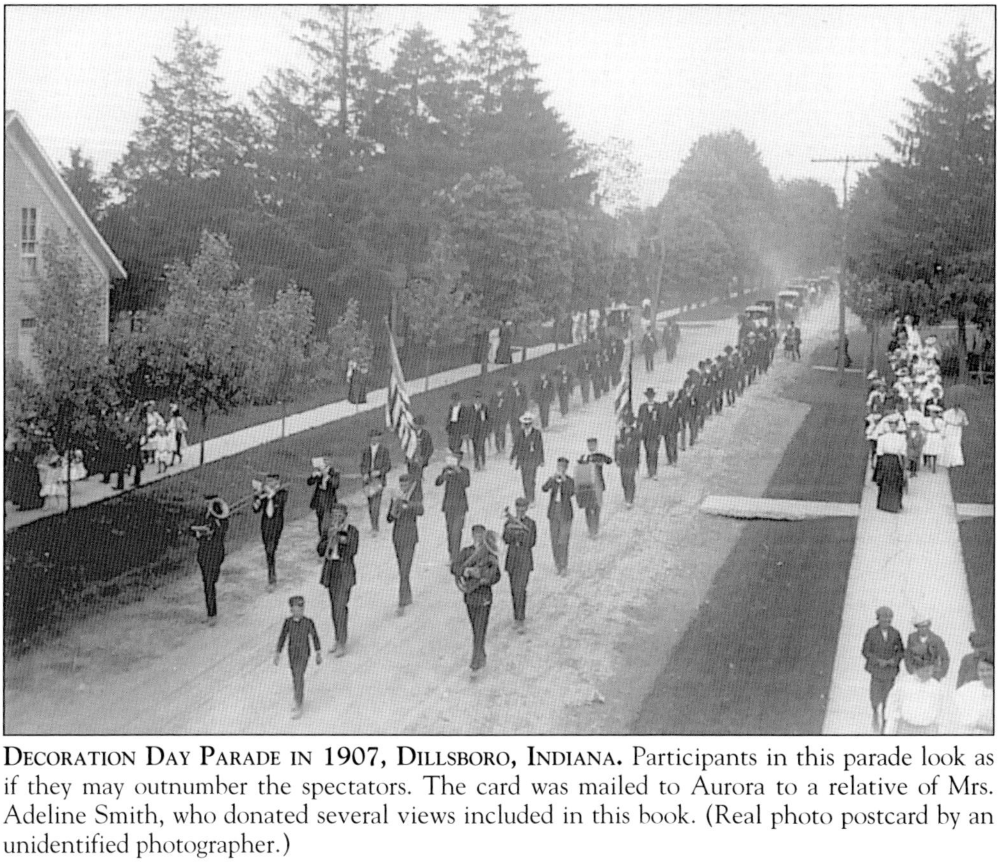

Decoration Day Parade in 1907, Dillsboro, Indiana. Participants in this parade look as if they may outnumber the spectators. The card was mailed to Aurora to a relative of Mrs. Adeline Smith, who donated several views included in this book. (Real photo postcard by an unidentified photographer.)

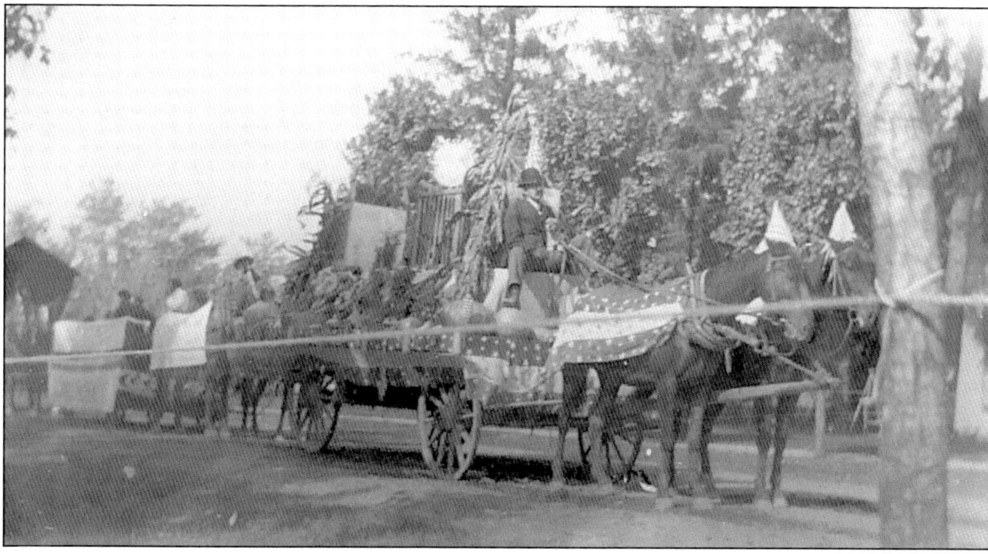

Parade Entry, Dillsboro, Indiana. These parade entries were probably lined up to participate in one of the early Dillsboro Farmer's Fall Festivals that started in 1906. (Real photo postcard by an unidentified photographer.)

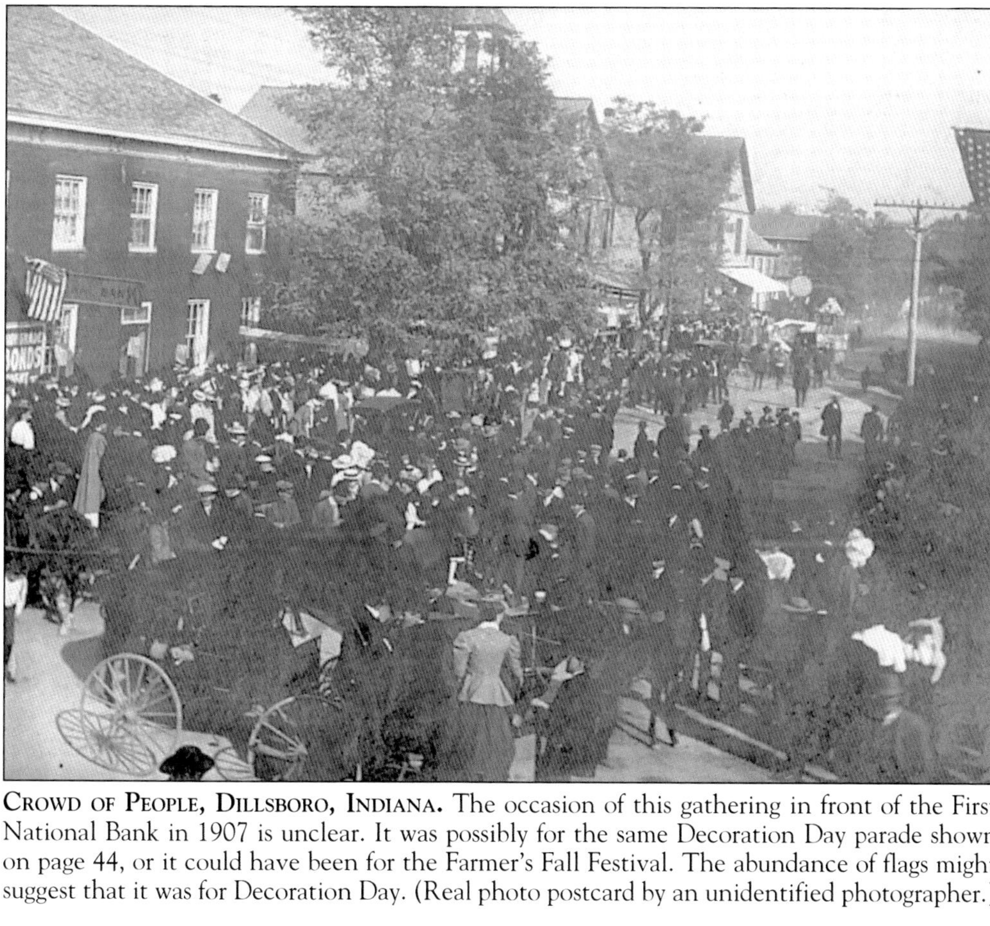

Crowd of People, Dillsboro, Indiana. The occasion of this gathering in front of the First National Bank in 1907 is unclear. It was possibly for the same Decoration Day parade shown on page 44, or it could have been for the Farmer's Fall Festival. The abundance of flags might suggest that it was for Decoration Day. (Real photo postcard by an unidentified photographer.)

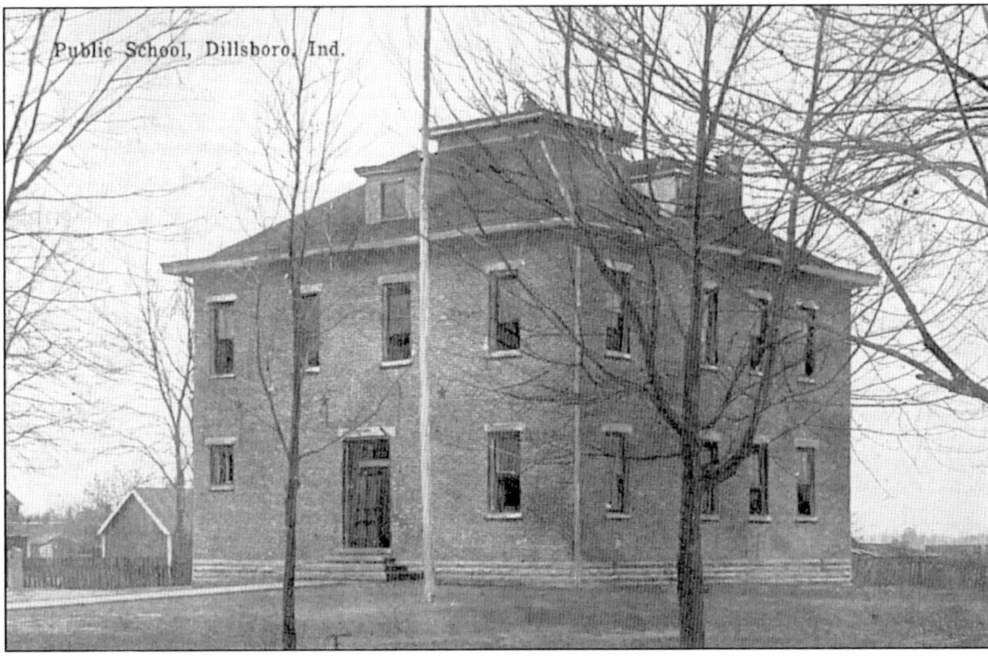

PUBLIC SCHOOL, DILLSBORO, INDIANA. Also called School #2, this building was located on the site of the current city hall and firehouse. The 1921 postmark on the back of this card indicates that it was mailed just one year before construction started on a new high school building. (Published by G.A. Triplett.)

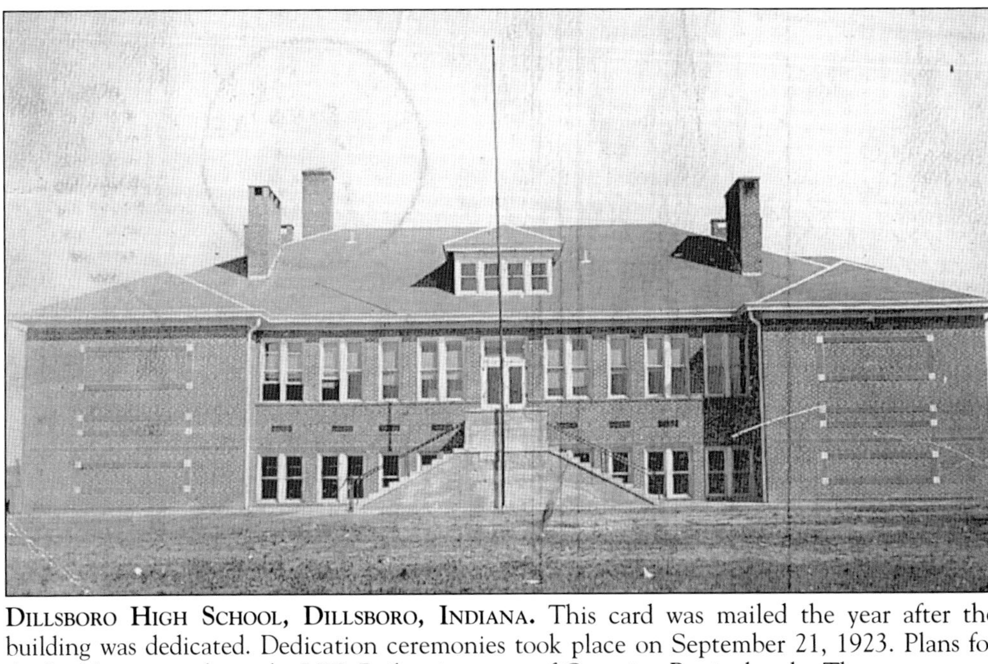

DILLSBORO HIGH SCHOOL, DILLSBORO, INDIANA. This card was mailed the year after the building was dedicated. Dedication ceremonies took place on September 21, 1923. Plans for the building were drawn by J.W. Bailey, in a sort of Georgian Revival style. The cornerstone was laid on September 28, 1922. In 1990, the contents of the cornerstone box were removed when construction on a new building was started. (Unidentified publisher.)

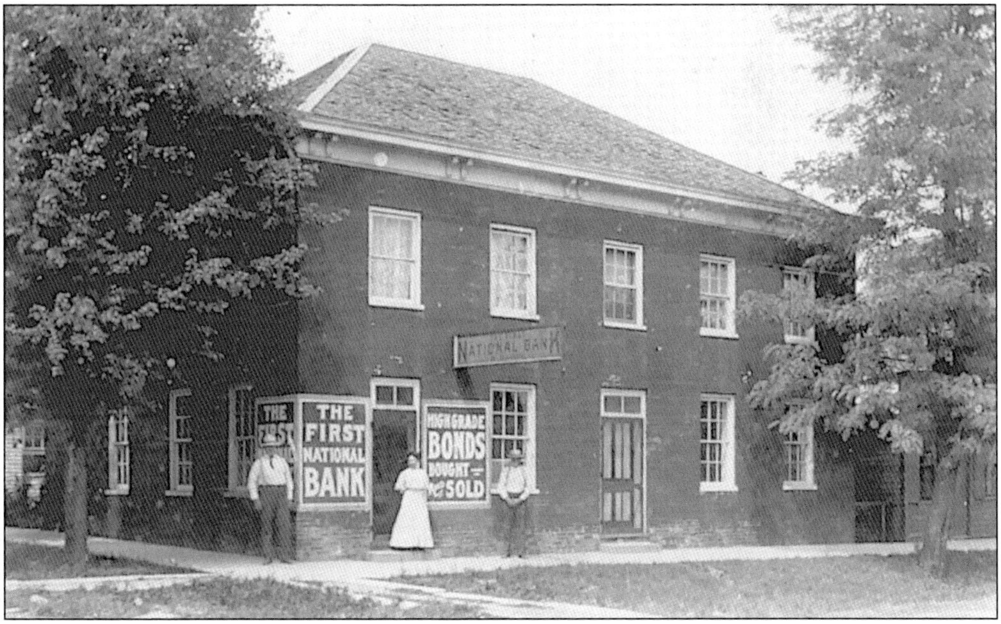

First National Bank, Dillsboro, Indiana. This card was postmarked in 1909. Officers of the bank at the time were: W.J. Gray, president; John R. Woods, cashier; and Margaret Hess, assistant cashier. Directors were Henry Schulte, T.D. Blue, J.H. Fisse, William Ohlmanseik, Henry Vinup, F.W. Kamman, Henry Marlman Jr., and John W. Woods. (Real photo postcard by an unidentified photographer.)

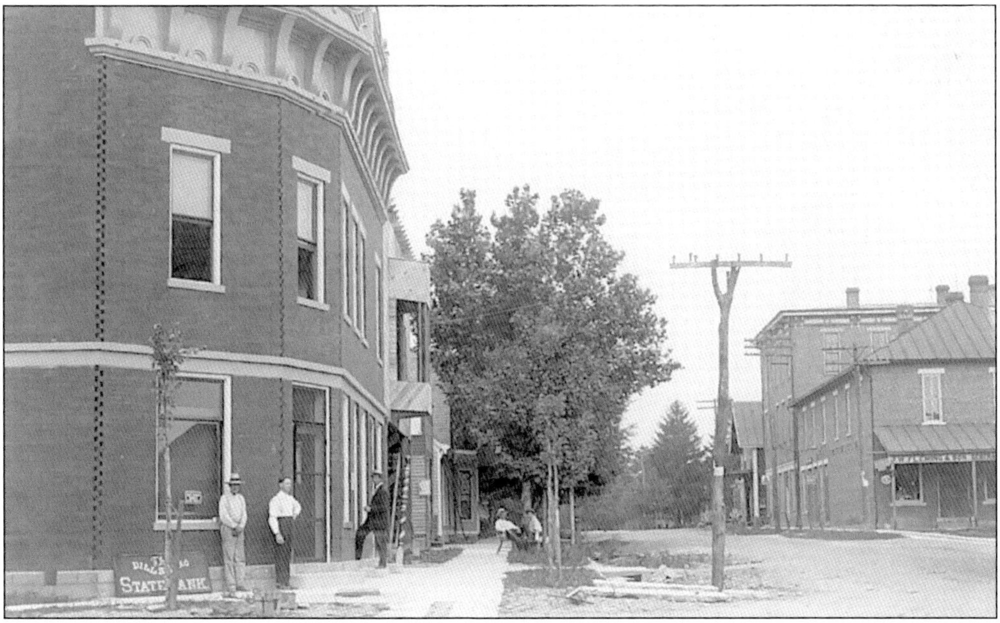

The Dillsboro State Bank. An advertisement for this bank in the 1908 Dearborn County Directory declared a capital stock of $25,000. Also in 1908, Henry Bulthaup was listed as president and Jesse J. Booster as cashier. The bank was located on North Street. J.W. Fleming's store is visible on the right side of the street, facing toward the cameraman. (Real photo postcard by an unidentified photographer.)

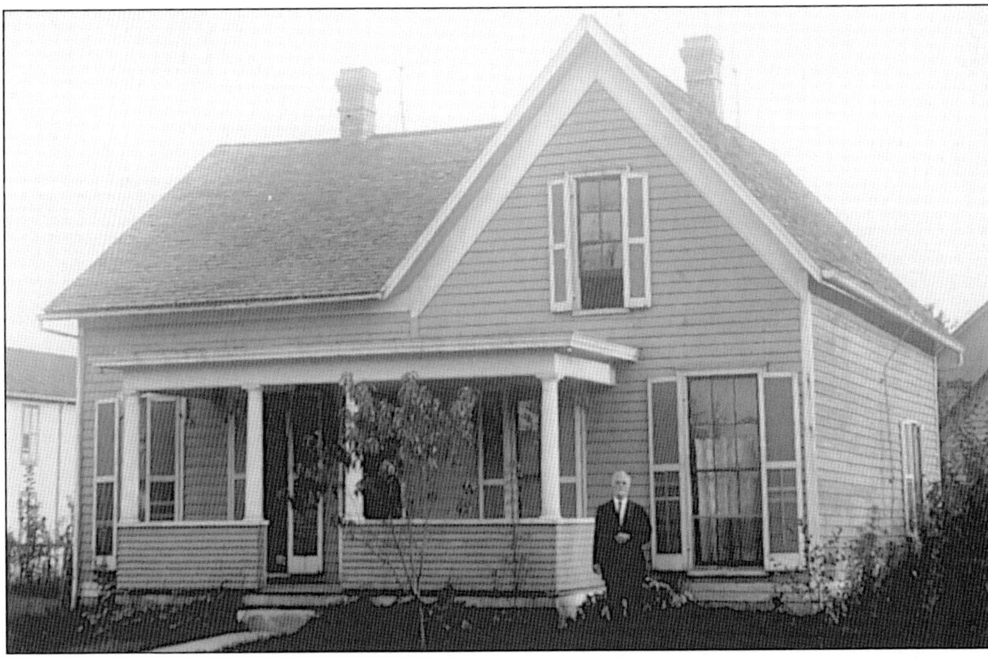

Evangelical Lutheran Church Parsonage, Dillsboro, Indiana. The original location of this structure was on old Highway #50, or North Street. It was moved to Lenover Street, c. 1930, by Harry Smith, who purchased the house from the church. In 1979 it was destroyed by fire. (Real photo postcard by an unidentified photographer.)

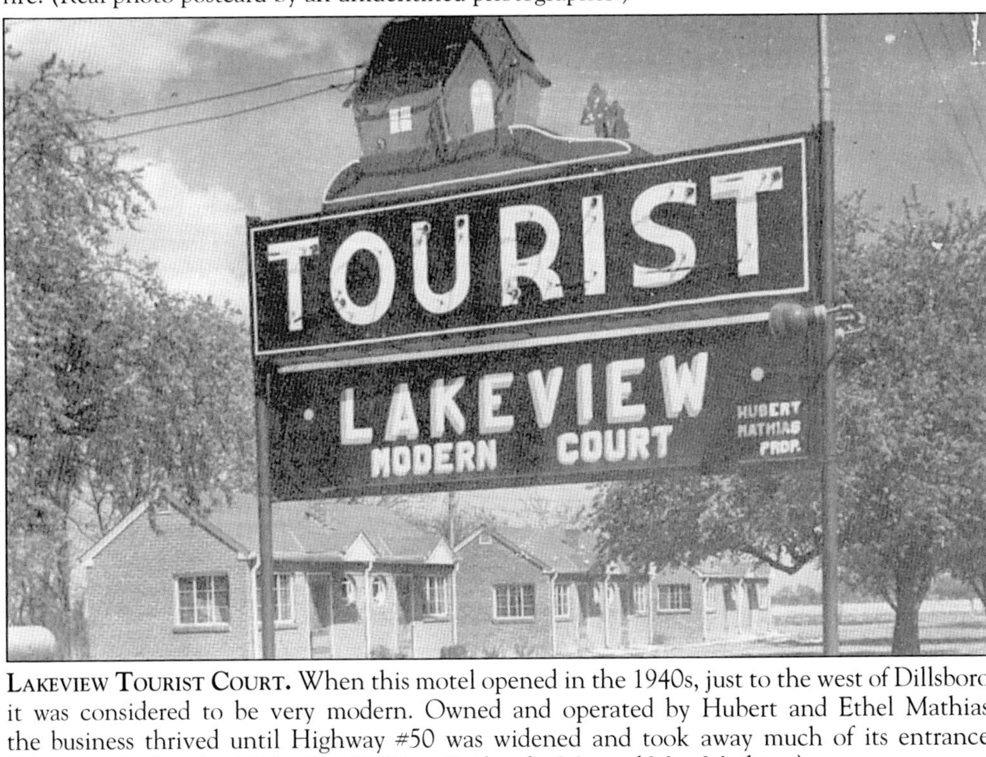

Lakeview Tourist Court. When this motel opened in the 1940s, just to the west of Dillsboro, it was considered to be very modern. Owned and operated by Hubert and Ethel Mathias, the business thrived until Highway #50 was widened and took away much of its entrance. (Photographed and published by William Krider, for Mr. and Mrs. Mathias.)

STREET SCENE, DILLSBORO, INDIANA. This 1907 postmarked picture shows the south side of North Street. In the foreground is Mulford's Blacksmith Shop. It was located where the post office now stands. Next to the blacksmith shop is the Masonic Lodge Building, which housed the Helms Drug Company at the time of the photograph. Apartments were housed in the upper floors of these buildings at the time of this picture, as indicated by the person that sent this card to Michigan. She mentions living "over the store." (Real photo postcard by an unidentified photographer.)

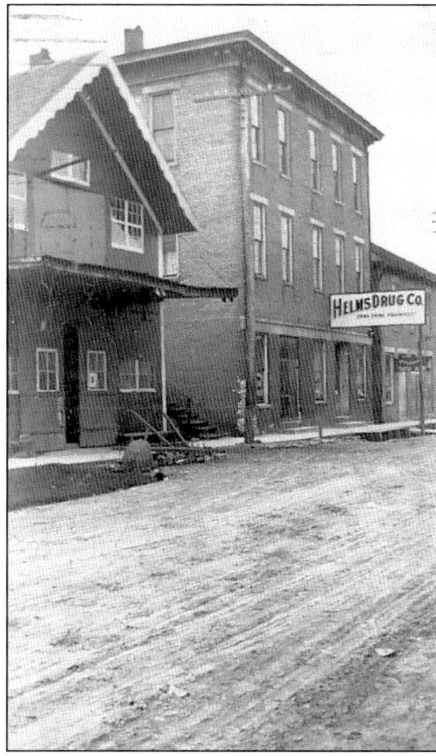

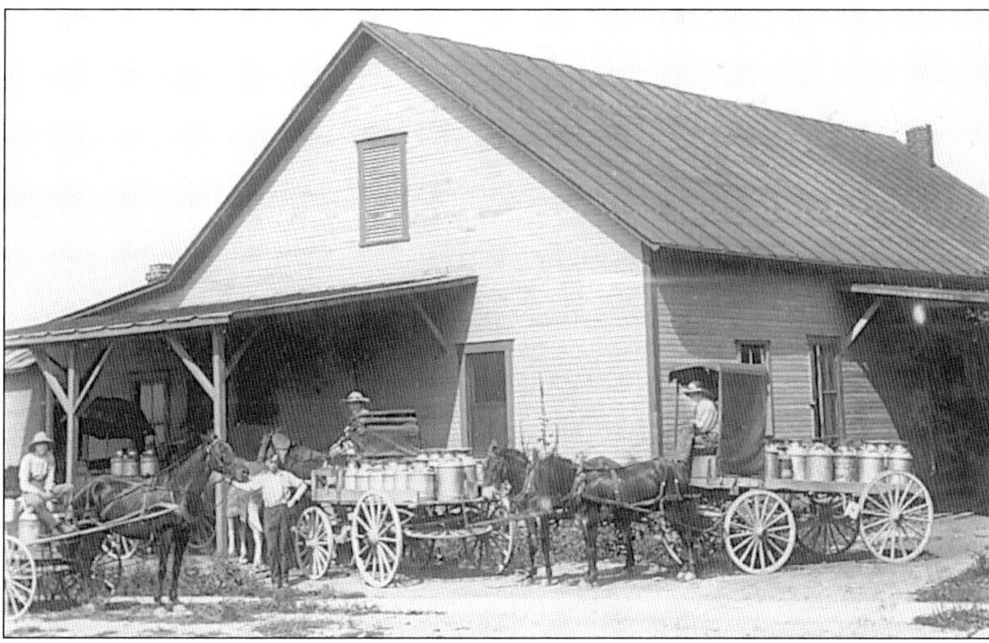

UNIDENTIFIED STORE. This store reportedly belonged to George Niemeyer at one time. It sold flour, feed, and, as indicated by the cans on the wagon, milk. Niemeyer's store was located on Highway #62, near the present site of the Dillsboro Elementary School. The card was not mailed, so the date of the photograph is unknown. (Real photo postcard by an unidentified photographer.)

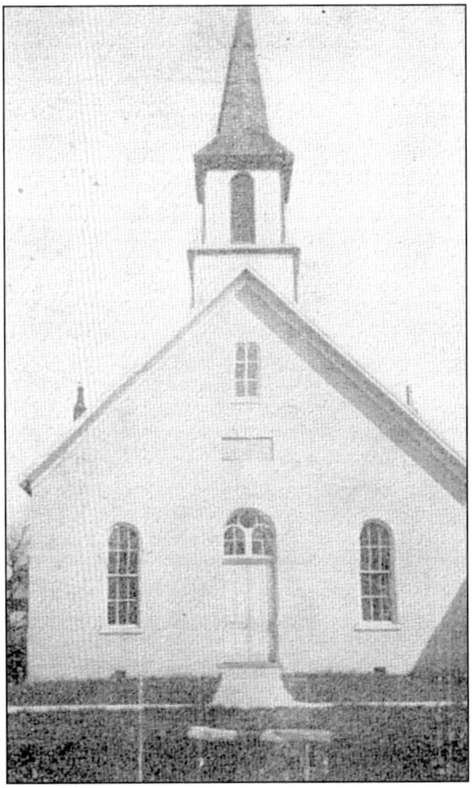

St. Peters Lutheran Church. The Saint Peters Lutheran Church is pictured in this photograph before it was remodeled into the building shown on the opposite page. Original construction on the building, completed in 1876, was in the Romanesque Revival style of architecture. It was constructed using wooden frames. In the first hundred years of the church's existence, it was served by 19 different pastors. (Unidentified printer and publisher.)

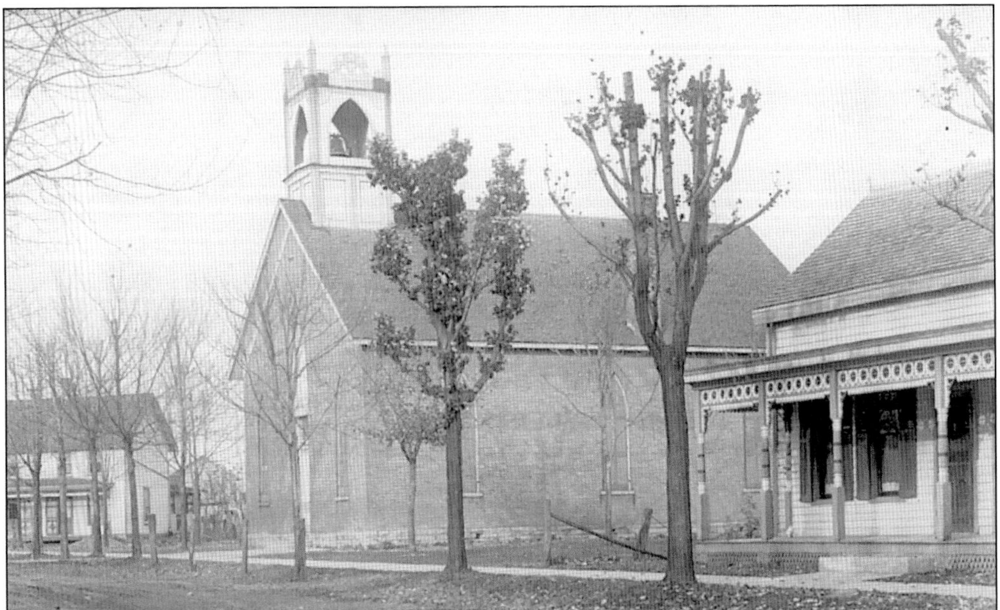

Methodist Church, Dillsboro, Indiana. The Gothic Revival-style building shown in this photograph was completed in 1871. It is located on Front Street and replaced an earlier 1838 building used by the Methodists on the same location. (Real photo postcard by an unidentified photographer.)

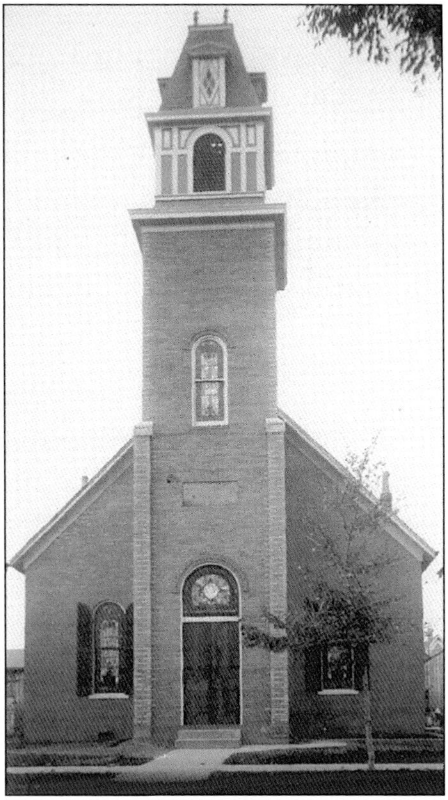

St. Peters Lutheran Church. In 1911, the building shown on the facing page was bricked over and remodeled into the building pictured here. Except for a few paint color changes and other minor cosmetic differences, the building remains today much as it is here. The building is located at 12963 North Street, Dillsboro, Indiana. (Real photo postcard by an unidentified photographer.)

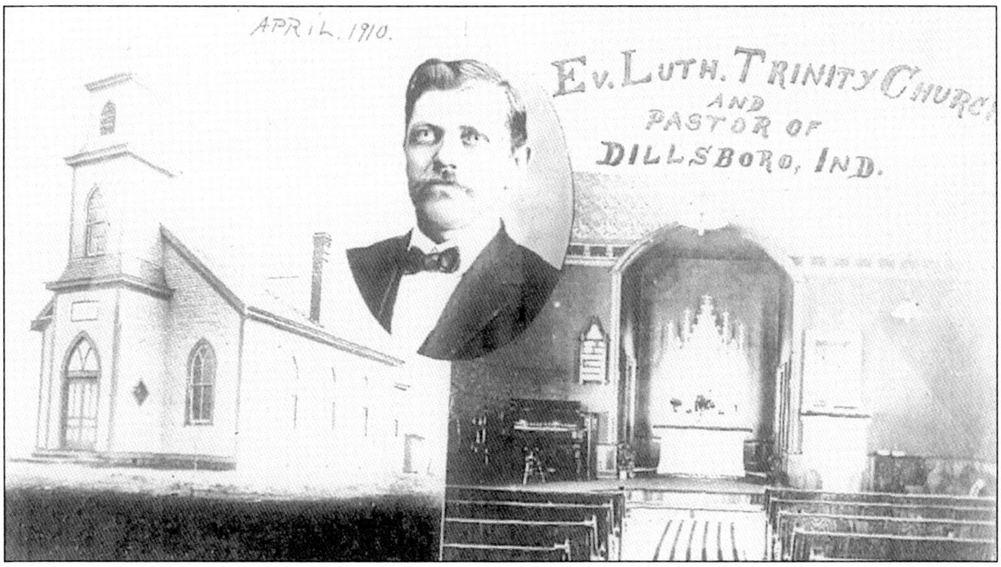

Evangelical Lutheran Trinity Church and Pastor, Dillsboro, Indiana. Produced in 1910, this card shows the building shortly after its dedication on December 5, 1909. The pastor, Reverend E. Herzberg, ministered to the congregation from 1909 to 1914. The building was erected at a cost of $3,000. It has now been replaced by a new building on Central Avenue. (Real photo postcard by an unidentified photographer.)

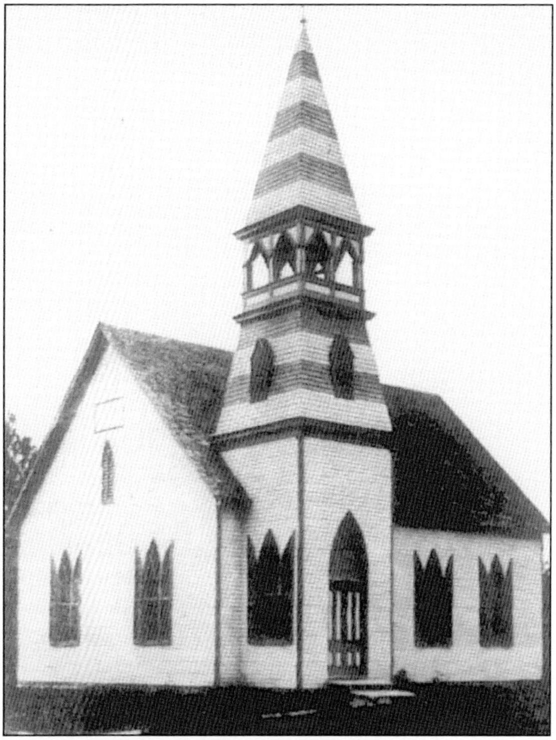

Hopewell Presbyterian Church. Located at 12644 North Street, Dillsboro, Indiana, the building of the Hopewell Presbyterian Church was completed in 1888 and dedicated on April 22nd. The architectural style of the building is Gothic Revival. Only minor changes in the building's appearance have taken place in the 111 years of its use. (Real photo postcard by an unidentified photographer.)

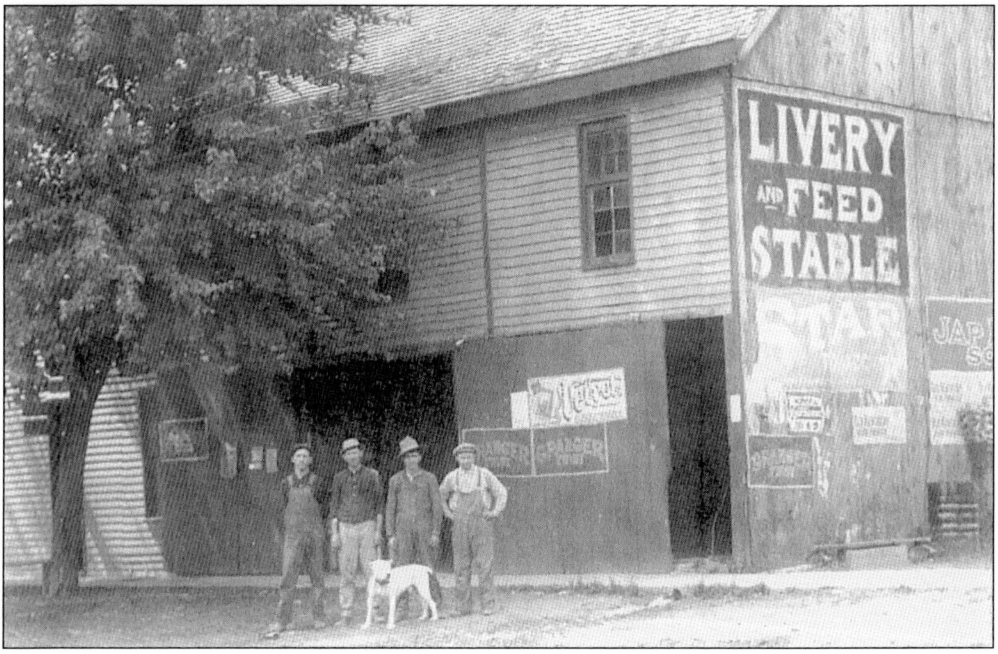

Niebrugge Livery Stable, Dillsboro, Indiana. Charles F. Niebrugge operated this business at the corner of North Street and Western Row. His advertisement in the 1908 Dearborn County Directory promotes Livery and Feed stables as well as the selling of coal. It also mentions that he gave "Special Attention to Commercial Men." Niebrugge later sold the business to Chub Berner. (Real photo postcard by an unidentified photographer.)

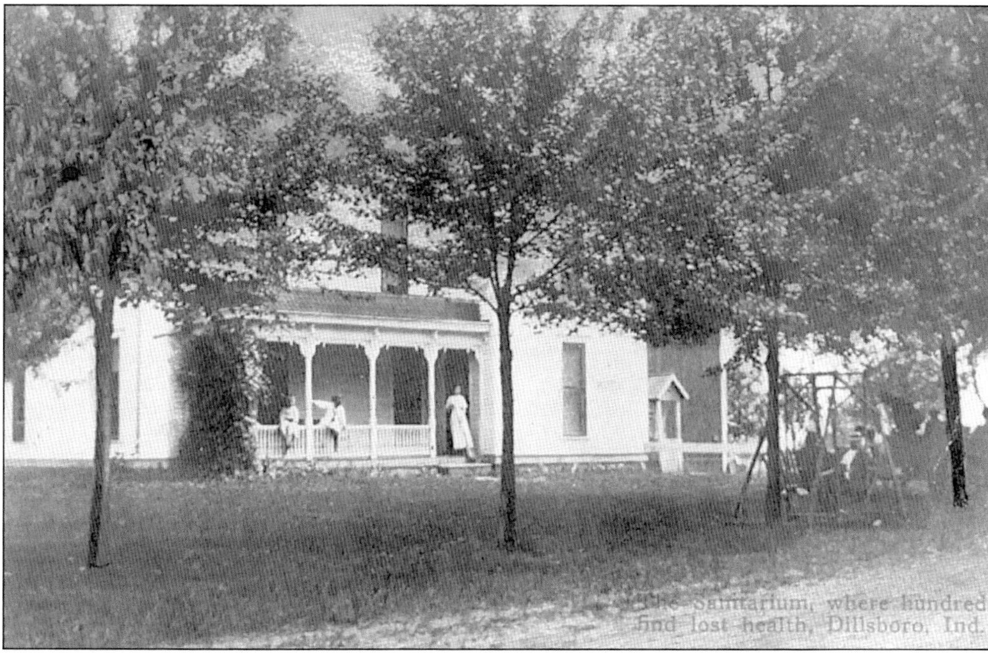

THE SANITARIUM, WHERE HUNDREDS FIND LOST HEALTH, DILLSBORO, INDIANA. The first site of the Dillsboro Sanitarium was in a house on Lenover Street owned by Dr. A.G. Miller. The discovery of water at this site was made shortly after attempts to drill for a gas well in 1905 failed. (Unidentified printer and publisher.)

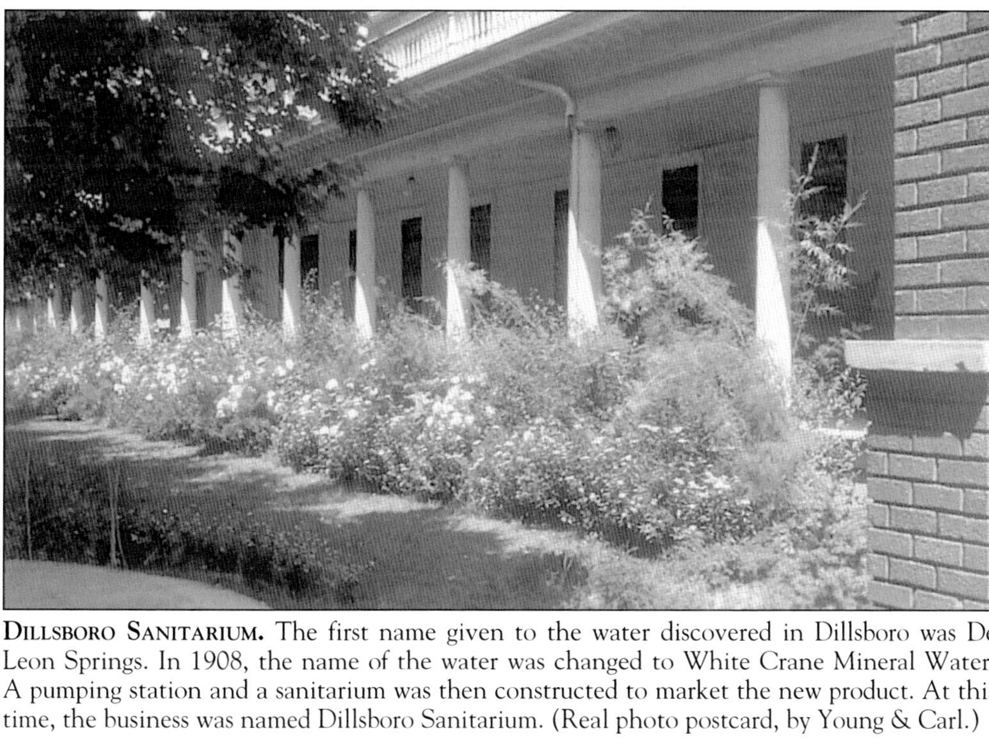

DILLSBORO SANITARIUM. The first name given to the water discovered in Dillsboro was De Leon Springs. In 1908, the name of the water was changed to White Crane Mineral Water. A pumping station and a sanitarium was then constructed to market the new product. At this time, the business was named Dillsboro Sanitarium. (Real photo postcard, by Young & Carl.)

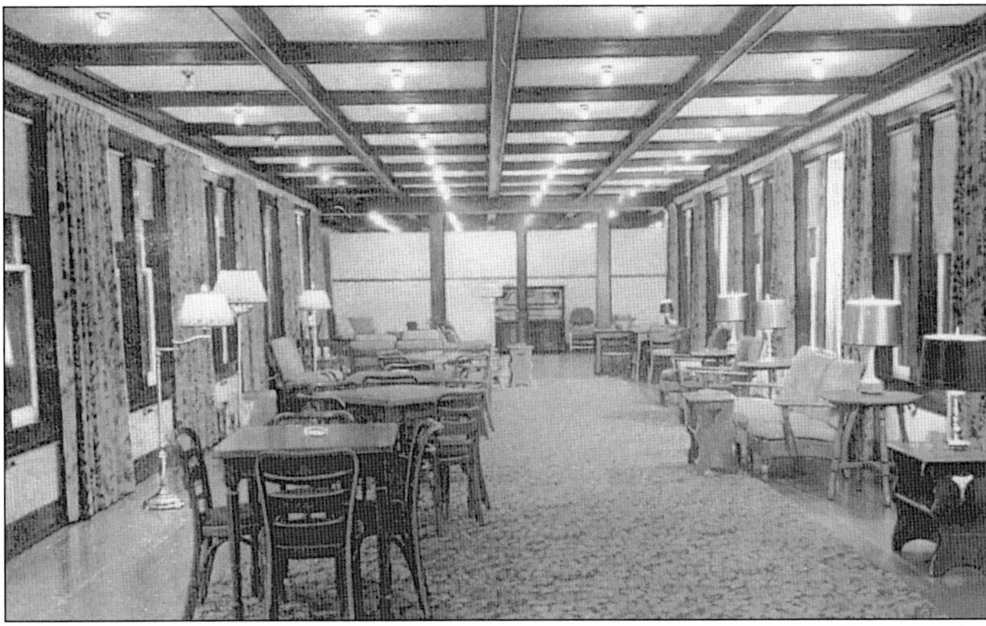

Solarium, Dillsboro Health Resort. As the sanitarium business prospered, the need to expand the business became necessary. In 1922, a larger structure was added on to the old building. It was a mostly-brick structure. In the late 1930s, the name was changed from Dillsboro Sanitarium to Dillsboro Health Resort. (Produced by Curt Teich Co., Chicago, Illinois, for the Dillsboro Health Resort.)

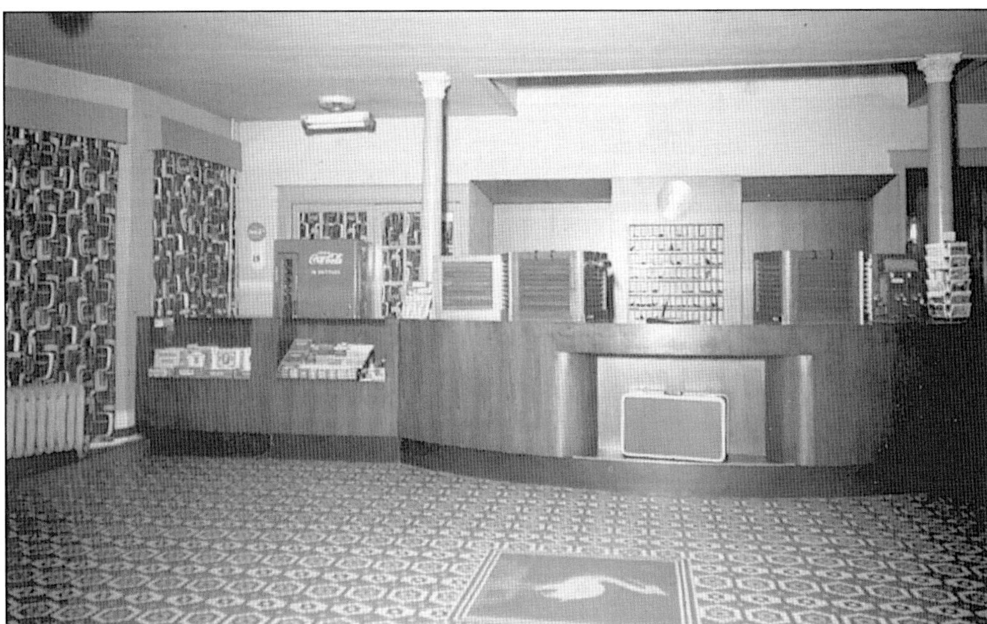

Lobby, Dillsboro Health Resort. This more modern, standard-sized chrome postcard was produced *c.* 1955, after Dellas Ross became the manager. In 1965, mineral baths were ceased, and the property became a nursing home. (Produced by W.M. Cline Co., Chattanooga, Tennessee—color photograph by Frank Shannon, for the Dillsboro Health Resort.)

Three

Greendale

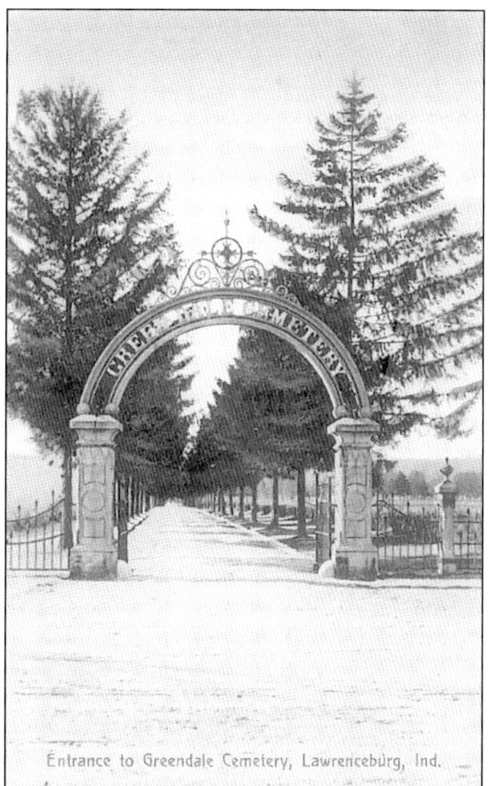

Entrance to Greendale Cemetery. Shortly after the Greendale Cemetery Association was formed in 1866, Benjamin Grove, an engineer from Louisville, Kentucky, was hired to draw plans for a cemetery. In 1867, landscape planning was done by a Mr. Ihle. The entrance gate pictured above was originally planned for the Ridge-Avenue entrance. At some later date the gate was moved to the Nowlin-Avenue entrance, where it now remains. (Produced by Kraemer Art Co., Cincinnati and Berlin.)

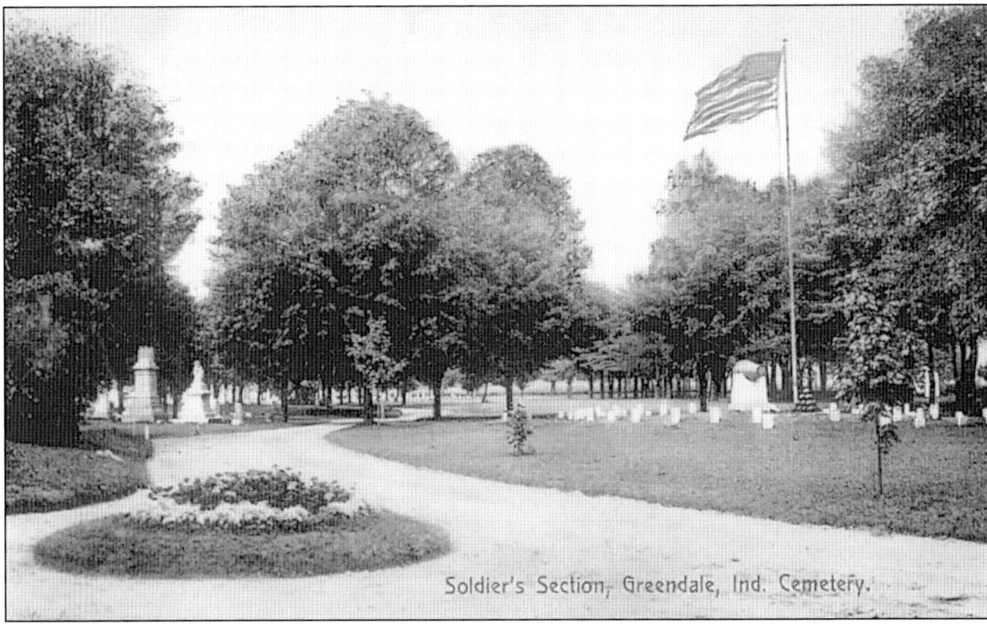

SOLDIER'S SECTION, GREENDALE, INDIANA CEMETERY. The first burial to take place in Greendale Cemetery was that of Hugh F. Smith, in section A on September 19, 1867. He was the first of 48 burials to take place in 1867. To date, nearly 13,000 burials have been made in the cemetery. (Produced by Kraemer Art Co., Cincinnati and Berlin, Germany.)

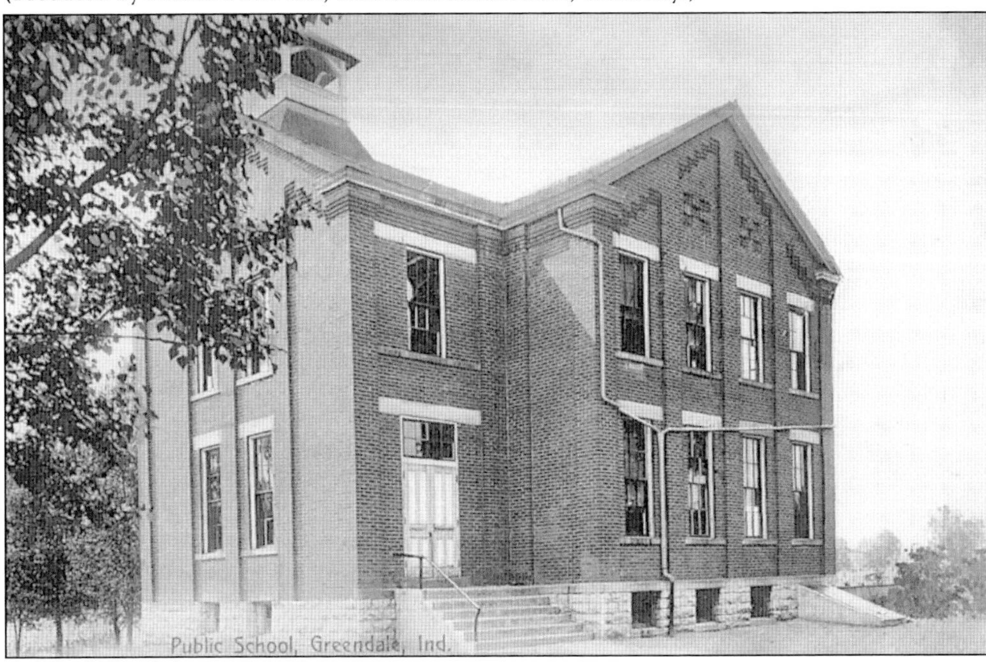

PUBLIC SCHOOL, GREENDALE, INDIANA. When constructed in 1870, this school building, commonly referred to as Homestead School, was a part of the county school system. Dorman Avenue, where the building was located, was later incorporated into Greendale. This building was replaced by a new building that was completed in 1917, from plans by Cincinnati architect Martin Fisher. (Produced by Kraemer Art Co., Cincinnati and Berlin, Germany.)

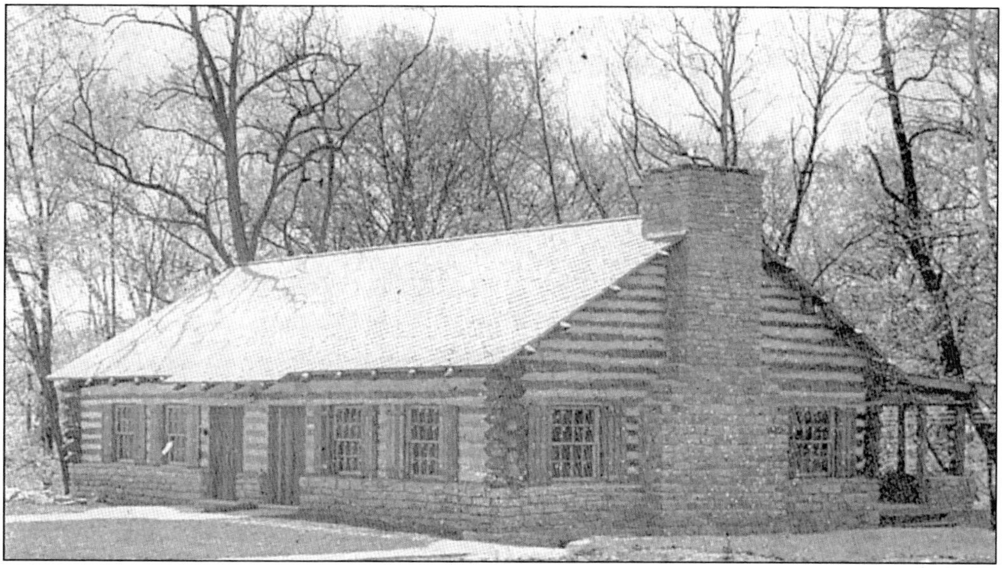

Cabin, Greendale Park. Dedicated on May 4, 1941, by Governor Henry F. Schricker, the cabin in Greendale Park was erected through the efforts of the Town of Greendale and the Lawrenceburg Conservation Club. The 1942 postmarked card pictured above was used to announce a meeting date of the Conservation Club. (Unidentified printer and publisher.)

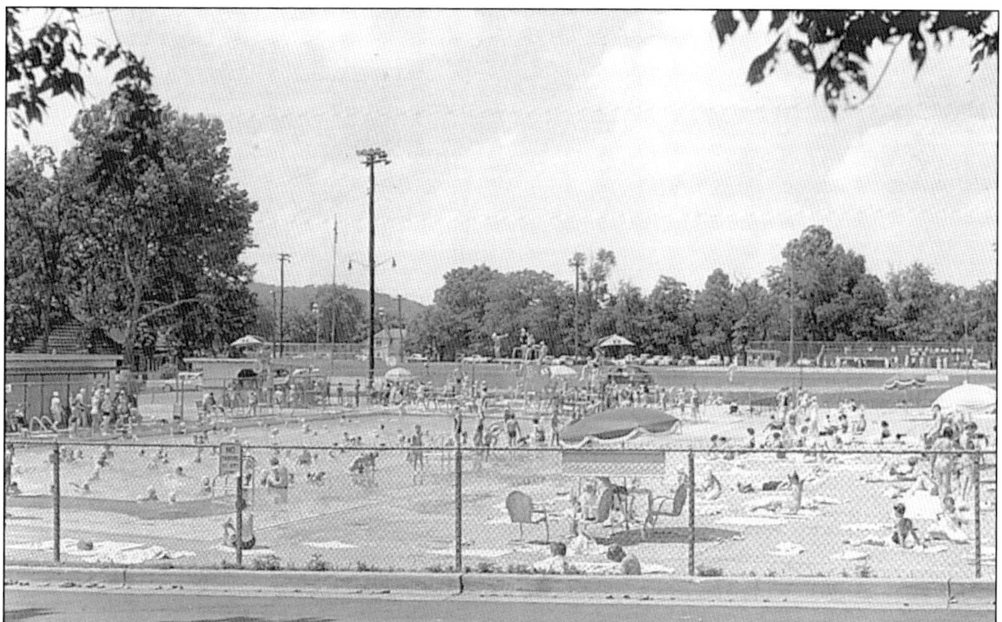

Recreation Center, Greendale Park. The pool in Greendale Park was dedicated on the fourth of July in 1950. The dedication ceremony included a 7:30 p.m. parade headed by the American Legion Color Guard and followed by Smittie's Band. After the parade and the dedication address, entertainment was provided by two swimming groups. (Photographed and published by FasFoto, Inc., Cincinnati, Ohio.)

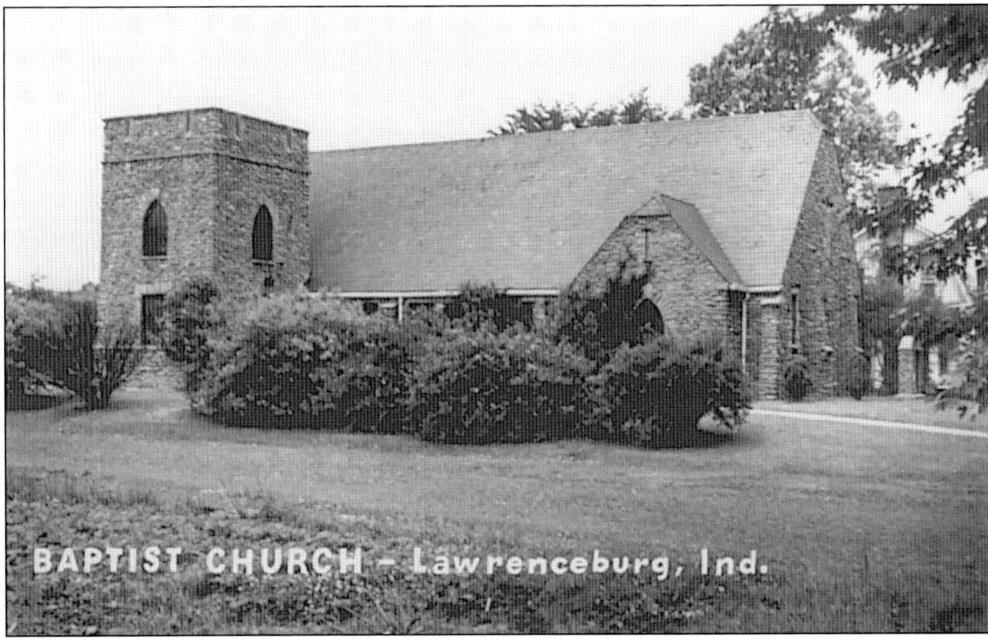

BAPTIST CHURCH, LAWRENCEBURG, INDIANA. This photograph shows the first of three phases of construction, just after completion of the first phase in 1938. Cincinnati architect F. William Bertsch drew the plans. The architectural style is English Provincial, but native stone was used in the building's construction. It was dedicated on May 29, 1938. (Real photo postcard by an unidentified photographer.)

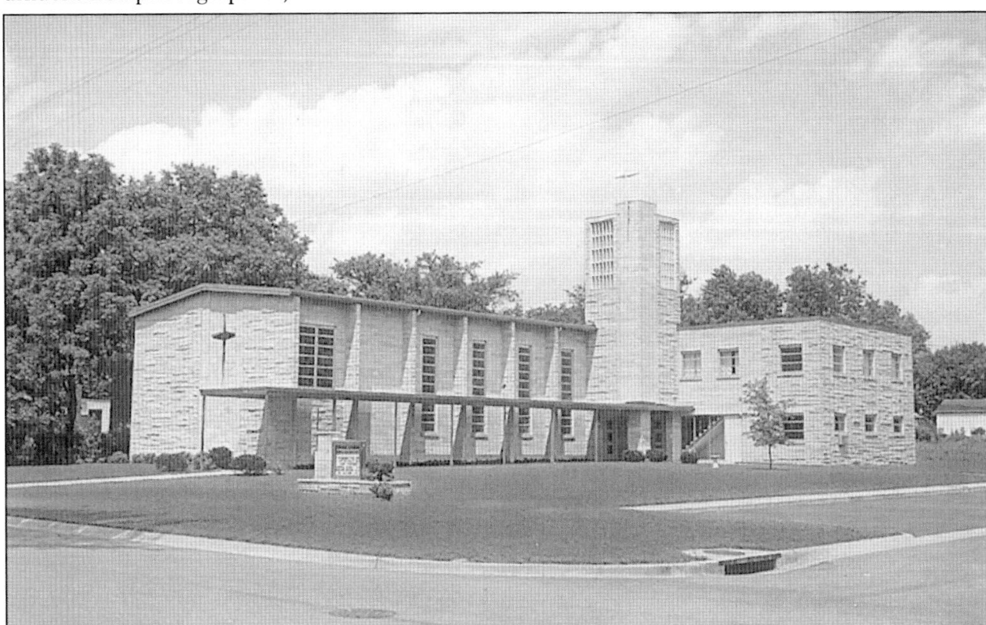

EMANUEL LUTHERAN CHURCH, GREENDALE. This standard-size chrome postcard was produced in the late 1950s to show the Lutheran Church recently completed in 1955. The building was designed by Arends & Arends of Cincinnati. It cost $66,000 to build. (Photographed and published by FasFoto, Inc., Cincinnati, Ohio.)

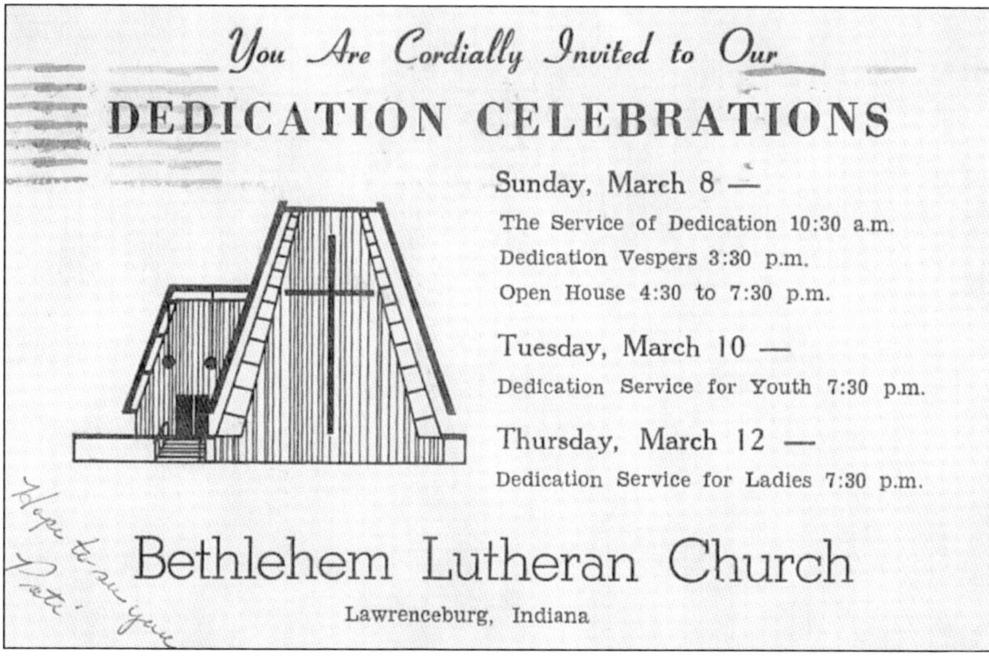

BETHLEHEM LUTHERAN CHURCH. Announcement postcards for various events have been common throughout the history of postcards. This card was produced for the 1970 dedication celebrations of the Bethlehem Church at 495 Ludlow Street. It is typical, in that most announcement cards were printed inexpensively with one color of ink. (Unidentified publisher, for the Bethlehem Lutheran Church.)

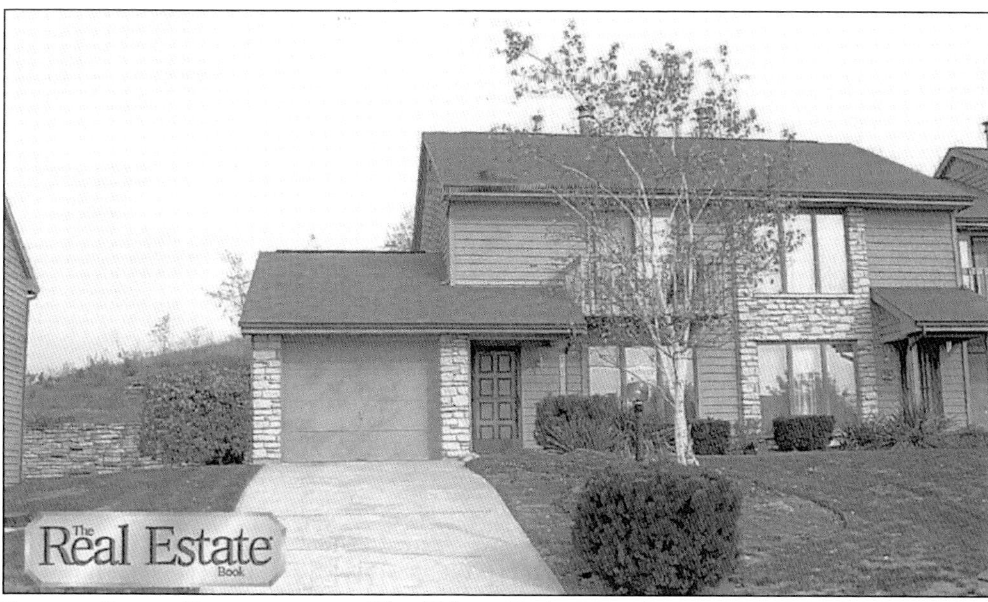

FALCON RIDGE CONDOMINIUMS. The Falcon Ridge Condominiums were the first major condominium development in Dearborn County. They were constructed in phases from 1984 through 1996 by Rupel Development Corporation. The 1998 card shown here is a computer-generated card sent out to indicate inclusion in a real estate sales book (The Real Estate Book, unidentified photographer.)

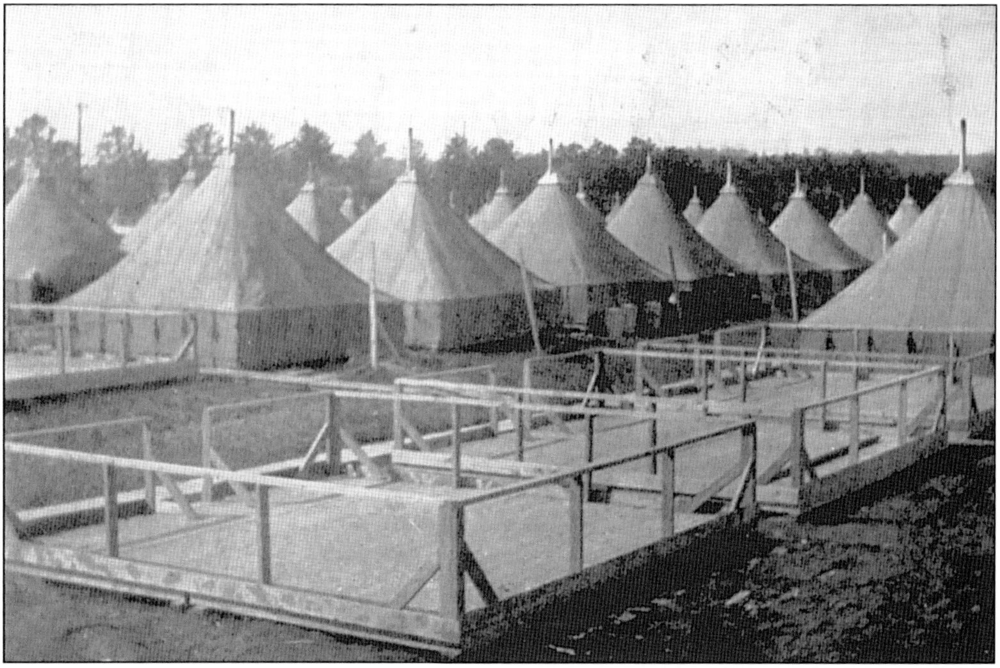

Tent City, Greendale, Indiana. Erected and operated by the Red Cross for the refugees who lost their homes during the flood of 1937, this tent city was located on Ridge Avenue near the entrance to the Greendale Cemetery. At one point the "city" consisted of nearly four hundred tents and wooden buildings. (Probably photographed and published by M.O. Whitney.)

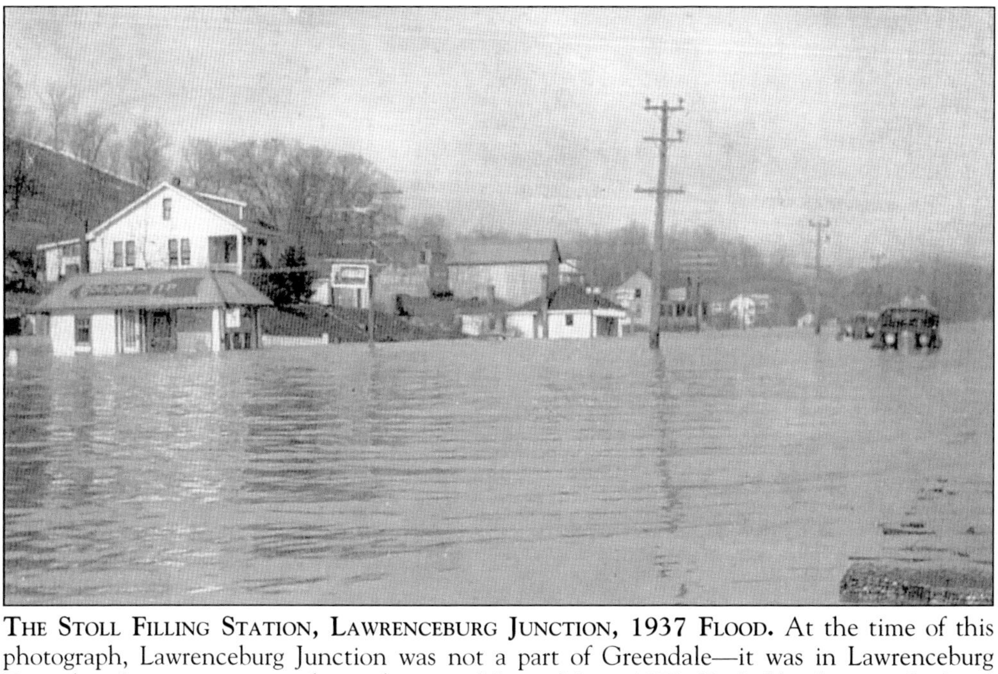

The Stoll Filling Station, Lawrenceburg Junction, 1937 Flood. At the time of this photograph, Lawrenceburg Junction was not a part of Greendale—it was in Lawrenceburg Township. It was incorporated into the city of Greendale in 1997. (Probably photographed and published by M.O. Whitney.)

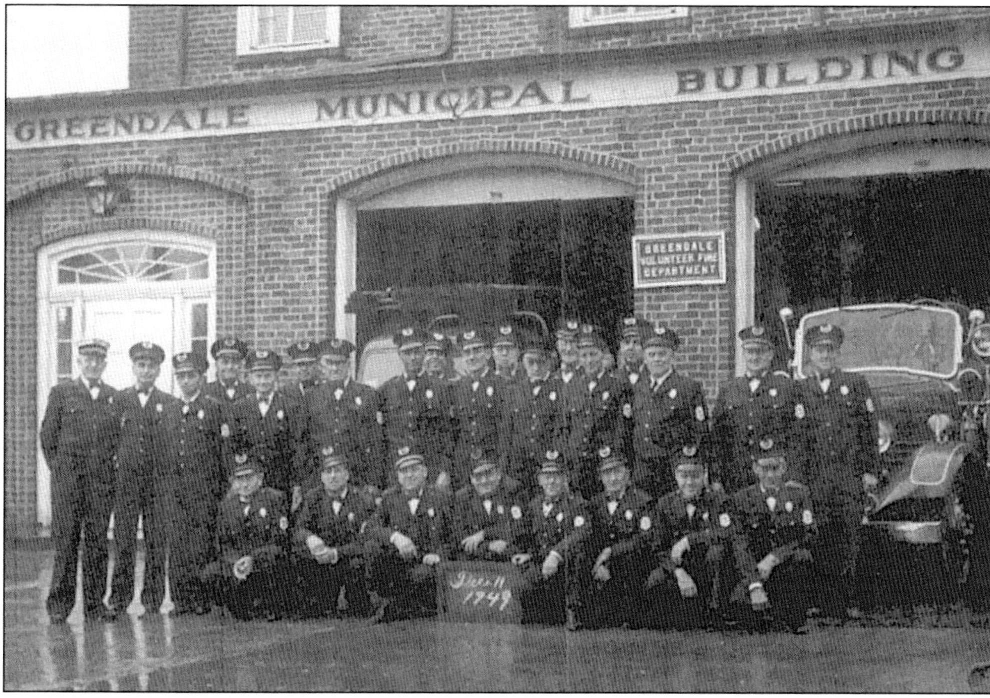

FIRE DEPARTMENT AND GREENDALE MUNICIPAL BUILDING. In 1915, when the Greendale Fire Department was first formed, they did not have a building to house their fire-fighting equipment—they used space at one of the local distilleries. In 1936, the building shown in this picture was constructed to house the municipal fire and police departments. (Real photo postcard by an unidentified photographer.)

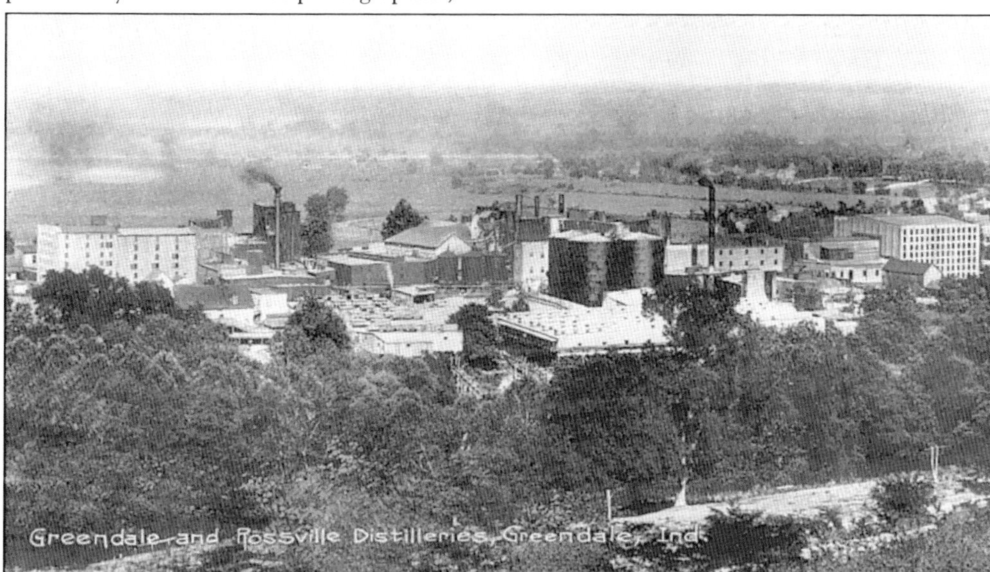

GREENDALE AND ROSSVILLE DISTILLERIES. Taken from Ludlow Hill, this after-the-turn-of-the-century view shows the plants of the Greendale Distilling Company on the left, and the Rossville Distilling Company on the right. Both plants were later sold out to other business interests. (Produced by Kraemer Art Co., Cincinnati and Berlin, Germany.)

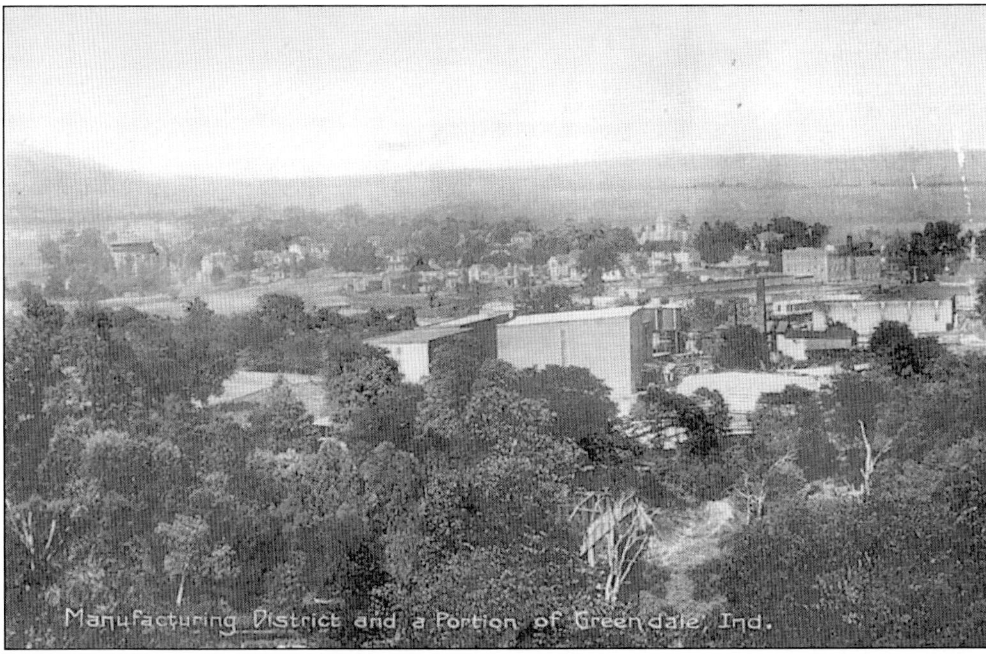

MANUFACTURING DISTRICT AND PORTION OF GREENDALE, INDIANA. Stephen Ludlow planned the community of Greendale in 1852. At first, development was slow. Only a few manufacturing structures and a sparse sprinkling of residences constituted the town. By the early 1900s, however, the town took off and grew rapidly. When the postcard above was made, the town was a thriving community with several large manufacturing plants and many large residences. (Produced by Kraemer Art Co., Cincinnati and Berlin, Germany.)

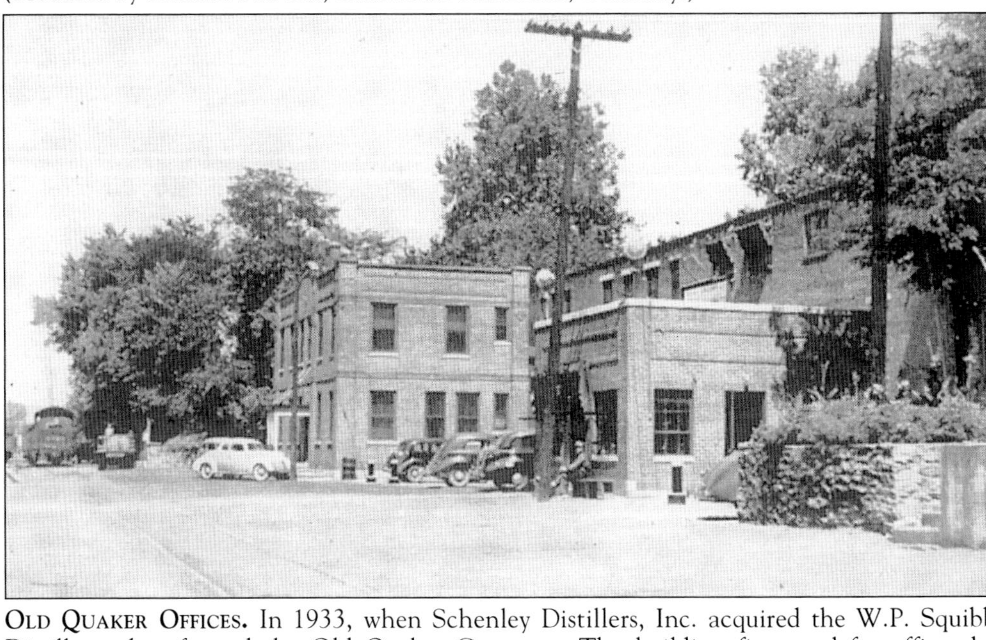

OLD QUAKER OFFICES. In 1933, when Schenley Distillers, Inc. acquired the W.P. Squibb Distillery, they formed the Old Quaker Company. The building first used for offices by the new company is shown in the above postcard. (Published by the Whitney Studio, Lawrenceburg, Indiana.)

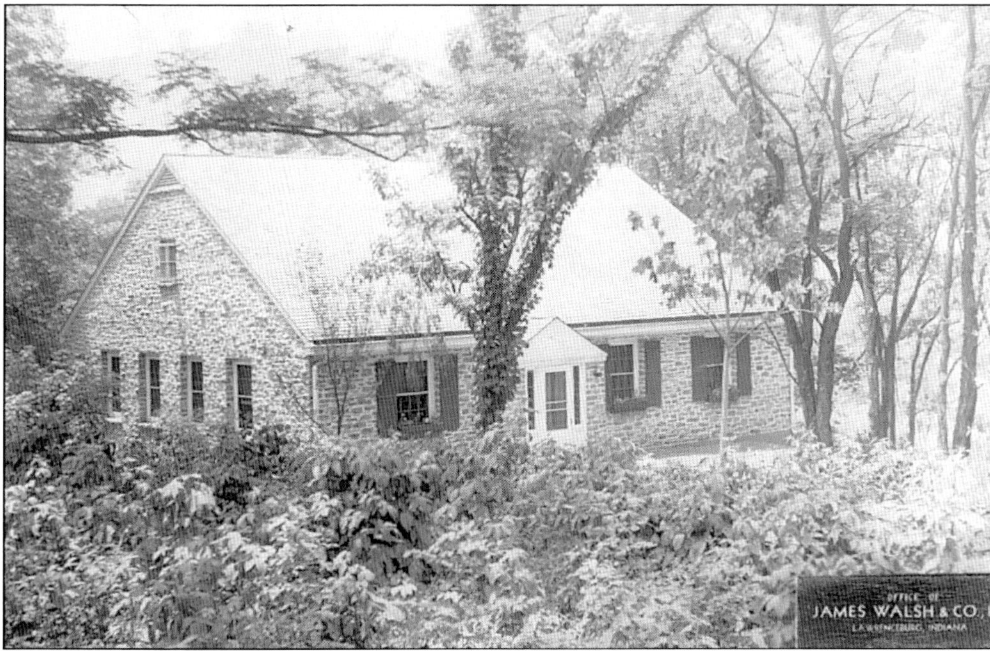

Office of James Walsh & Company, Inc. Used as a thank-you card to send to customers, the above postcard depicts the office building of James Walsh & Company of Lawrenceburg. The distillery, owned and operated by the O'Shaughnessy Brothers, maintained their offices at the end of Probasco Street in Greendale until 1965. (Real photo postcard by an unidentified photographer.)

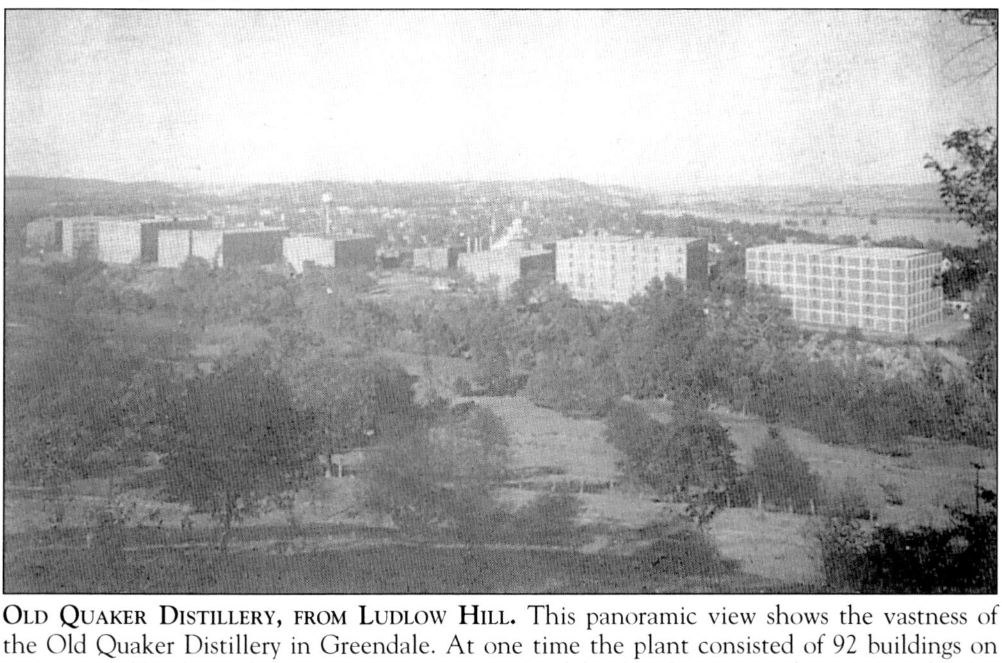

Old Quaker Distillery, from Ludlow Hill. This panoramic view shows the vastness of the Old Quaker Distillery in Greendale. At one time the plant consisted of 92 buildings on 226 acres of land. By the time operations in Greendale closed in September 1988, Schenley Distillers, Inc. was the fourth largest employer in Dearborn County. (Produced by Whitney Studio, Lawrenceburg, Indiana.)

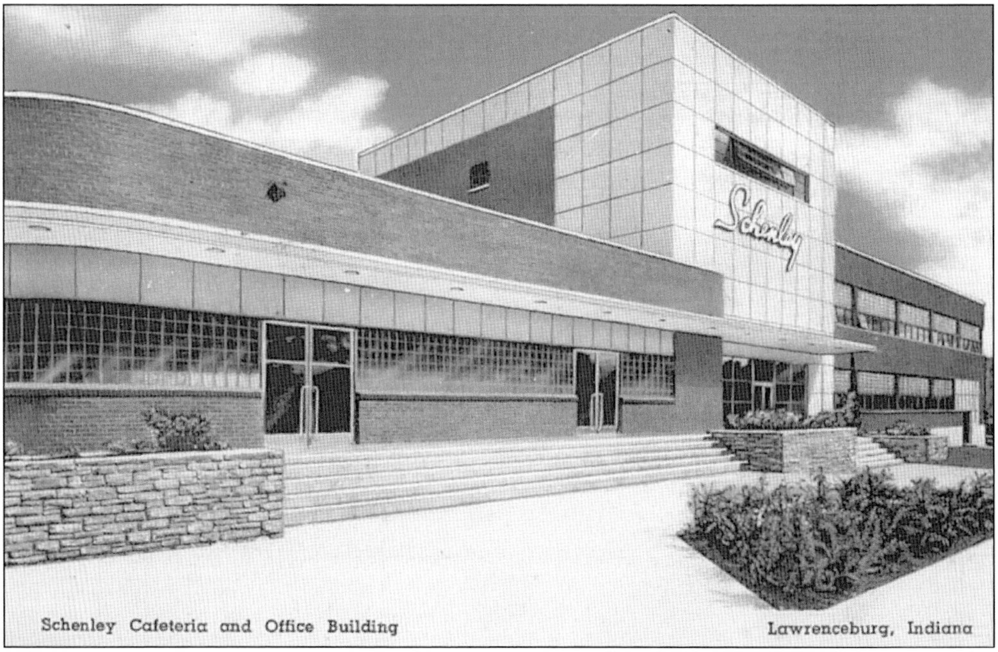

SCHENLEY CAFETERIA AND OFFICE BUILDING. Art Deco styling dominates this building on Mary Street, used as offices for Schenley Distillers, Inc. Plans for the building were drawn in 1946 by the firm of Carl J. Kiefer, Inc. of Cincinnati, Ohio. (Produced by Curt Teich & Company, Chicago, for Schenley Distillers, Inc.)

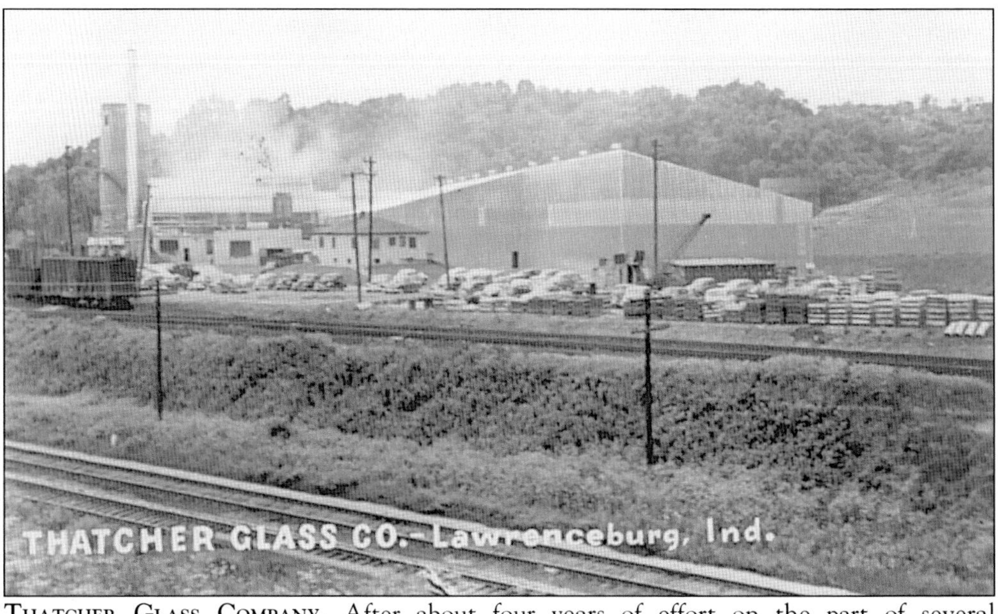

THATCHER GLASS COMPANY. After about four years of effort on the part of several Lawrenceburg city officials, ground was broken for this new plant in Greendale in 1950. On April 11, 1951, the first glass bottle was produced by the plant. In 1959, the plant was expanded; in 1986 the name changed to Diamond-Brathurst Inc.; and, in 1988, the name changed to Anchor Glass Container Company. (Real photo postcard by an unidentified photographer.)

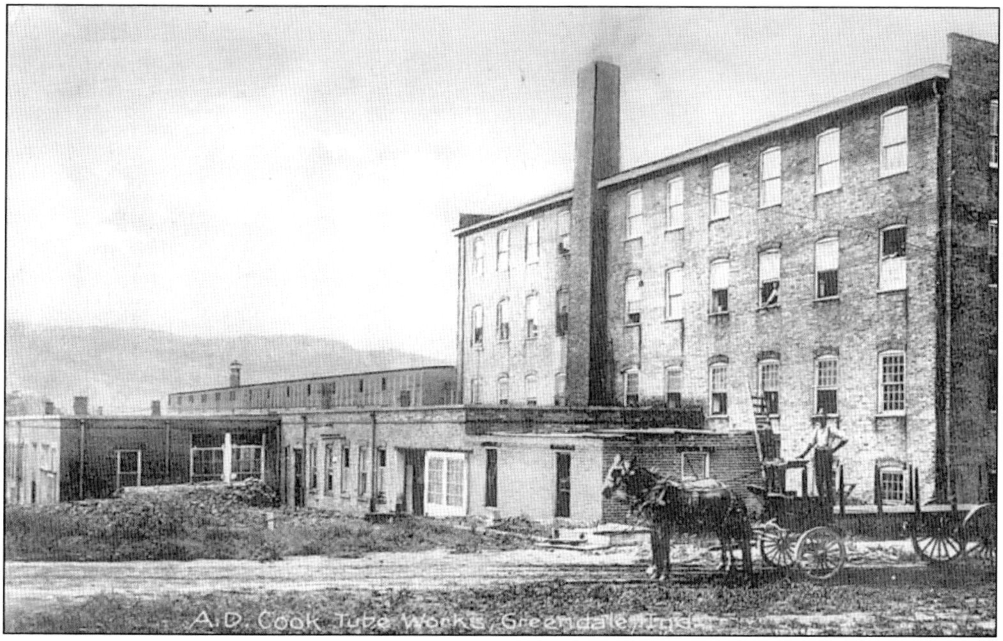

A.D. Cook Tube Works. August D. Cook, along with his father, started the Cook Well Pump Works factory in Lawrenceburg in 1870. After several expansions in three different Lawrenceburg locations, the plant moved to Greendale in 1901. In 1921, when the company incorporated, Mr. Cornelius O'Brien, son-in-law of A.D. Cook, became president. (Produced by Kraemer Art Co., Cincinnati and Berlin, Germany.)

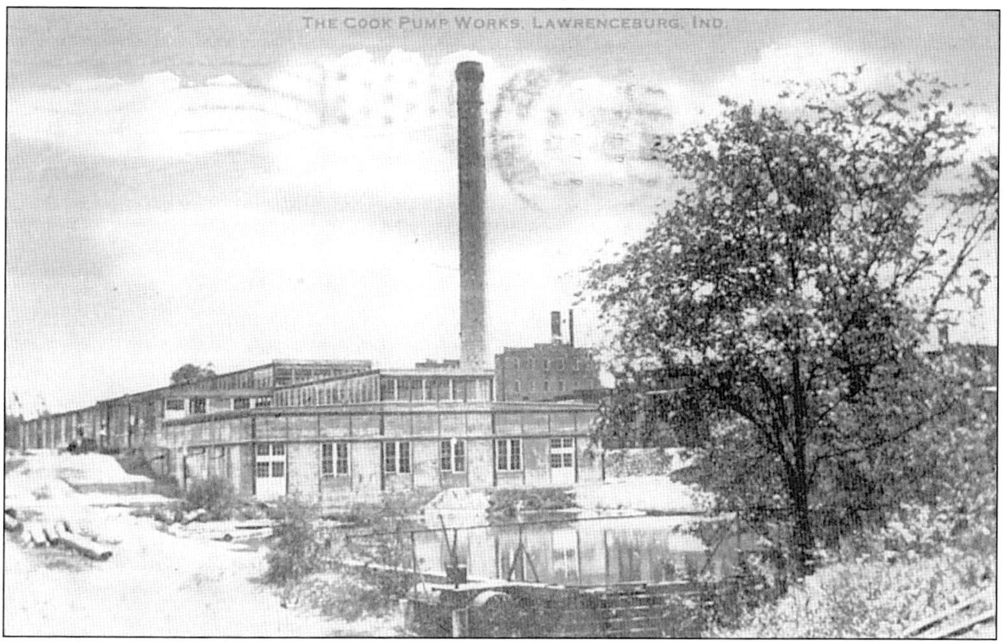

The Cook Pump Works. In 1947, the A.D. Cook factory was sold to American Steel & Pump Company. In 1950, Bardes Forge & Foundry Company of Cincinnati became the owners. When the factory moved to Tulsa, Oklahoma in 1964, it was known as Byron Jackson Pump Co., Inc. of Indiana. (Produced by Auburn Post Card Mfg. Co., Auburn, Indiana.)

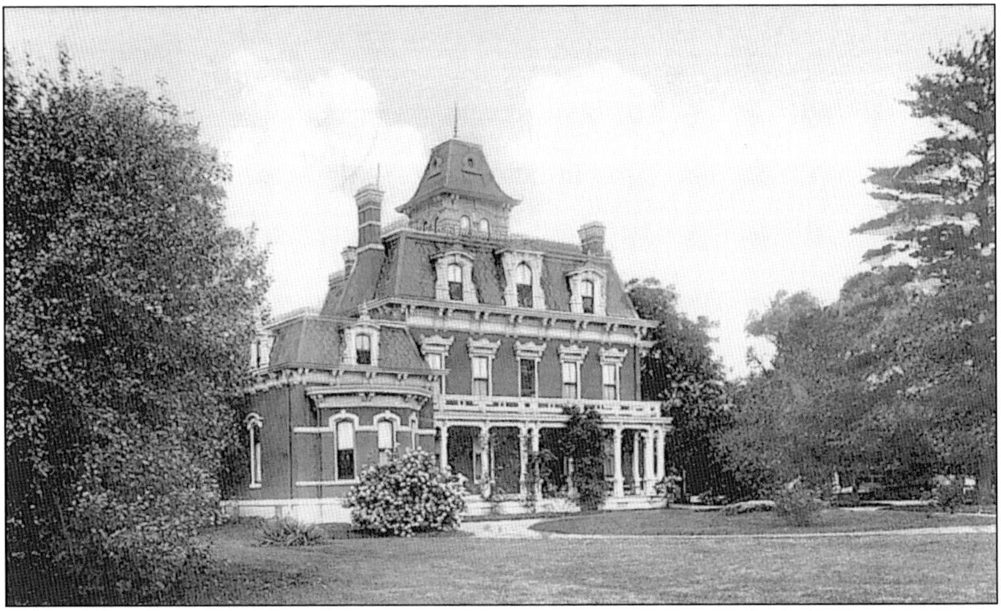

The Cook Residence. This 1852 house at 423 Ridge Avenue was built by Ezra G. Hayes just after his October 22, 1851 marriage. In 1877, when the house was owned by A.D. Cook, Hannaford & Hannaford of Cincinnati was hired to draw plans to enlarge and redesign the house. It was remodeled into the Italianate Second Empire-style house pictured here. In 1976, the house was torn down to make room for a church, and another historic landmark was lost. (Produced by Kraemer Art Co., Cincinnati and Berlin, Germany.)

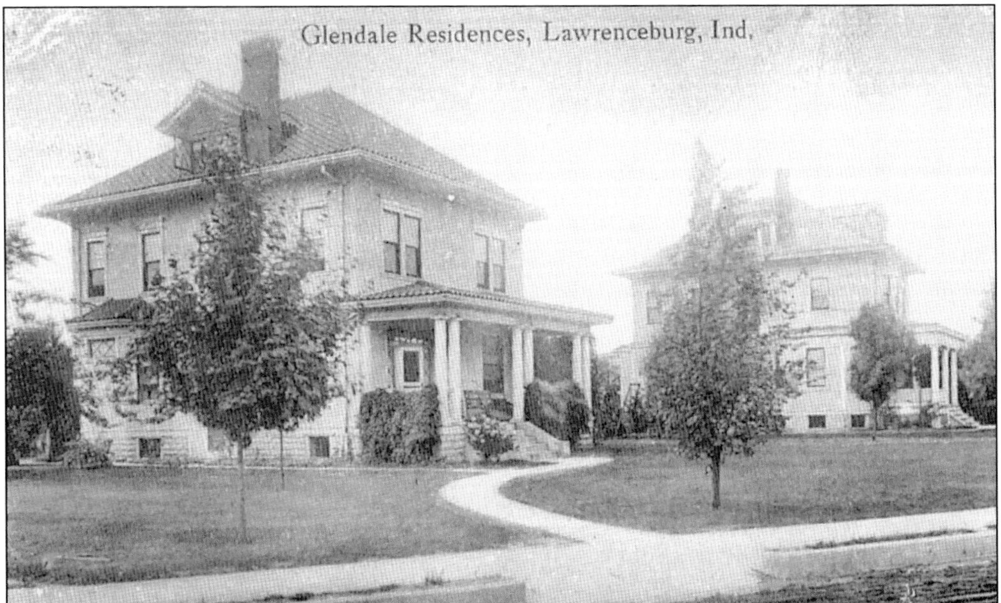

Ridge Avenue Residences, Greendale, Indiana. The two houses pictured on this postcard are located at 607 and 619 Ridge Avenue. They were constructed in 1902 by William P. Squibb from plans drawn by Cincinnati architects Boll & Taylor. He built the houses for his two sons, Nathaniel and George. (Produced by Kraemer Art Co., Cincinnati and Berlin, Germany.)

Four

LAWRENCEBURG

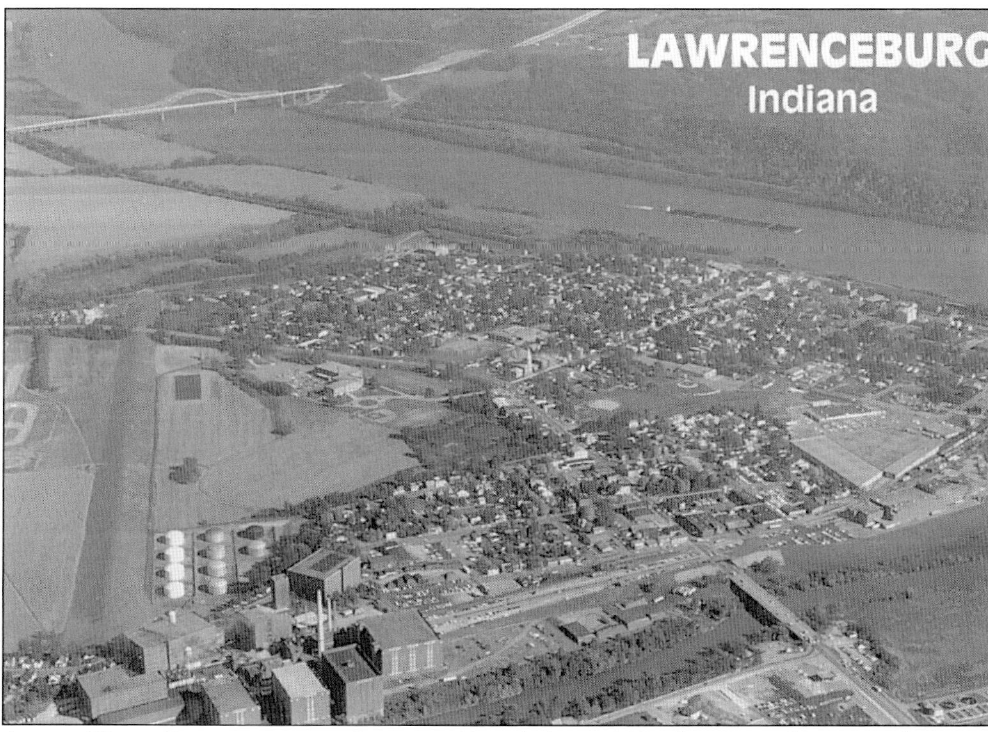

AERIAL VIEW, LAWRENCEBURG, INDIANA. Founded in 1803, the City of Lawrenceburg was named by Captain Samuel C. Vance in honor of his wife, whose maiden name was Lawrence. Today, Lawrenceburg is a thriving community located adjacent to the western edge of the I-275 Cincinnati beltway. It is the county seat of Dearborn County, which now has a population of nearly 40,000 inhabitants. The continental-size chrome postcard pictured above was published in 1988 from a photograph taken a year or two earlier. (Photograph by William Krider, published by Tri-State Visuals.)

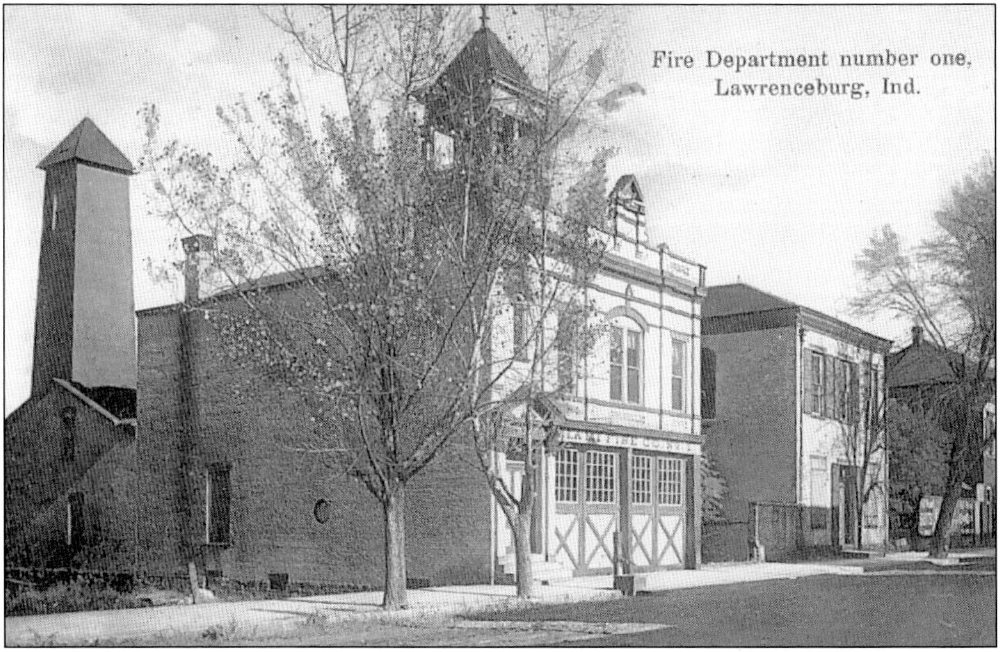

FIRE DEPARTMENT NUMBER ONE. The building pictured above, in the foreground, is located at 124 Short Street. When the Queen Anne-style building was first completed *c.* 1885, it housed both a firehouse and chambers for the city council. Just beyond the firehouse is the early site of the Peoples Bank. (Produced by Kraemer Art Co., Cincinnati, Ohio.)

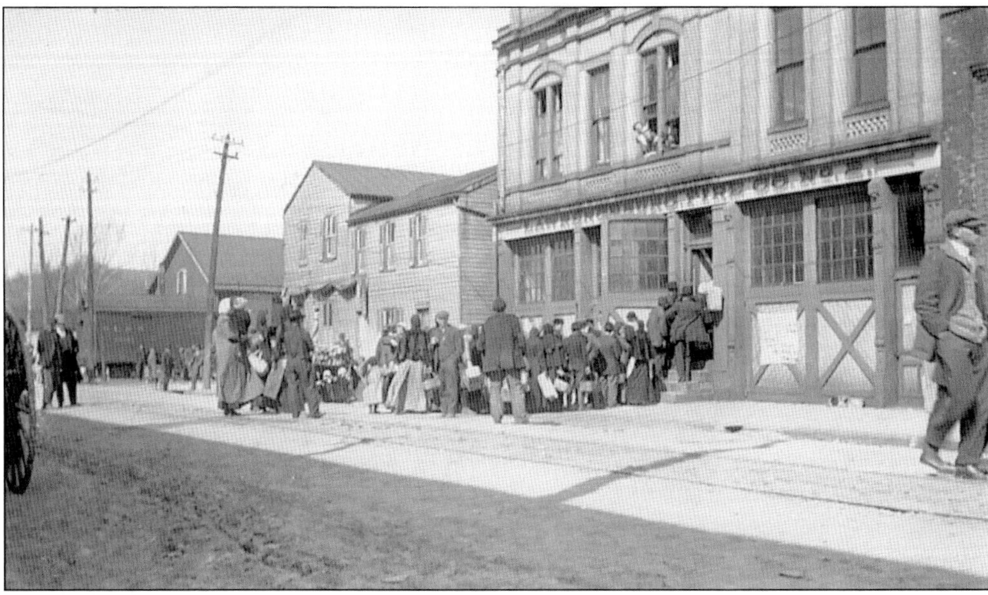

FIRE DEPARTMENT NUMBER TWO. When this picture was taken in 1913, Lawrenceburg Fire Station Number Two was being used to accommodate people affected by the flood. The message on the back of the card states, "over 30 people were accommodated in the room where you see the heads out the window—I will be here at least two months longer. The line usually stretches across the street and then some." (Real photo postcard by an unidentified photographer.)

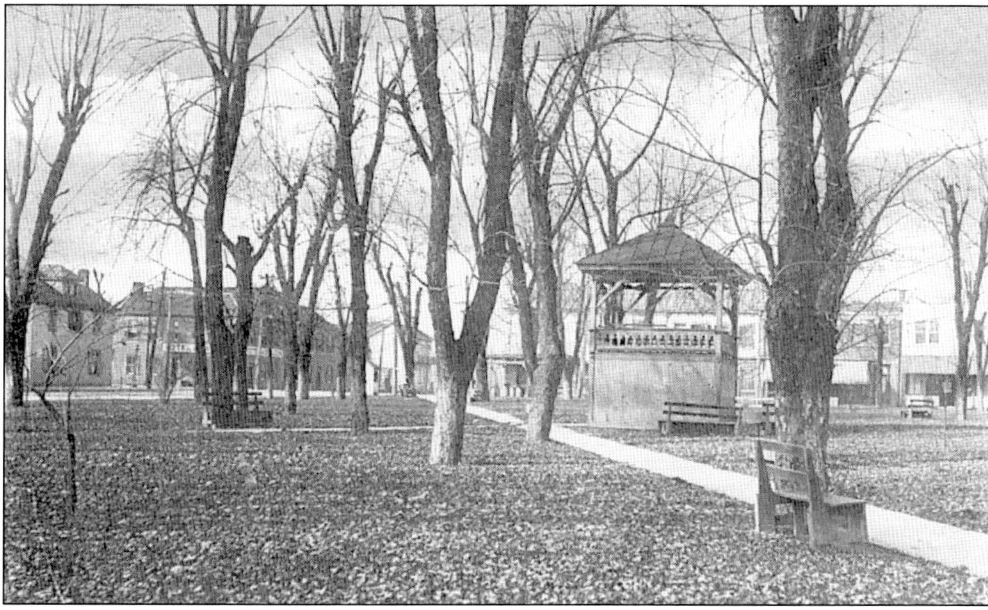

NEWTOWN PARK. Before there was a fountain, there was a bandstand in Newtown Park. Marked off in Isaac Dunn's 1819 original plat of what is known as Newtown, this block was to be maintained in perpetuity as a public park. Today, the park is named Eads Park, in honor of James Buchanan Eads, one of Lawrenceburg's most famous sons. The bandstand was torn down in 1923. (Produced by Auburn Post Card Mfg. Co., Auburn, Indiana.)

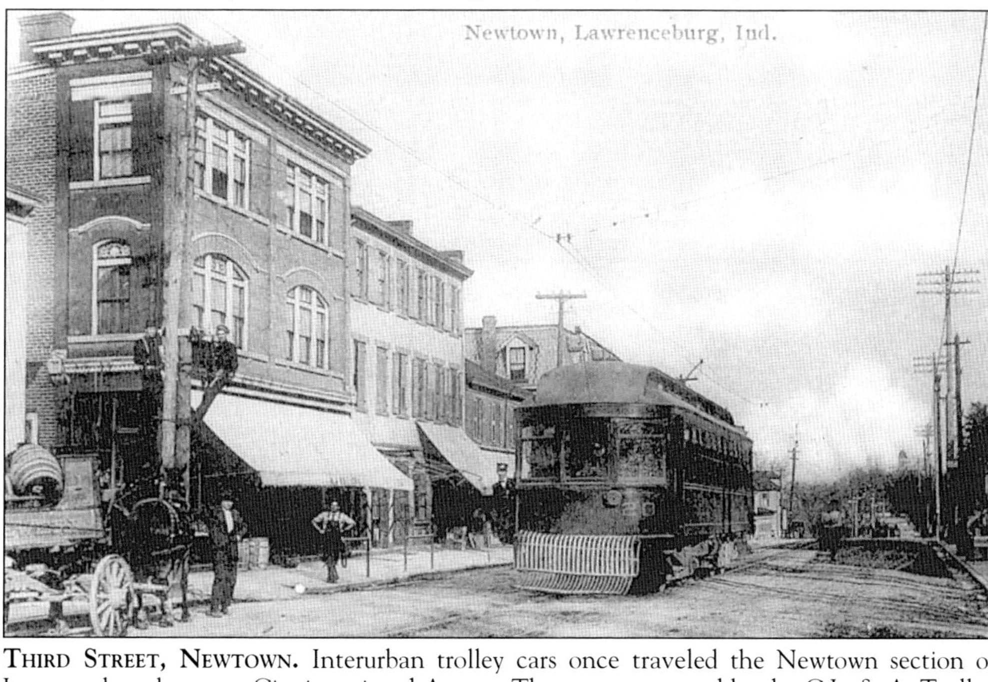

THIRD STREET, NEWTOWN. Interurban trolley cars once traveled the Newtown section of Lawrenceburg between Cincinnati and Aurora. They were operated by the C.L. & A. Trolley Company. Third Street was later renamed Eads Parkway. The two prominent buildings shown in this scene are now part of the United Community Bank. (Unidentified photographer and publisher.)

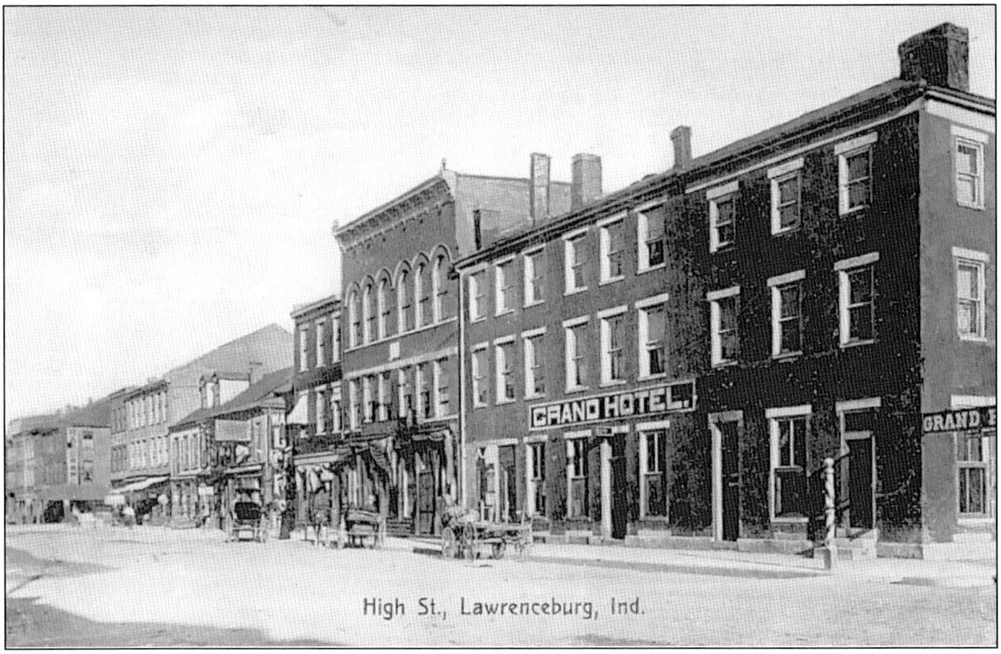

High Street. The south side of east High Street is pictured here just after the turn of the century. The Grand Hotel, pictured in the foreground, was originally built as the Hunt House Hotel, and is located on the southeast corner of High and Walnut Streets. (Produced by Kraemer Art Co., Cincinnati and Berlin, Germany.)

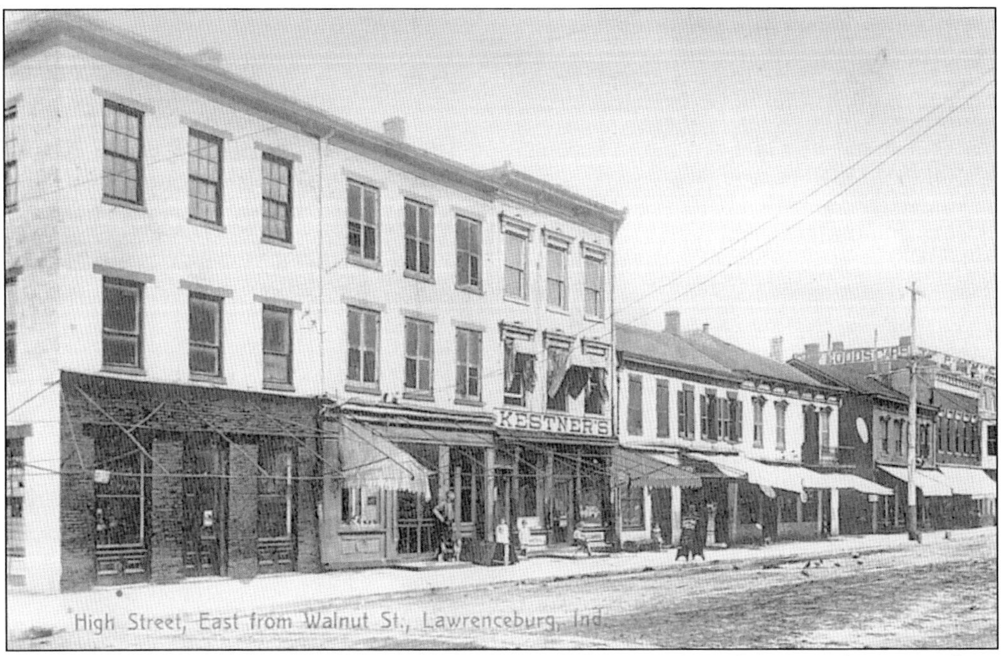

High Street, East from Walnut Street. This is a scene directly across the street from the scene illustrated at the top of this page. Both were photographed from the center of the intersection of High and Walnut Streets. They were also both taken before High Street was covered over with bricks. (Produced by Kraemer Art Co., Cincinnati and Berlin, Germany.)

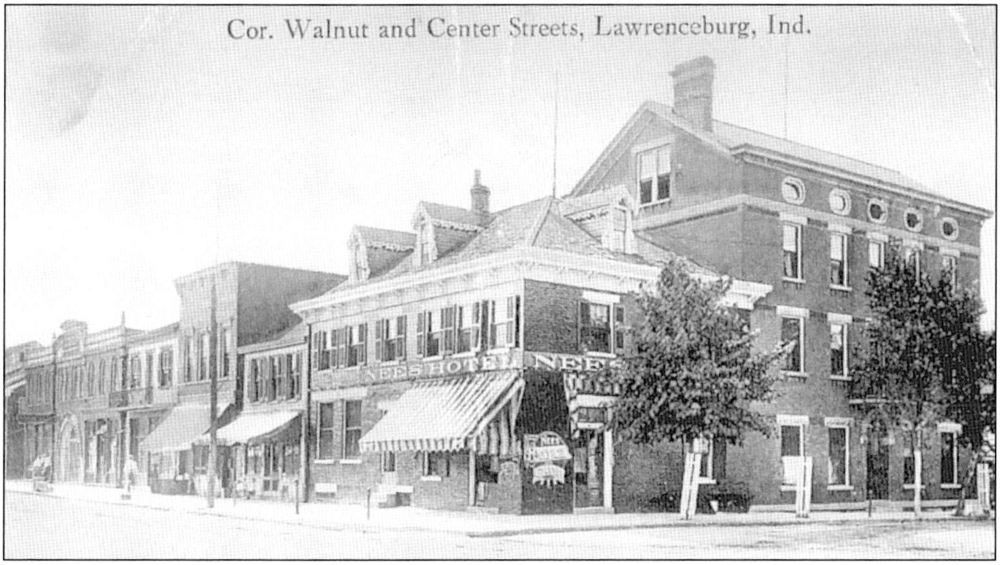

CORNER, WALNUT AND CENTER STREETS. The Nees Hotel once occupied the northeast corner of this intersection in Lawrenceburg. It was owned and operated by Thomas Nees. Prior to being the Nees Hotel, it was known as the Bartholome House Hotel. A 1939 bank building, built by Peoples National Bank (now a Firstar Bank Branch), now stands on the site. (Produced by Kraemer Art Co., Cincinnati and Berlin, Germany.)

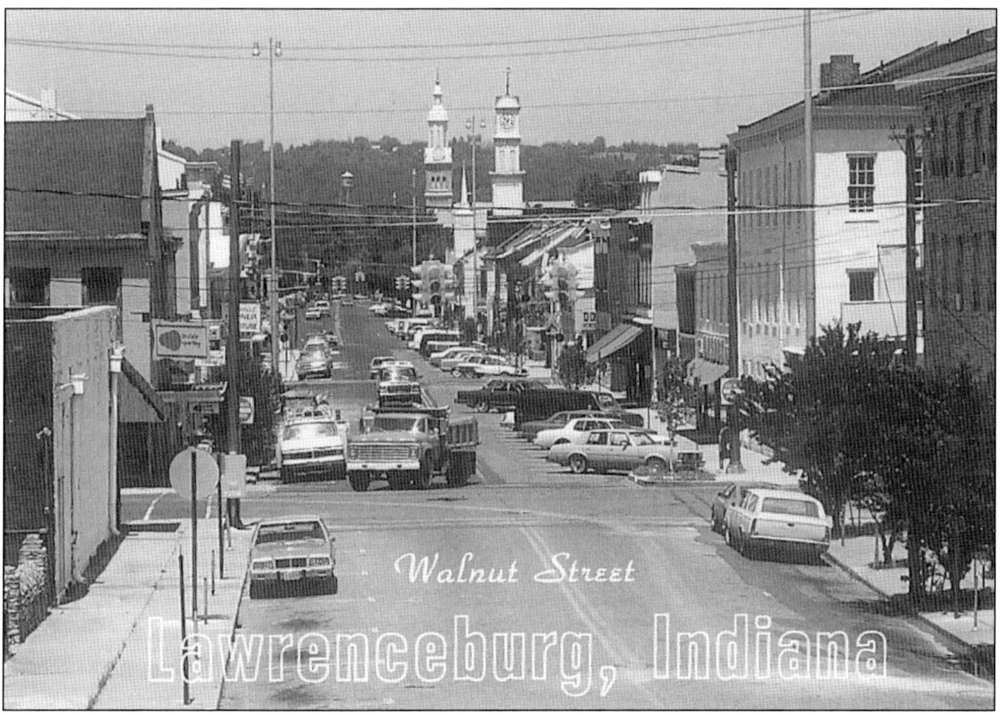

WALNUT STREET, LAWRENCEBURG, INDIANA. In 1987, this photograph was taken with a telephoto lens from the top of the Ohio River levee. Trees that were planted just before the photograph was taken now stand higher than most of the buildings that they front. (Photograph by Milt Masing, published by Tri-State Visuals.)

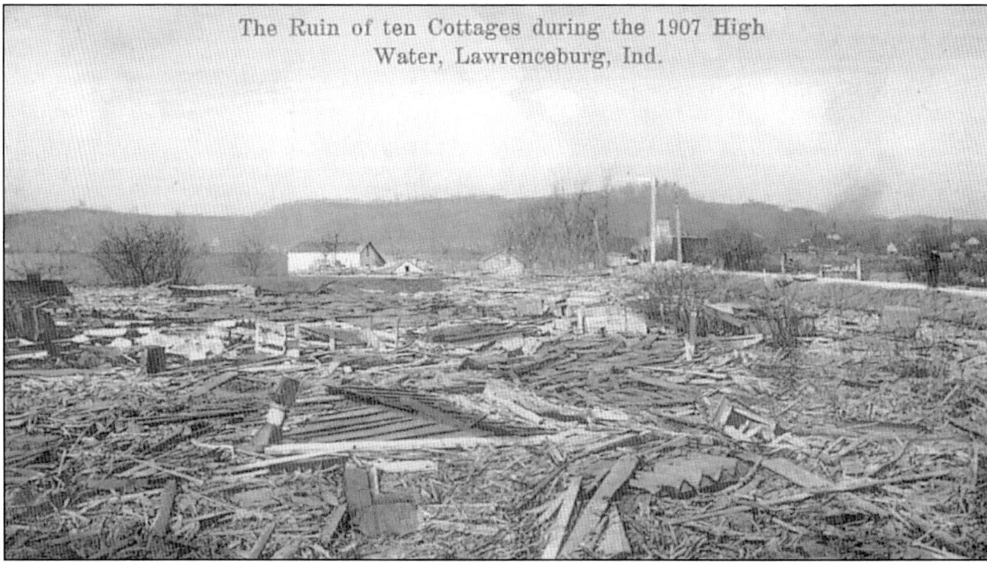

THE RUIN OF TEN COTTAGES DURING THE 1907 HIGH WATER. On Monday, January 21, 1907, water reached a height of 66 feet—just high enough, by a few inches, to come over the top of the levee. When the water did come over it, the levee sank a little, and the citizens were rallied by Mayor Bielby to work to save the city. Most of the water was kept out of the city, but it was too late for at least ten cottages pictured on the above postcard. (Produced by Kraemer Art Co., Cincinnati, Ohio.)

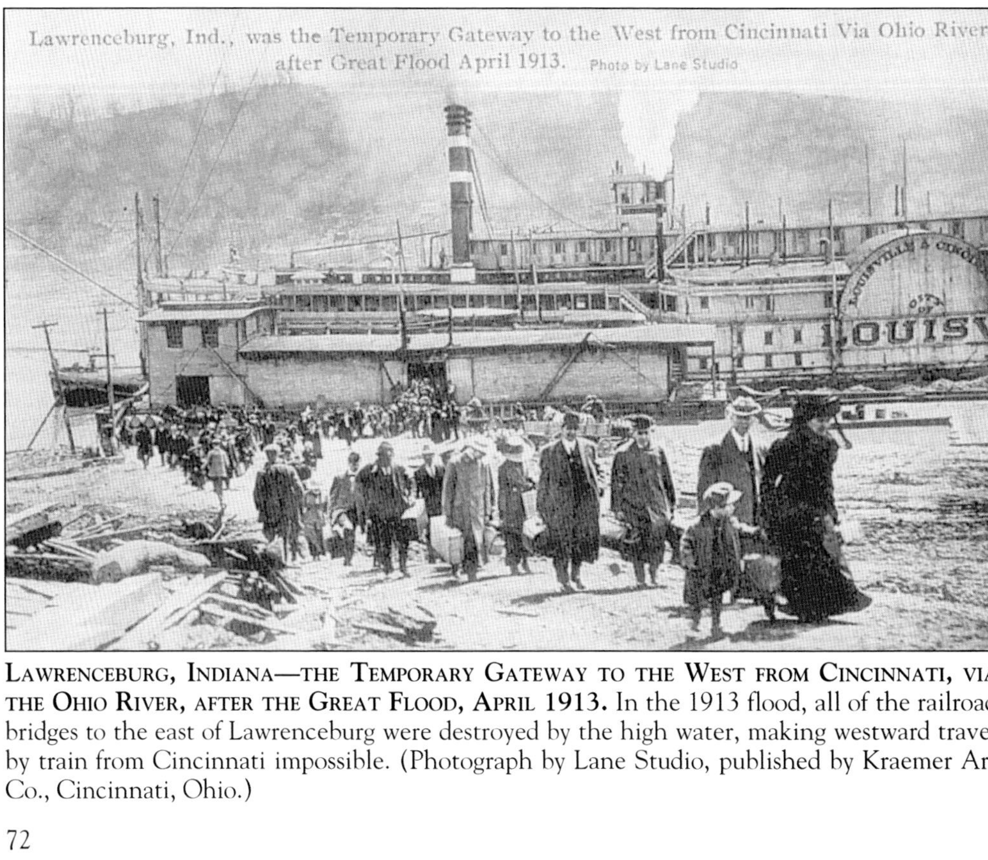

LAWRENCEBURG, INDIANA—THE TEMPORARY GATEWAY TO THE WEST FROM CINCINNATI, VIA THE OHIO RIVER, AFTER THE GREAT FLOOD, APRIL 1913. In the 1913 flood, all of the railroad bridges to the east of Lawrenceburg were destroyed by the high water, making westward travel by train from Cincinnati impossible. (Photograph by Lane Studio, published by Kraemer Art Co., Cincinnati, Ohio.)

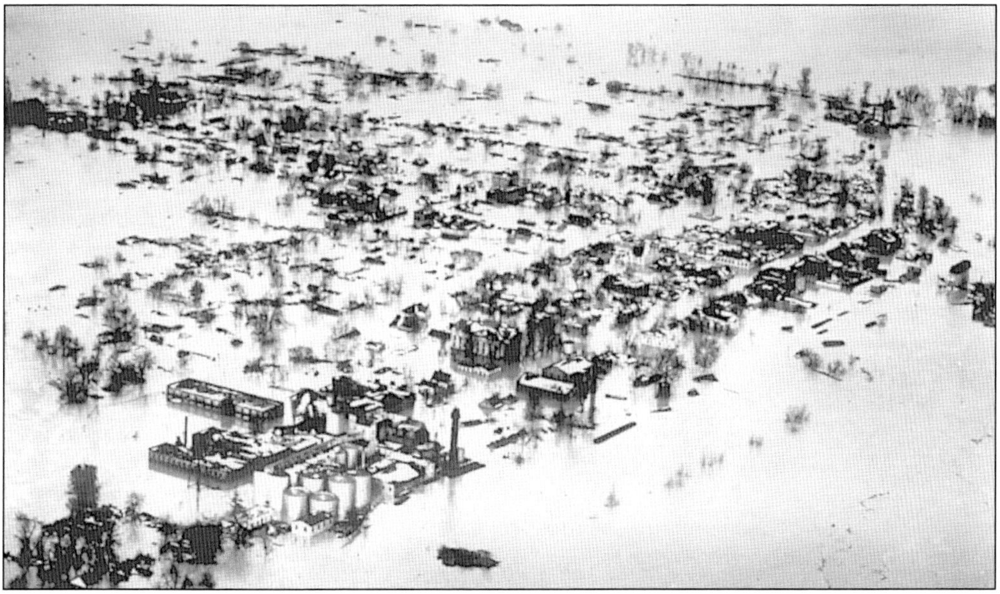

LAWRENCEBURG, INDIANA, GREAT FLOOD OF JANUARY 1937. In 1937, flood records of all time were broken. The water at Lawrenceburg reached a height of 82 feet and 6 inches. The city remained submerged in this water for two weeks, with every home in the city flooded. Downtown Lawrenceburg is pictured here. (Real photo postcard, photograph by Dan Henry.)

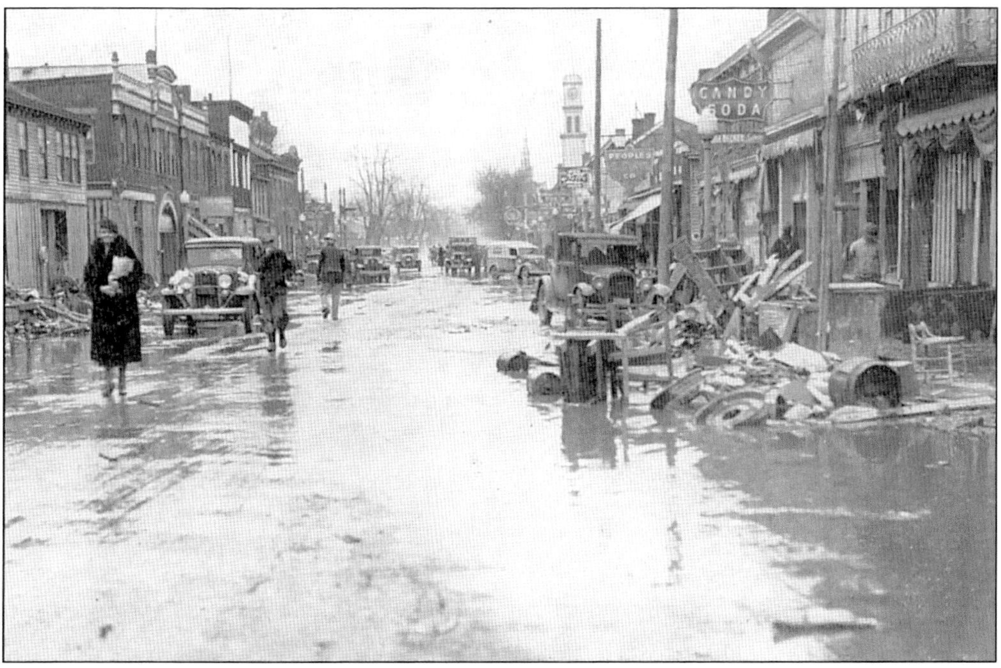

WALNUT STREET, IMMEDIATELY AFTER THE FLOOD OF 1937. One of the big problems after the flood was what to do with the refuge thrown out on the streets. This view of the 200 block of Walnut Street depicts some of the problem. (Photograph by M.O. Whitney, published by Whitney's Studio.)

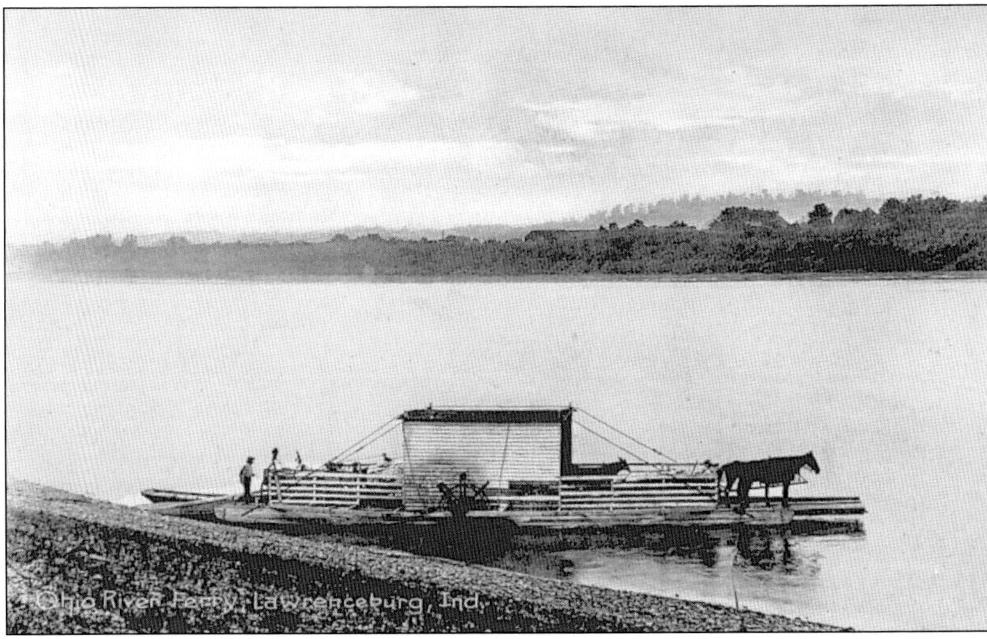

Ohio River Ferry. In the early history of Dearborn County, ferry boats were commonly used to cross the many streams that fed into the Ohio River. As bridges were constructed across these streams during the 1800s, only the ferries across the Ohio River remained. The above photograph was taken *c.* 1915. (Produced by Kraemer Art Co., Cincinnati and Berlin, Germany.)

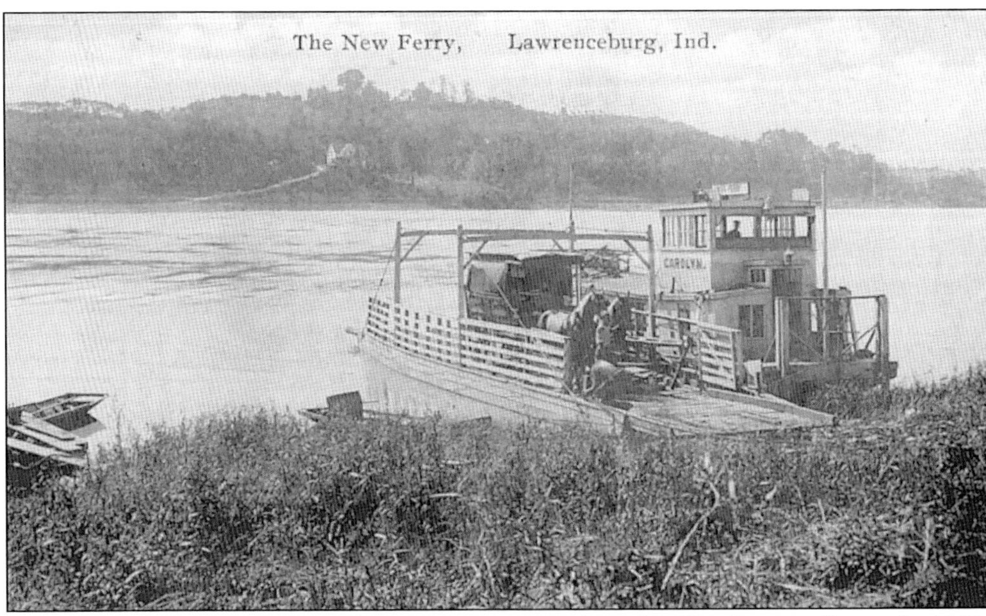

The New Ferry. Horse-powered ferries were common along the Ohio River well into the 1920s. This view shows the boat *Carolyn* docked at the Indiana shore, ready to dismiss its passengers. Carolyn was operated by the Lawrenceburg Ferry Company. This card was postmarked with a railroad postmark in 1921. (Produced by Kraemer Art Co., Cincinnati.)

B & O Railroad Bridge, East of Lawrenceburg, Indiana. Constructed to carry the B & O Railroad line across the Great Miami River to the east, toward Cincinnati, this bridge was probably constructed to replace the one lost during the 1913 flood. The card is not postmarked, so the date cannot be substantiated by the card. Other cards from this series in the author's collection carry postmarks of 1914 and 1915. (Produced by Indianapolis Post Card Co., Indianapolis, Indiana, for Jackson's Dry Good Store.)

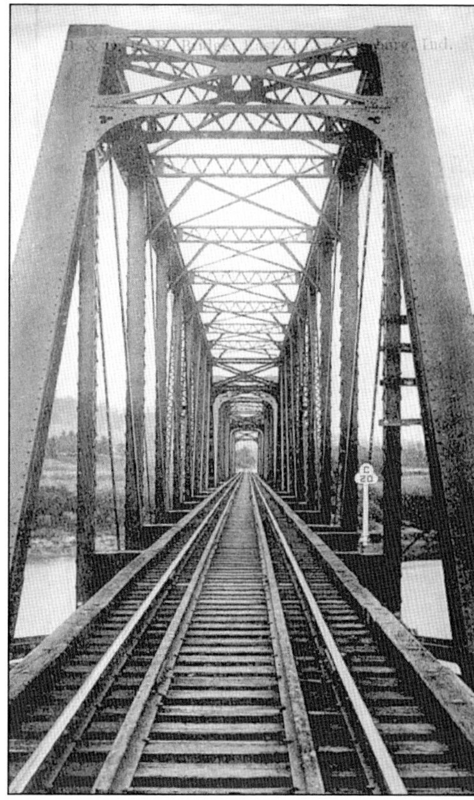

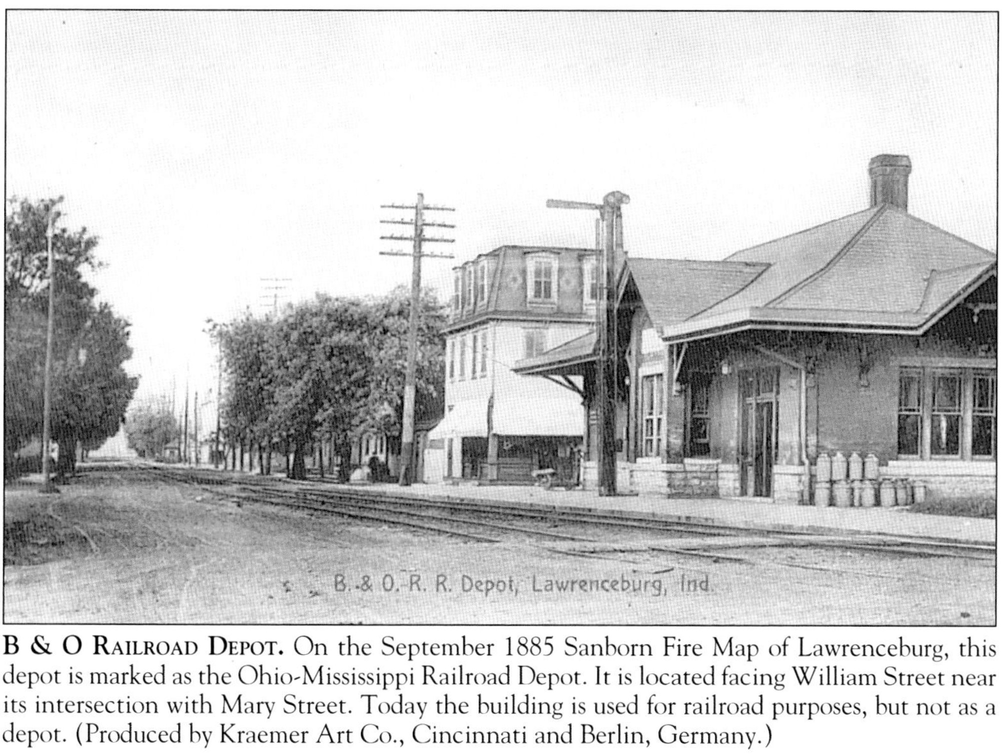

B & O Railroad Depot. On the September 1885 Sanborn Fire Map of Lawrenceburg, this depot is marked as the Ohio-Mississippi Railroad Depot. It is located facing William Street near its intersection with Mary Street. Today the building is used for railroad purposes, but not as a depot. (Produced by Kraemer Art Co., Cincinnati and Berlin, Germany.)

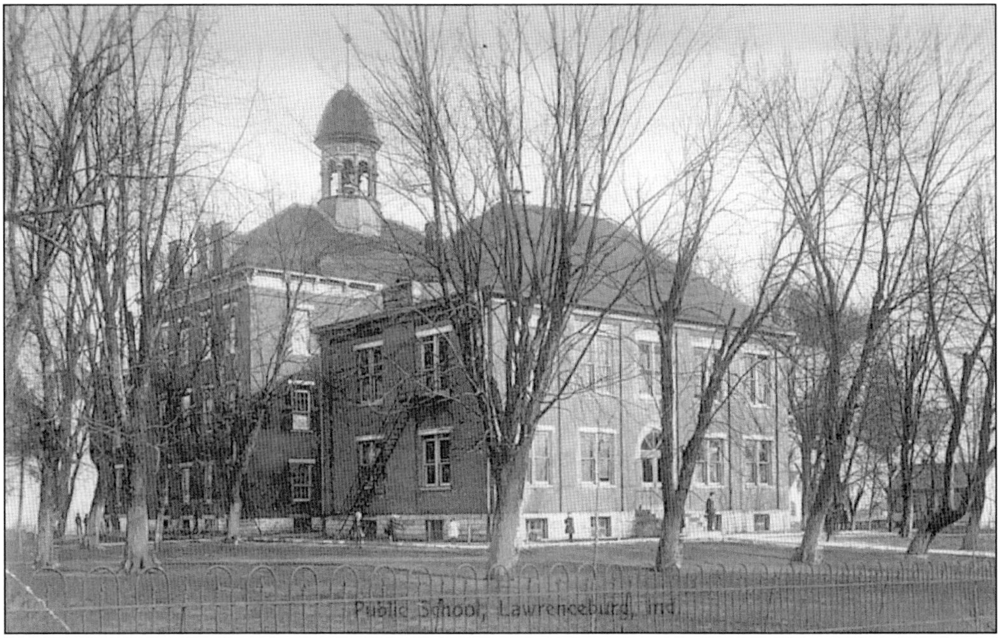

LAWRENCEBURG PUBLIC SCHOOL. Constructed originally as a high school in 1859, this building has had a history of mixed use for all of the grades. In 1904, an addition was constructed that made the building appear as shown in the above postcard. The building was demolished in June and July of 1958, as the Central Elementary School neared completion. (Produced by Kraemer Art Co., Cincinnati and Berlin, Germany.)

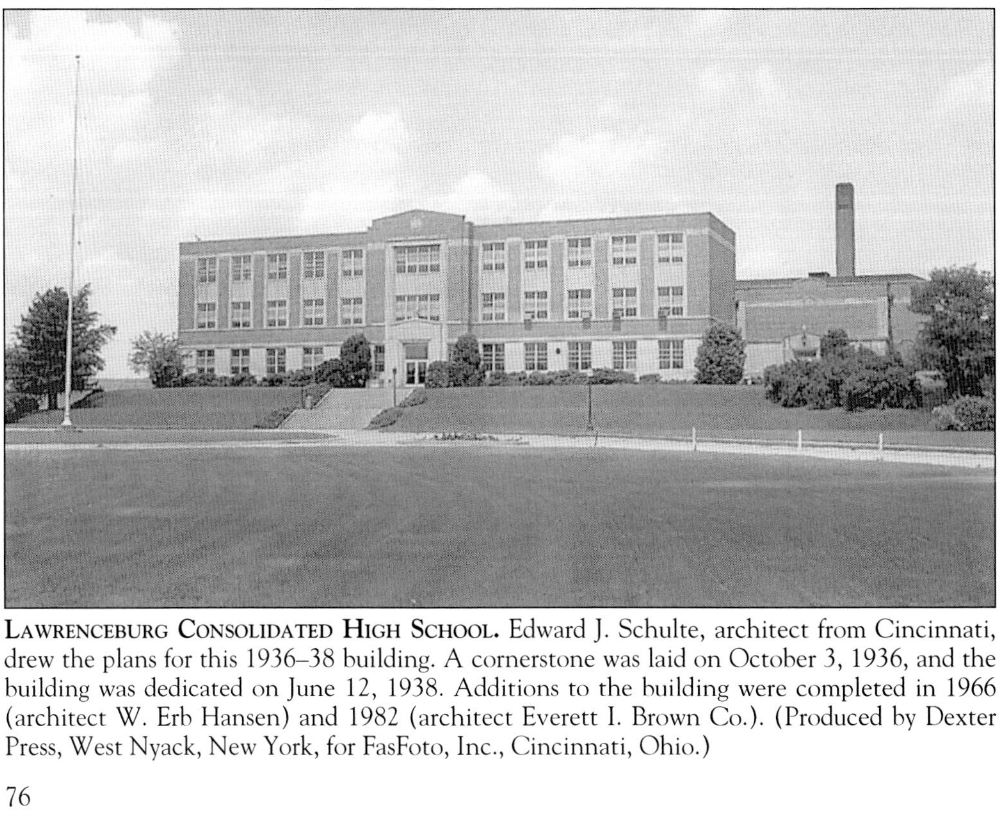

LAWRENCEBURG CONSOLIDATED HIGH SCHOOL. Edward J. Schulte, architect from Cincinnati, drew the plans for this 1936–38 building. A cornerstone was laid on October 3, 1936, and the building was dedicated on June 12, 1938. Additions to the building were completed in 1966 (architect W. Erb Hansen) and 1982 (architect Everett I. Brown Co.). (Produced by Dexter Press, West Nyack, New York, for FasFoto, Inc., Cincinnati, Ohio.)

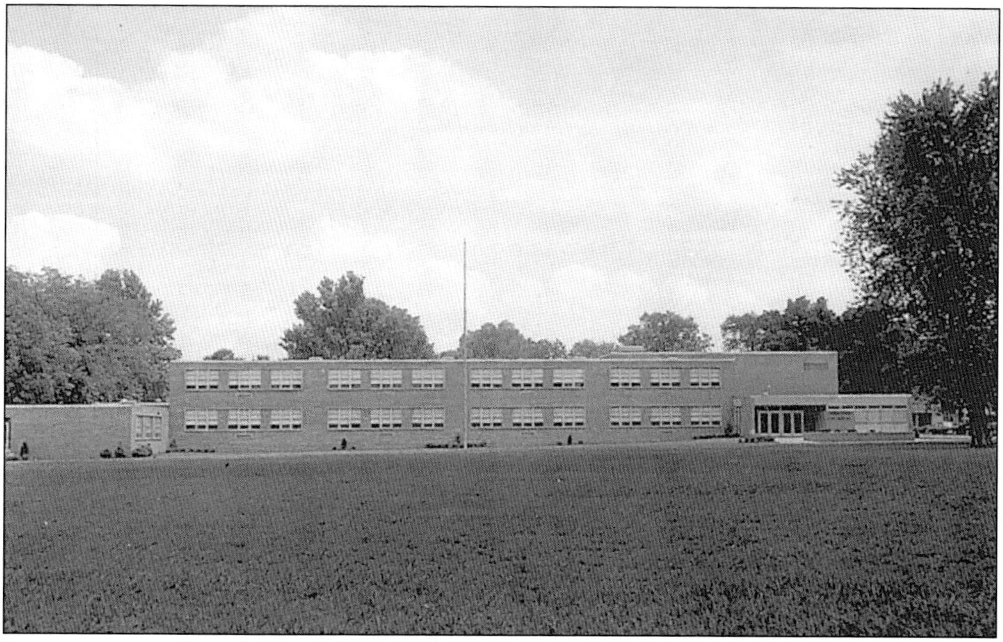

LAWRENCEBURG CITY SCHOOL. Central Elementary School was completed at a cost of just over one million dollars, in time for the 1958 school year. McGuire, Shook, Compton, Richey, and Associates of Indianapolis were the architects. Dedication ceremonies were held on September 21 and 22, 1958. F.W. Owen Co., of Louisville, Kentucky, was the contractor. (Produced by Dexter Press, West Nyack, New York, for FasFoto, Inc., Cincinnati, Ohio.)

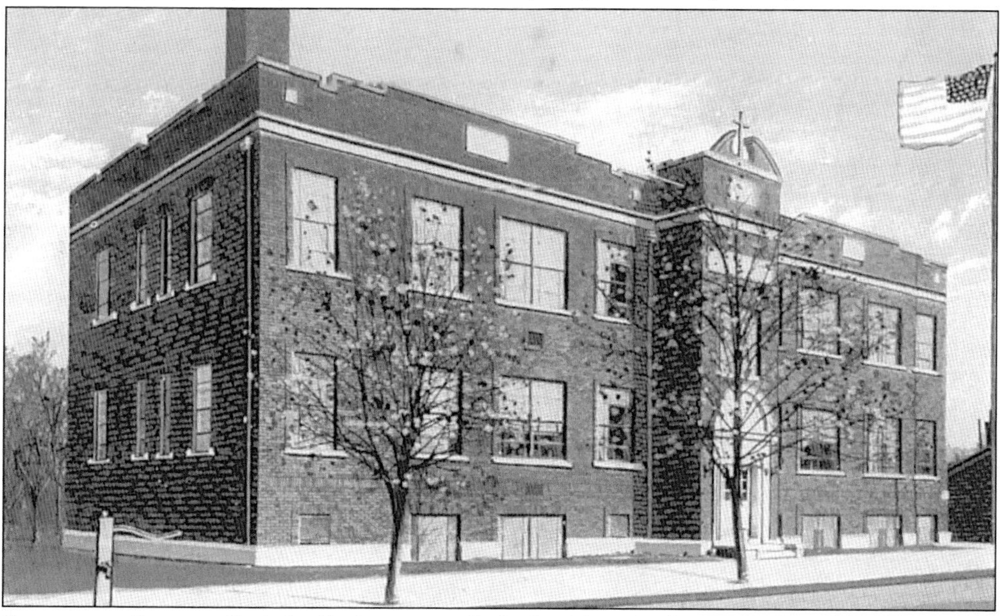

PAROCHIAL SCHOOL. Built by St. Lawrence Catholic Church, this somewhat classical building was completed in 1927 and dedicated on November 20th. Cornerstone ceremonies were held on June 22, 1927. Connersville, Indiana architect Karl P. Henkle drew the plans for the building. The school is operated by the Sisters of St. Francis. (Produced by Curt Teich & Co., Chicago, Illinois.)

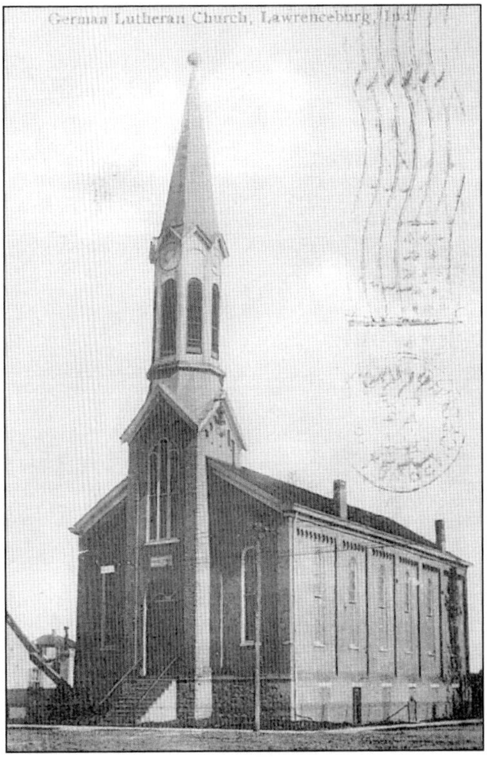

GERMAN LUTHERAN CHURCH. This Gothic Revival Church, built by the Lutherans of Lawrenceburg, Indiana, is located at 500 Main Street in Newtown. The cornerstone for the building was put in place on July 14, 1867. The building was finished in 1869, and dedicated on August 22nd. The cost of the building was upward of $16,000, including a brick main portion measuring 40 by 80 feet, a 120-foot-high steeple, and a stone basement. During the 1937 flood the building sustained major damage to the interior, with water reaching 10 feet into the parsonage. The church was repaired at considerable expense and was again put to use. On November 2, 1953, the church building caught fire and suffered considerable damage again. At this time the congregation decided to move to a different location in Greendale. At that time, the church changed its name to Emanuel Evangelical Lutheran Church. (Unidentified printer and publisher.)

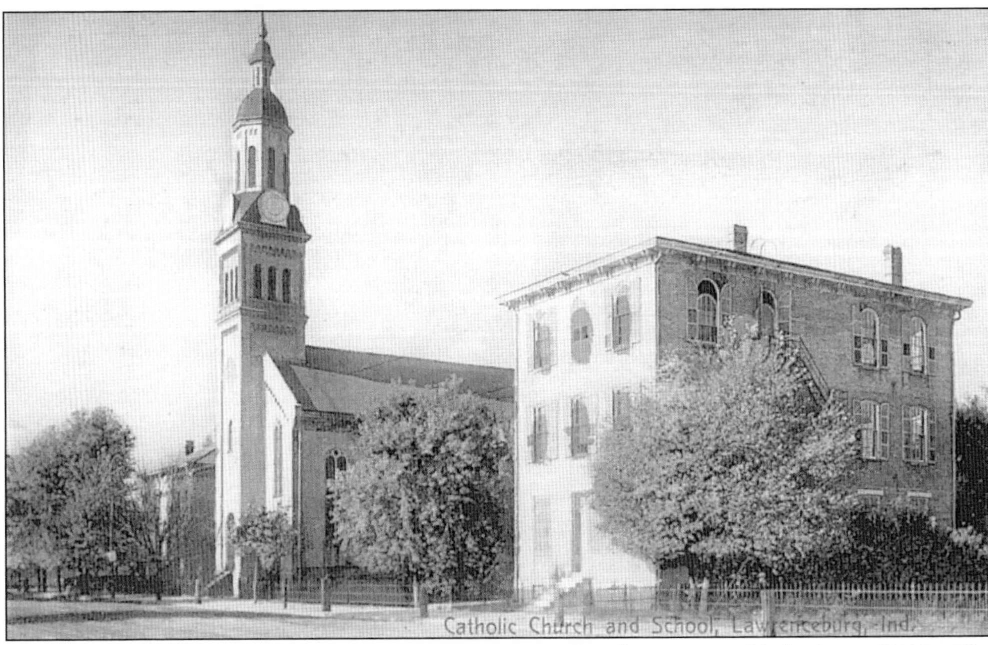

CATHOLIC CHURCH AND SCHOOL. St. Lawrence Parish was established in 1840. The Romanesque-style church pictured above was completed in 1867, from plans drawn by Louis (Ludwig) Riedinger, a resident of Yorkville, Indiana at the time. A dedication ceremony for the building was held on June 2, 1867. The building is still in use today and is in excellent condition. (Produced by Kraemer Art Co., Cincinnati and Berlin, Germany.)

HAMLINE CHAPEL, M.E. CHURCH. A marker on the pediment below the front roof of this structure dates the building to 1847. Records, however, show that Hamline Chapel was dedicated on July 2, 1848. Services for the occasion were performed by Reverend Dr. Simpson and Reverend S.T. Gillett. Reverend Simpson preached in the forenoon, while Reverend Gillett preached in the afternoon. The chapel was named in honor of Leonidas L. Hamline, bishop of the area that included Lawrenceburg. The presiding elder at the time of the church's construction was Enoch G. Wood. Charles B. Davidson was station preacher. Hamline Chapel is located on the southwest corner of High and Vine Streets. The building is in excellent condition and still in use today by the Methodists of Lawrenceburg. (Produced by Kraemer Art Co., Cincinnati, Ohio.)

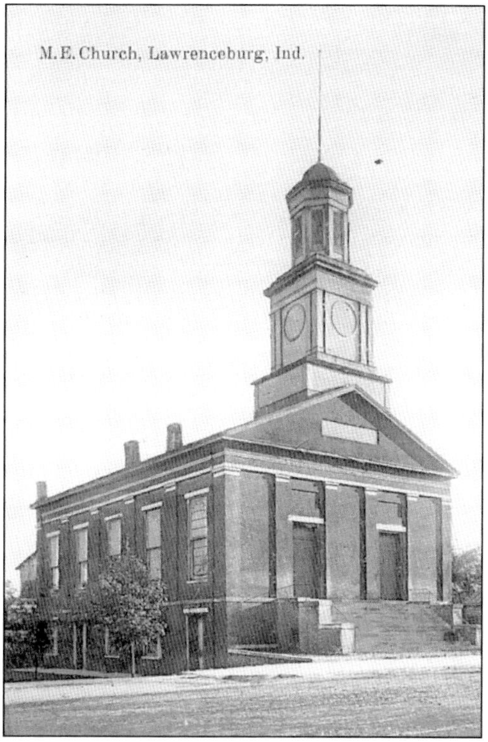

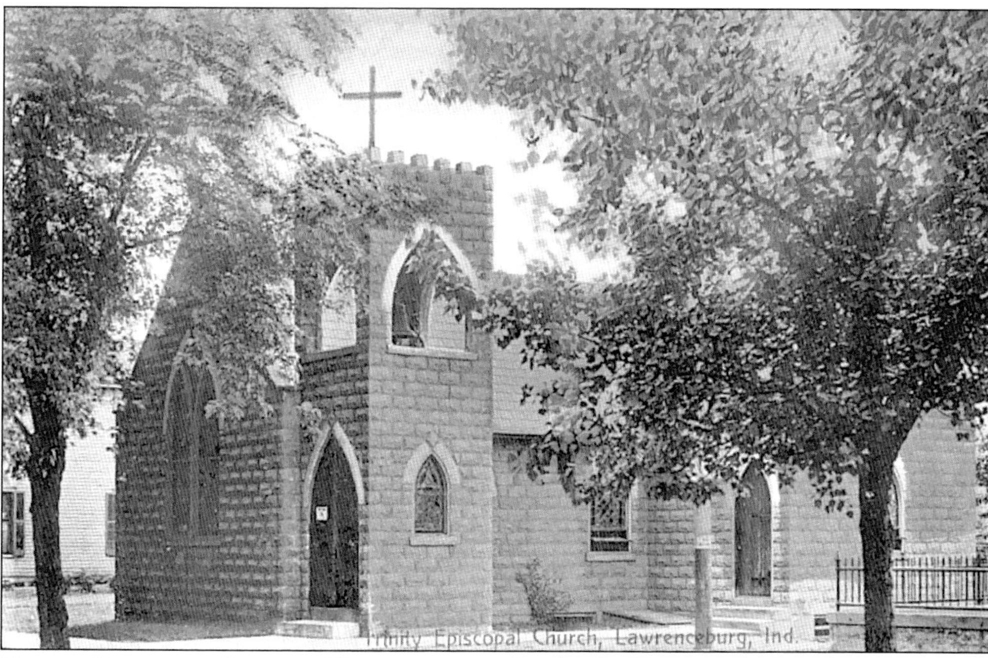

TRINITY EPISCOPAL CHURCH. The cornerstone for this building was laid in the fall of 1905, and bears the inscription, "Bishop Knickerbocker Memorial." It was completed in 1906. In 1936, a new addition to the parish was started. In 1937, while the addition was still under construction, the record-breaking flood occurred. Everything was lost, and the building had to be repaired. (Produced by Kraemer Art Co., Cincinnati and Berlin, Germany.)

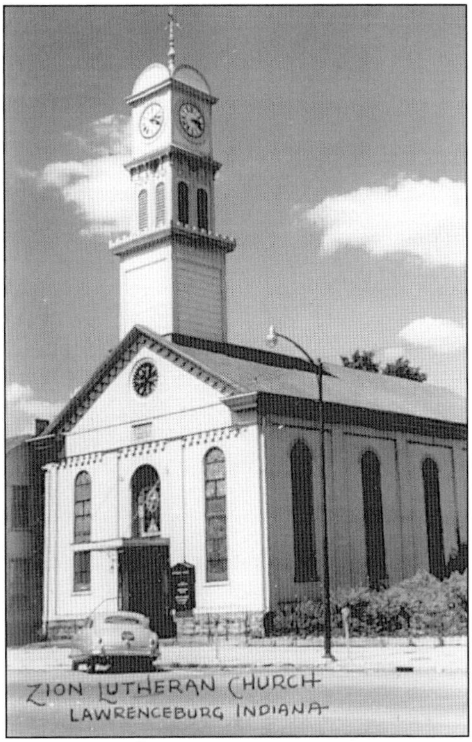

ZION LUTHERAN CHURCH. The cost of this building, along with a parsonage, was $14,000 once it was completed in 1867. On November 24, 1867, the building was consecrated. At the time the building was completed, the church joined the German Evangelical Synod of North America, resulting in a change of the name to the Zion Evangelical Church of Lawrenceburg. The German language was used exclusively in all services and meetings of the congregation, until 1901, when some English services were introduced. By 1905, all services were held in English. In 1910, the steeple of the church was struck by lightning and badly damaged. As a part of the needed repairs, the town clock was installed at a cost of $800. Several alterations and repairs have taken place since this time, including noticeable changes in 1929, 1946, and 1973. (Real photo postcard by an unidentified photographer.)

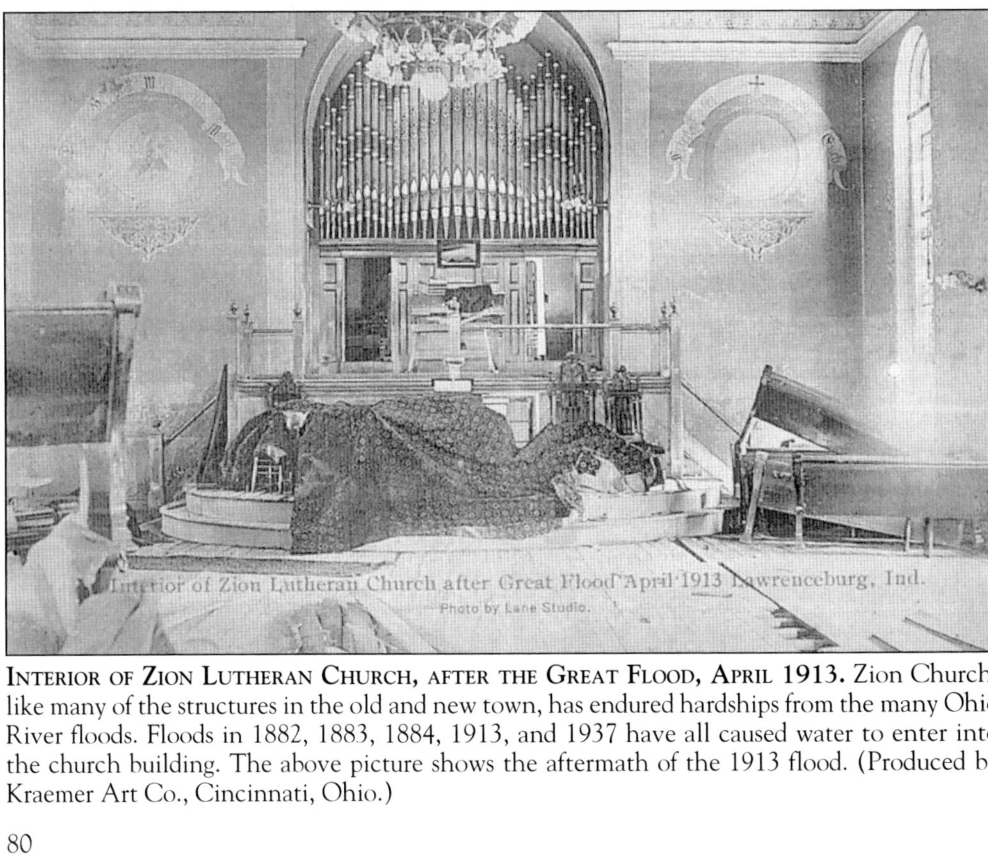

INTERIOR OF ZION LUTHERAN CHURCH, AFTER THE GREAT FLOOD, APRIL 1913. Zion Church, like many of the structures in the old and new town, has endured hardships from the many Ohio River floods. Floods in 1882, 1883, 1884, 1913, and 1937 have all caused water to enter into the church building. The above picture shows the aftermath of the 1913 flood. (Produced by Kraemer Art Co., Cincinnati, Ohio.)

PRESBYTERIAN CHURCH AND PARSONAGE. The First Presbyterian Church of Lawrenceburgh was first organized Sabbath morning, September 27, 1829, with Reverend Sylvester Scovel in charge. In April 1882, after the 1831 church pictured below was taken down, construction of the building pictured to the right was begun. On September 24, 1883, the building was dedicated. The total cost of the structure was $10,768. The bell in the tower was purchased by the children of the Sunday school at a cost of $232. The furniture of the pulpit was purchased by the young ladies of the church. In 1884, flood waters reached well into the second floor level, destroying all that was below. In 1929, during the church's 100-year celebration, the building's name was changed to Beecher Presbyterian Church to honor Reverend Beecher. (Produced by Kraemer Art Co., Cincinnati, Ohio.)

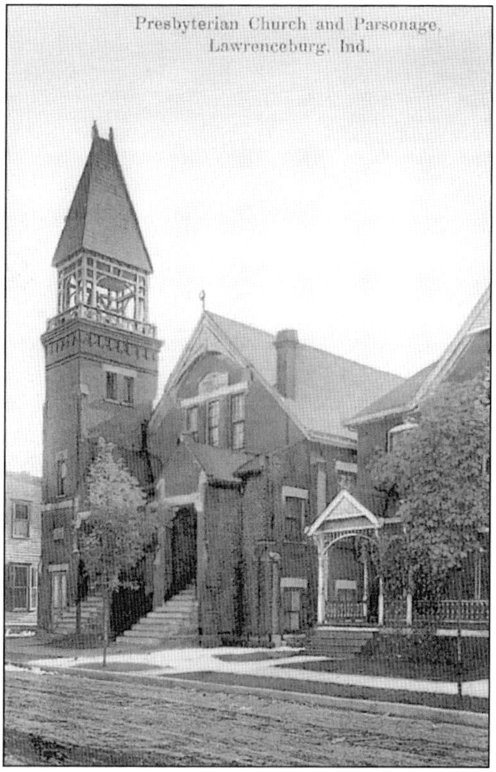

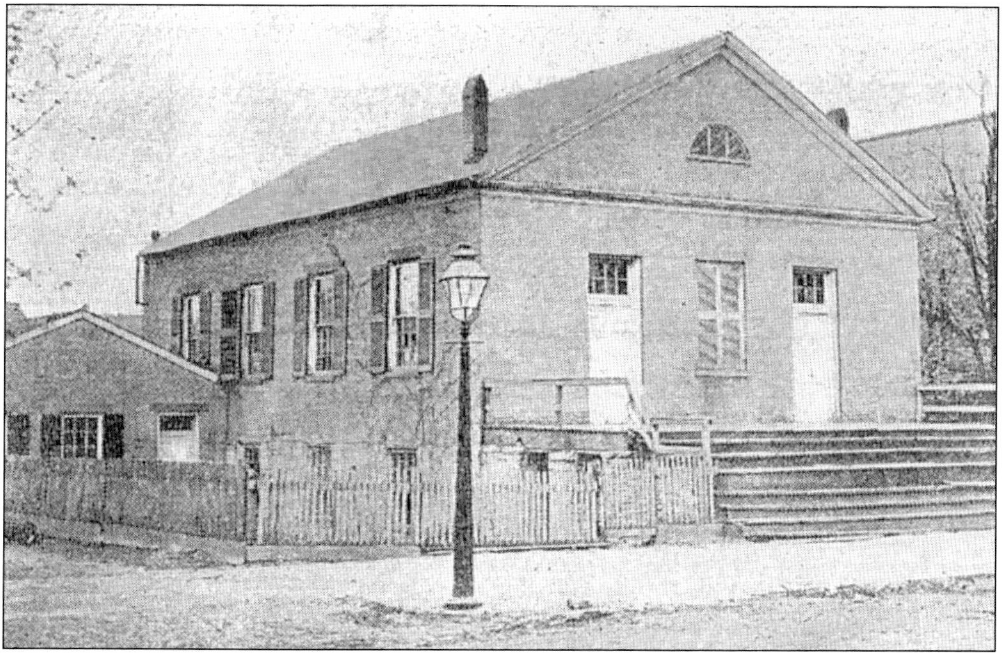

FIRST CHARGE OF REVEREND HENRY WARD BEECHER. Reverend Beecher served as pastor of the Lawrenceburgh Presbyterian Church from May 1837 until July 1839, at which time he moved to accept a position in Indianapolis. The church pictured above was constructed in 1831, with some work possibly being completed in 1832. (Photograph by E.M. Lee.)

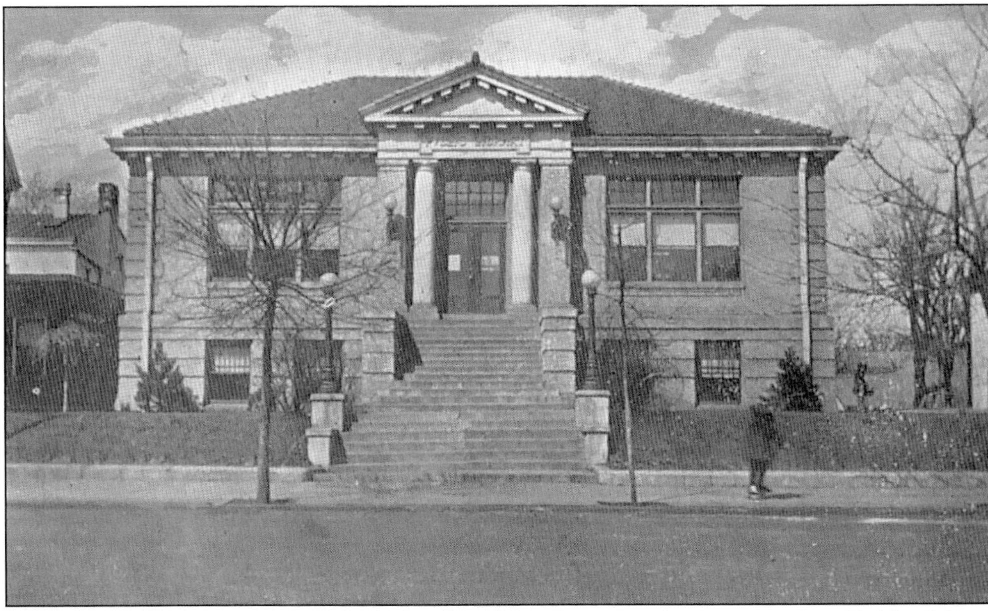

PUBLIC LIBRARY. In 1915, with the help of Andrew Carnegie, the Lawrenceburg Public Library opened in this building on West High Street. It was designed in the classic Revival style of architecture by True L. Brookie of Indianapolis. The $12,000 building was dedicated on October 9, 1915. (Produced by Auburn Post Card Mfg. Co., Auburn, Indiana.)

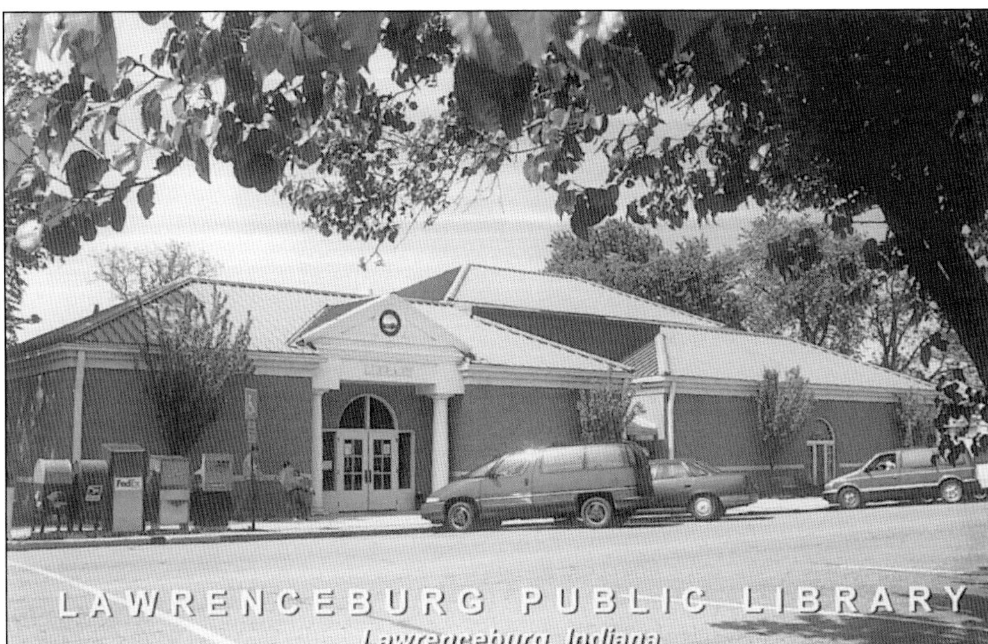

LAWRENCEBURG PUBLIC LIBRARY. In 1988, an addition constructed around the building pictured above was completed from plans prepared by the Interdesign Group of Indianapolis, Indiana. An earlier expansion of the library completed in 1959 was removed to make room for the new plans. (Photograph by Milt Masing, published by Tri-State Visuals.)

Miniature Sprinkler Demonstration. This photo postcard is from either the 1940s or 1950s, when Victor M. Drury was giving demonstrations of his miniature sprinkler invention. Mr. Drury was an employee of the Joseph E. Seagram & Sons Distillery in Lawrenceburg. He started at Seagrams as a chauffeur for Mr. Bronfman, and later became the chief of the plant fire department. It was while he was fire chief that he invented the miniature sprinkler shown here. In support of his achievement, Mr. Drury received many recognitions. In addition to having had the opportunity to demonstrate his device to the President of the United States, Mr. Drury was awarded, in 1979, the honor of being a "Sagamore of the Wabash" by Lieutenant Governor Robert Orr. In 1982, Mr. Drury was awarded the distinction of being a "Kentucky Colonel." (Real photo postcard by an unidentified photographer.)

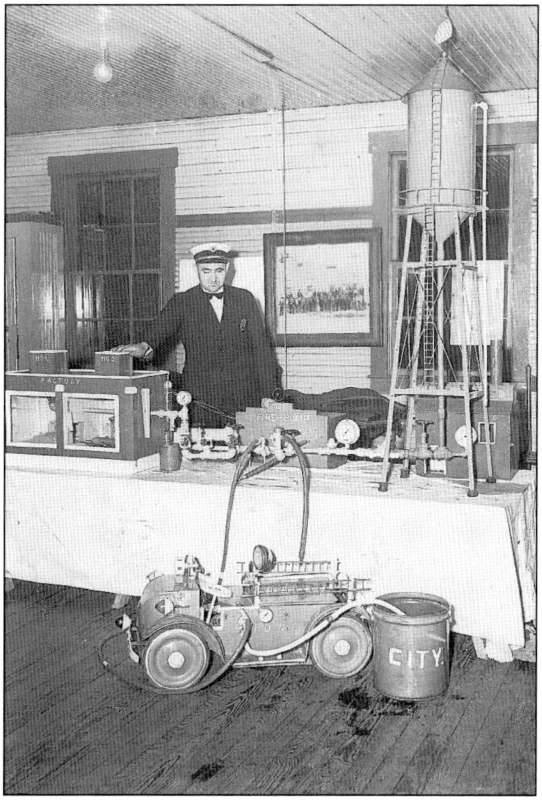

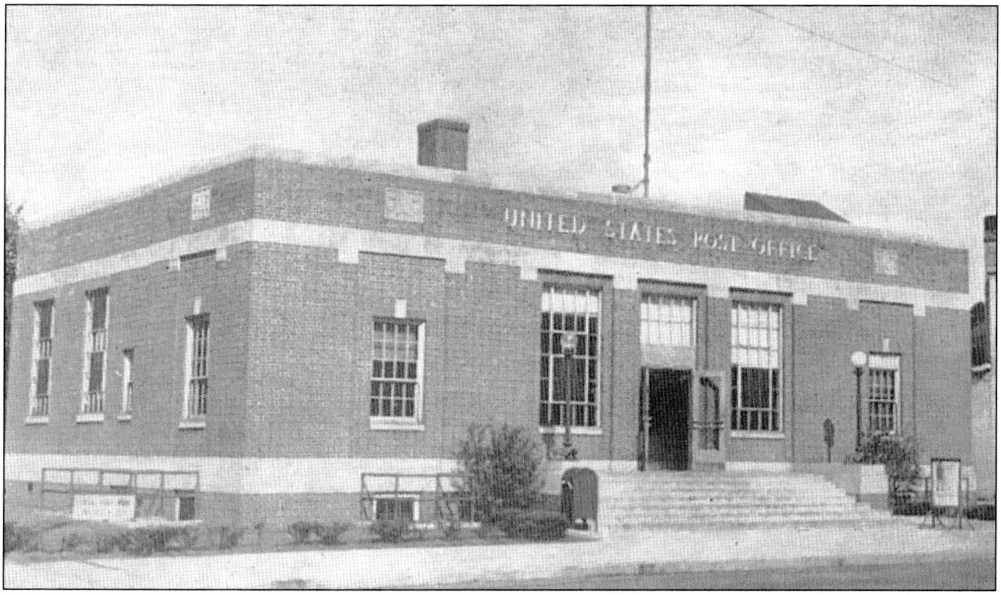

United States Post Office. Art Deco styling was a very popular style of architecture in the 1930s. In 1935, this Art Deco-style building was completed in Lawrenceburg from plans drawn by Louis A. Simon, government architect. The building cornerstone was placed in 1934, and the building was dedicated November 9, 1935. (Produced by Whitney's Studio, Lawrenceburg, Indiana.)

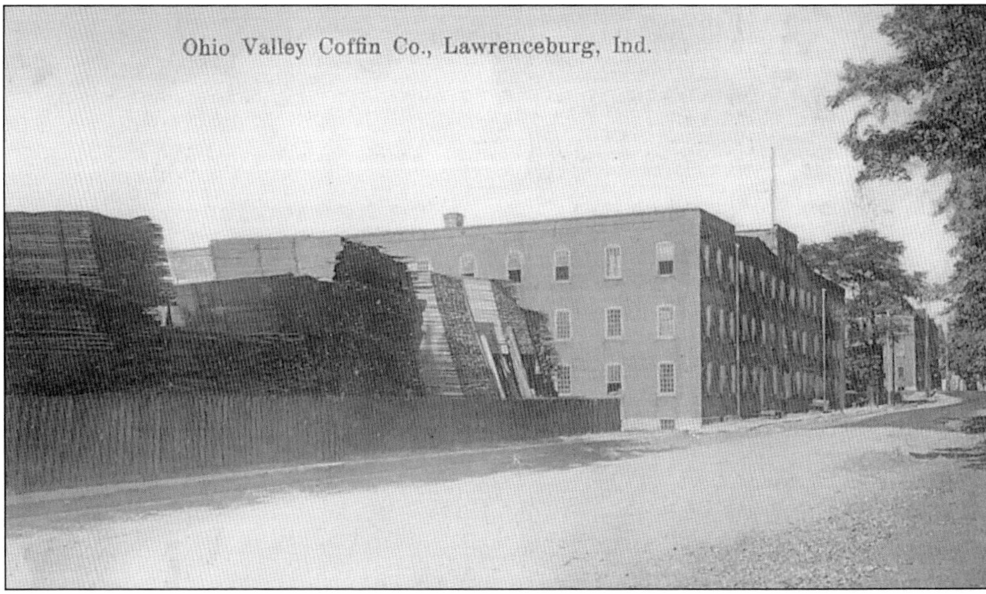

Ohio Valley Coffin Company. The coffin factory in Lawrenceburg was located on West High Street, at the intersection with Ash Street. The *c.* 1915 view above is looking east down High Street toward the buggy factory, courthouse, and town. The factory was organized on January 27, 1872. (Produced by Kraemer Art Co., Cincinnati, Ohio.)

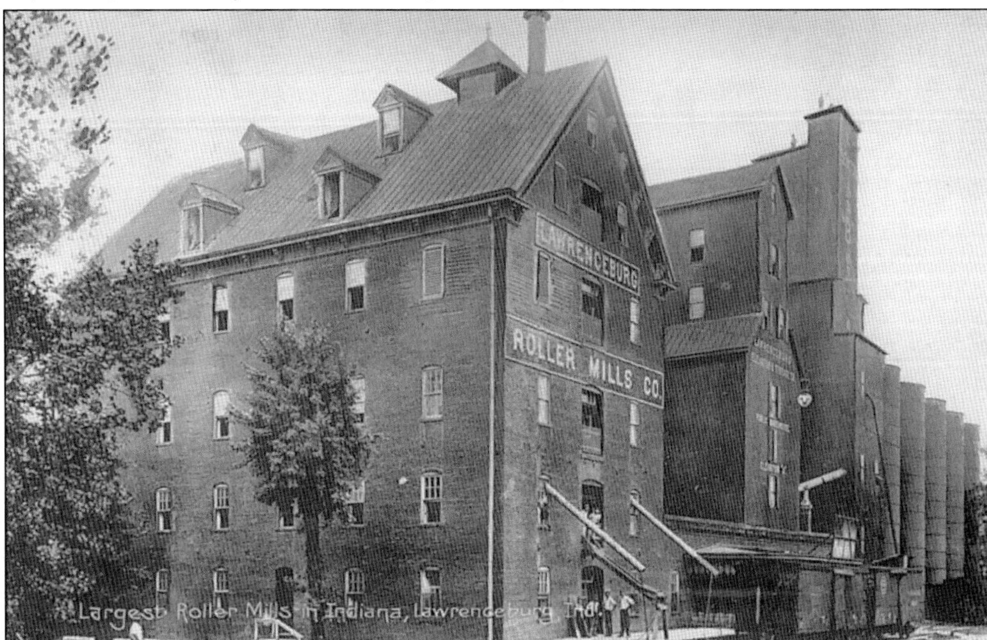

Largest Roller Mills in Indiana. At one time the largest roller mills in Indiana were located on West High Street in Lawrenceburg. Started in the 1870s as the G.Y. Roots Company Flour Mills, the factory later became known as the Lawrenceburg Roller Mills Company. In 1941, a major fire destroyed the buildings of the company. And, in 1997, the last part of the company was removed when the storage silos were torn down. (Produced by Kraemer Art Co., Cincinnati, Ohio.)

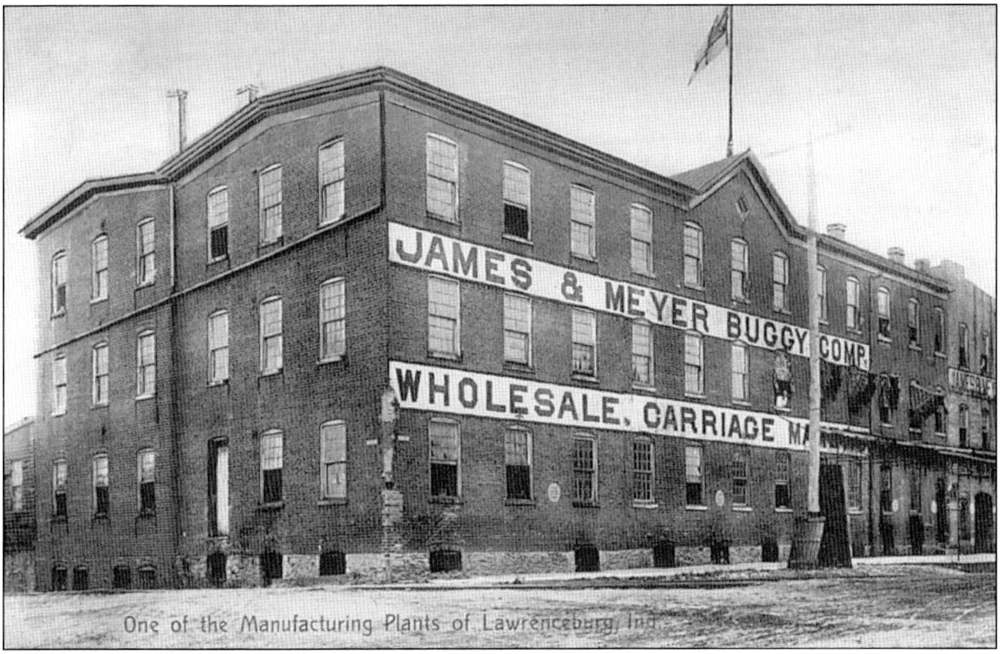

JAMES & MEYER BUGGY COMPANY. James & Meyer occupied the half block bounded by High Street, Maple Street, and William Street in what might be called the first Lawrenceburg "Industrial District." The postcard displayed above is postmarked 1911. In later years, the factory was known as Standard Vehicle Company. (Produced by Kraemer Art Co., Cincinnati and Berlin, Germany.)

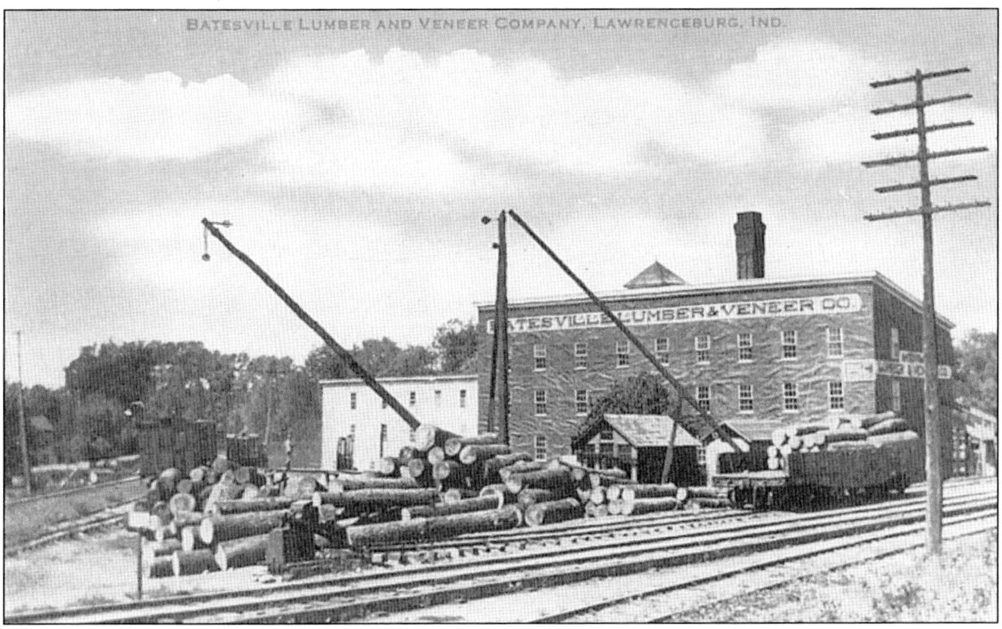

BATESVILLE LUMBER AND VENEER COMPANY. Located at the end of William Street, near the railroad tracks, this property was purchased from the A.D. Cook Company in 1906. The plant was later sold to the Pierson Hollowell Company. The location is now occupied by Argosy Resort. (Produced by Auburn Post Card Mfg. Co., Auburn, Indiana.)

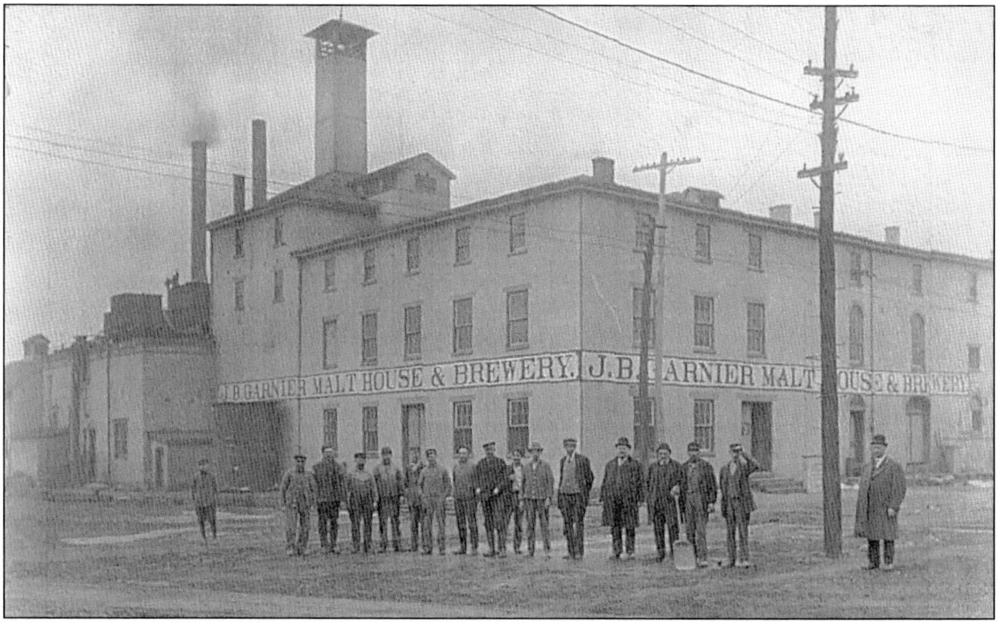

John B. Garnier Brewery. John B. Garnier, a native of Hummerdengen, Alsace-Lorraine, France, started a brewery on the southwest corner of Third and Shipping Streets in 1866. He previously owned a small brewery located nearby on Shipping Street. After Mr. Garnier died on March 7, 1897, his son-in-law, Victor Oberting, operated the business. The business closed after prohibition was passed. (Real photo postcard by an unidentified photographer.)

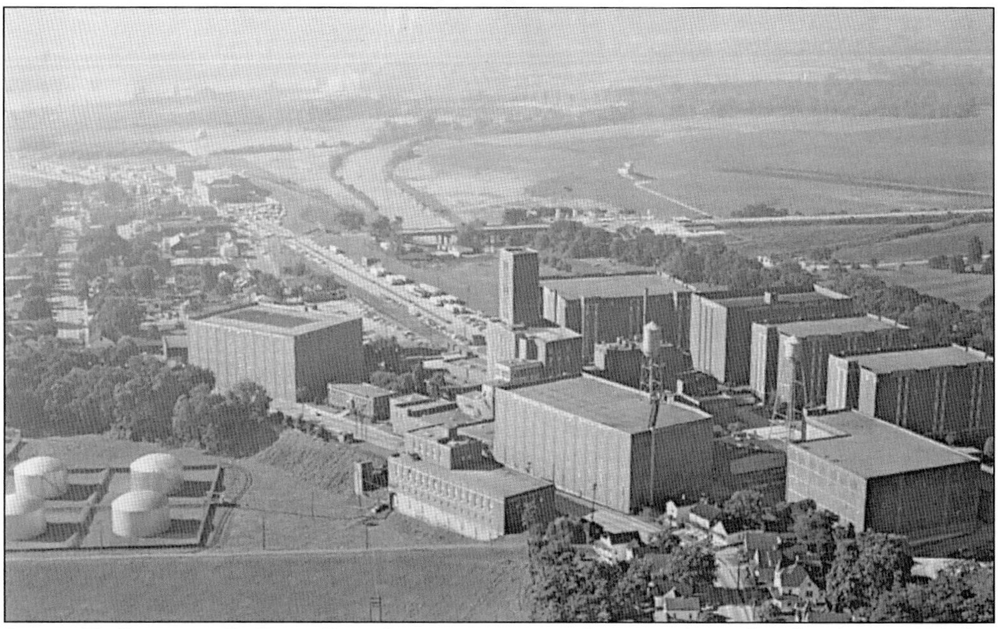

Joseph E. Seagram & Sons, Inc. Seagrams came to Lawrenceburg shortly after a 1933 fire destroyed the Rossville Distillery. On October 23, 1933, Seagrams was incorporated in Indiana to manufacture distilled spirits. Warehouse # 7, the large building in the foreground, was razed in 1991–92, and replaced by other structures. (Produced by Dexter Press, West Nyack, New York, for William Krider.)

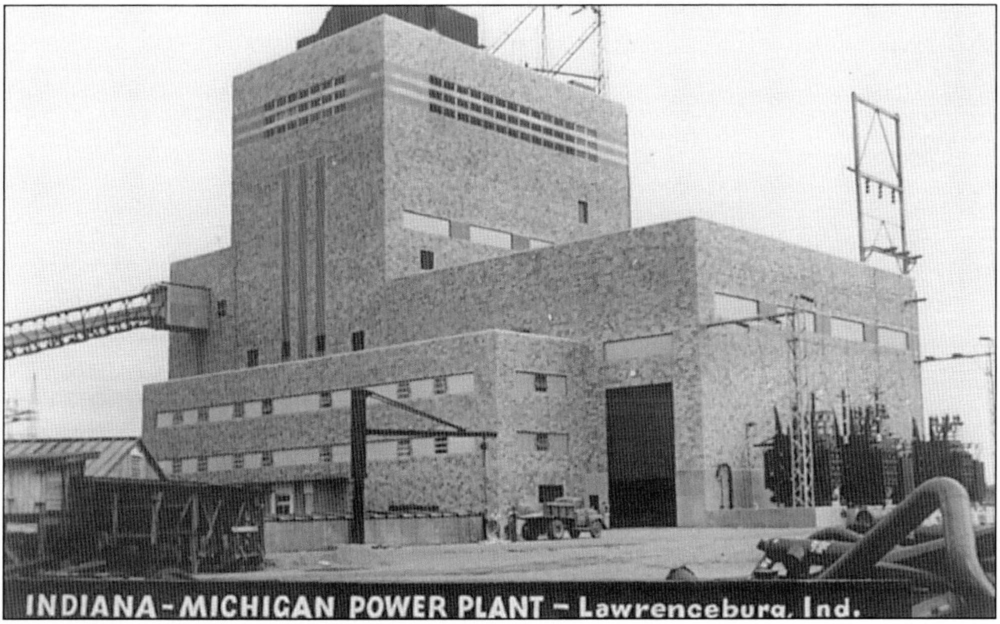

INDIANA-MICHIGAN POWER PLANT. I & M Electric Power Company has operated a power plant on the banks of the Ohio River, at the mouth of Tanners Creek, since 1949. In the following decades, the Lawrenceburg plant experienced steady growth. (Real photo postcard by an unidentified photographer.)

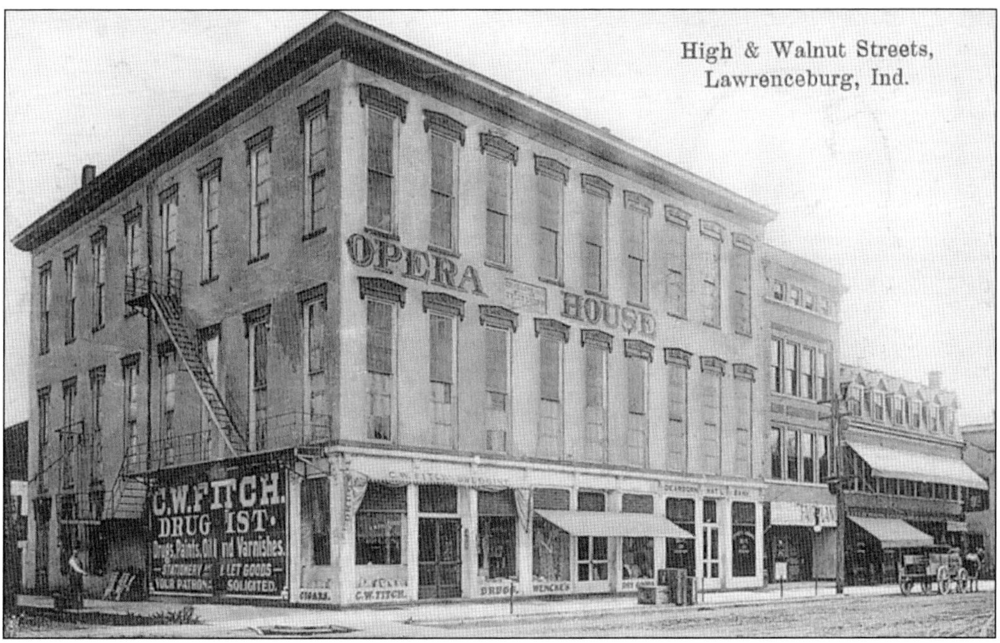

HIGH & WALNUT STREETS. In 1908, when this card was mailed, C.W. Fitch operated a drug store in the large 1853 Opera House building. The Italianate-style building was also the home of the International Order of Odd Fellows. A major fire in the 1970s caused considerable damage to the building, and later repairs eliminated the top two floors of the historic landmark. (Unidentified printer and publisher.)

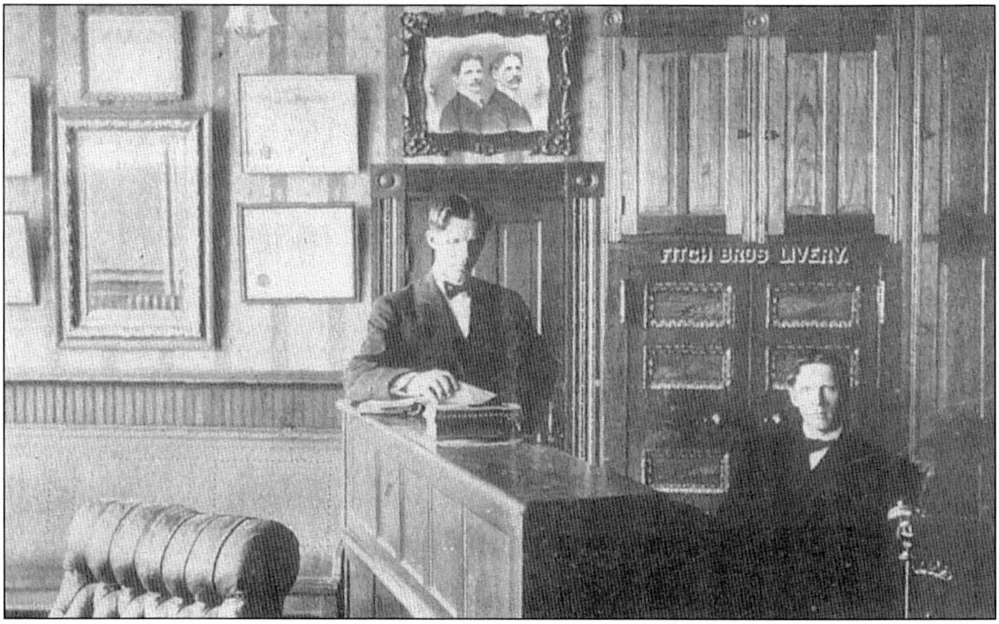

OFFICE, FITCH BROTHERS LIVERYMEN AND FUNERAL DIRECTORS. The Fitch Brothers Funeral Home and Livery Stable was first started in Lawrenceburg in 1888 by Thomas A. and Joseph T. Fitch. The business started as a livery stable in the rear of their home on the corner of West High and Mary Streets, later known as the American Legion Home. (Produced by Art Mfg. Co., Amelia, Ohio.)

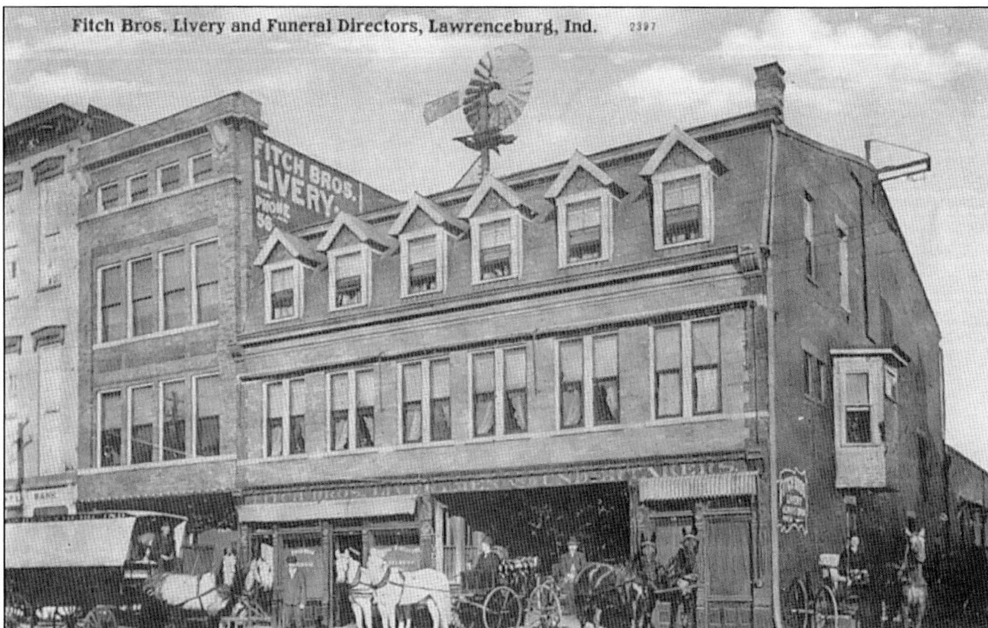

FITCH BROTHERS LIVERYMEN AND FUNERAL DIRECTORS. In 1910, Thomas and Joseph Fitch purchased the building pictured here from John F. Hornberger, a jeweler and optician. Theodore H. Fitch, son of Joseph, joined in the business in 1929, and his brother, Thomas, in 1940. Joseph H. Fitch died on July 27, 1939. (Produced by Art Mfg. Co., Amelia, Ohio.)

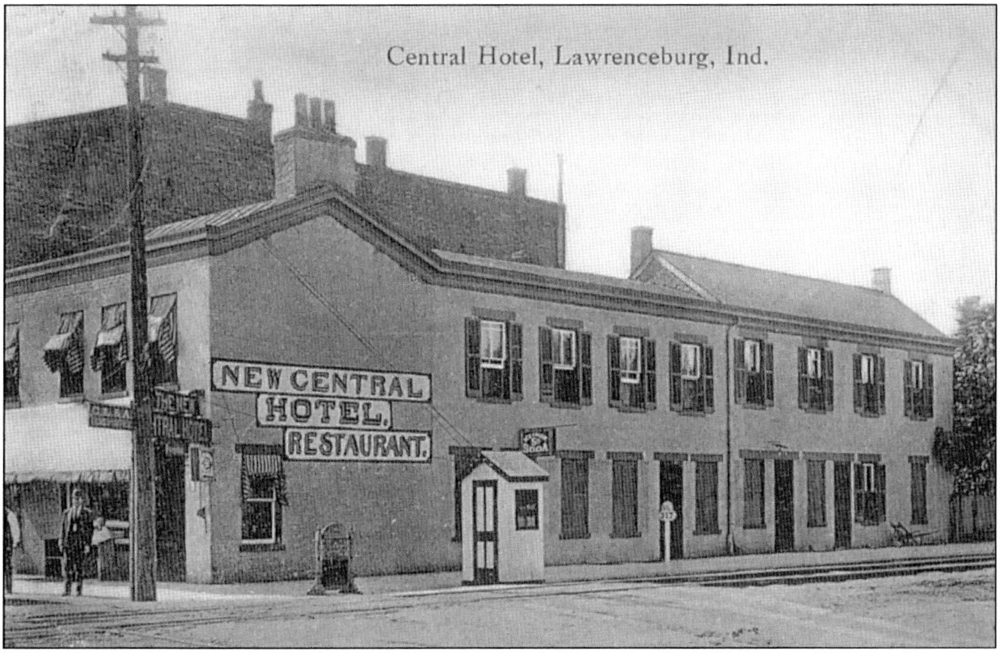

Central Hotel. The Central Hotel and Restaurant was located on the southwest corner of Walnut and William Streets. Before this was the site of the Central Hotel, it was occupied by a drug store and the Ragen Hotel. (Produced by Kraemer Art Co., Cincinnati and Berlin, Germany.)

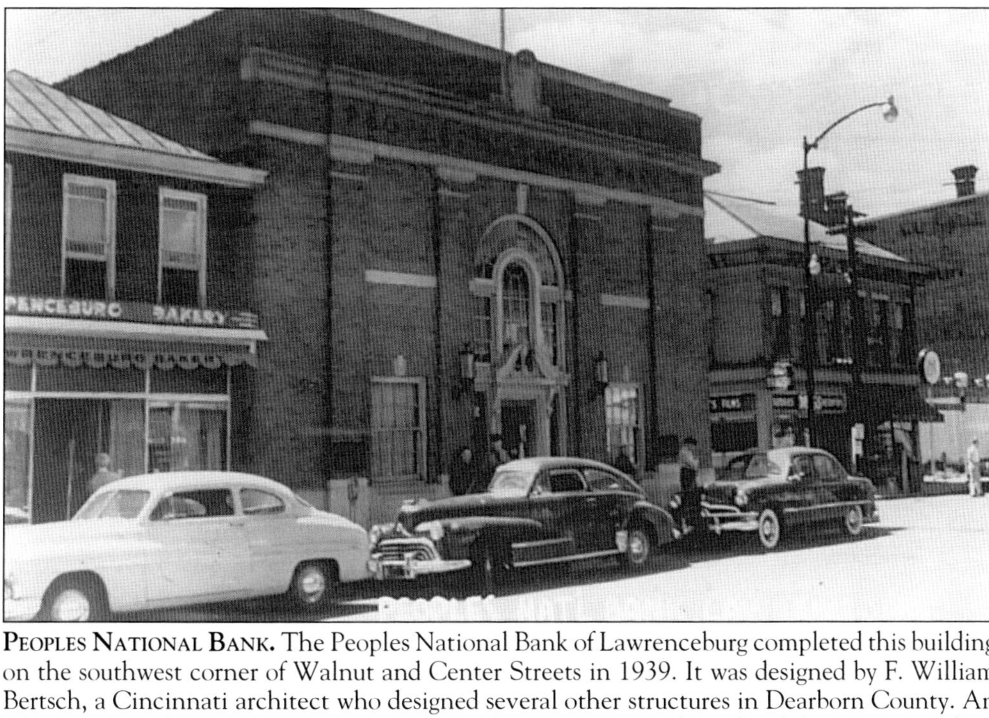

Peoples National Bank. The Peoples National Bank of Lawrenceburg completed this building on the southwest corner of Walnut and Center Streets in 1939. It was designed by F. William Bertsch, a Cincinnati architect who designed several other structures in Dearborn County. An addition was added onto the rear at a later date. It is now a branch of the Firstar Bank of Cincinnati, Ohio. (Real photo postcard by an unidentified photographer.)

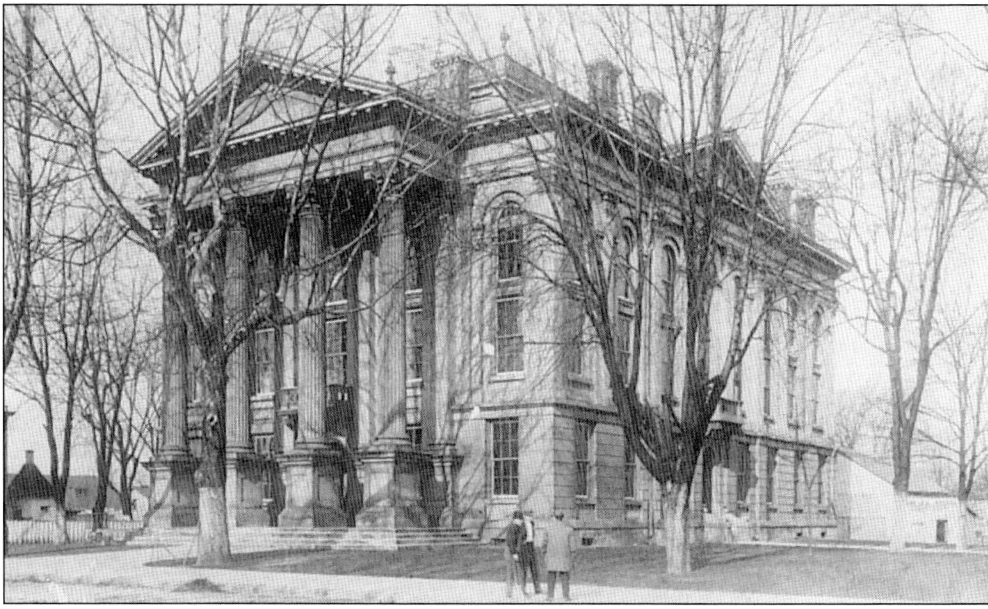

Dearborn County Courthouse. George H. Kyle, of Vevay, Indiana, was the architect for this Classic Revival structure completed in 1873. According to newspaper accounts, on April 13, 1871, a cornerstone for the building was laid with elaborate ceremony. Later efforts to locate the stone, however, have been unsuccessful. Construction costs for the building were $100,000. (Produced by Kraemer Art Co., Cincinnati, Ohio.)

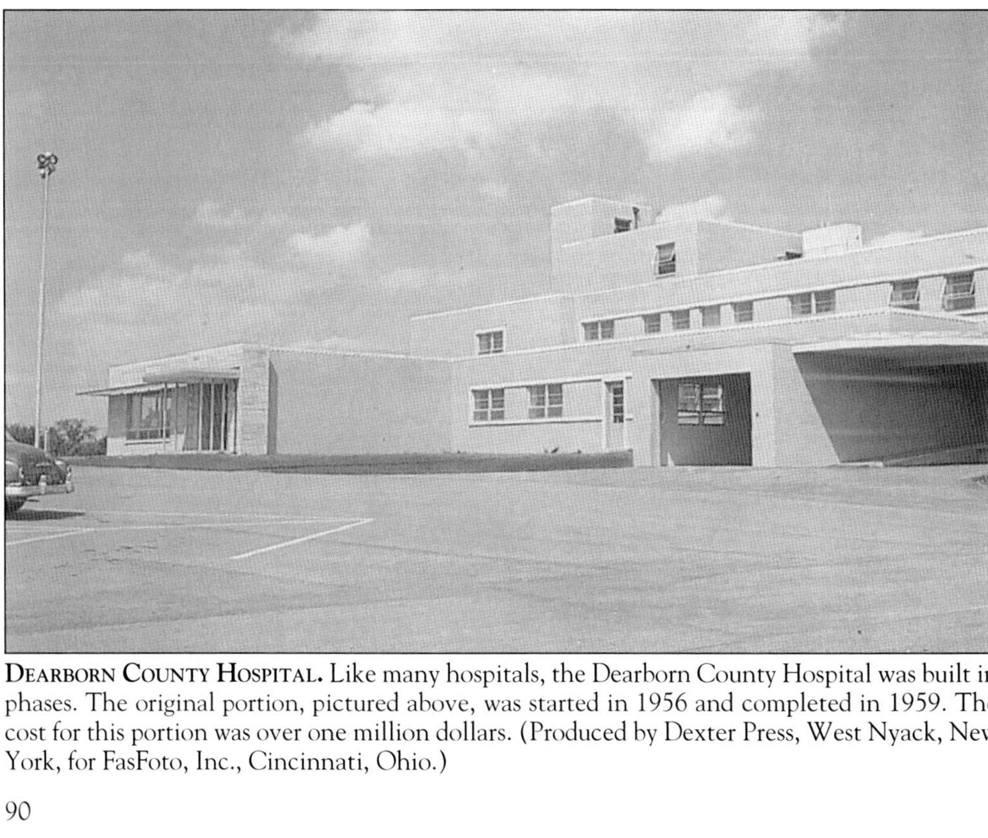

Dearborn County Hospital. Like many hospitals, the Dearborn County Hospital was built in phases. The original portion, pictured above, was started in 1956 and completed in 1959. The cost for this portion was over one million dollars. (Produced by Dexter Press, West Nyack, New York, for FasFoto, Inc., Cincinnati, Ohio.)

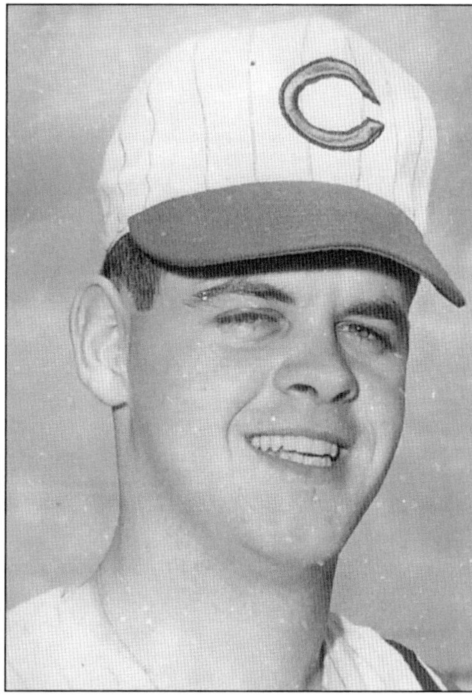

WILLIAM H. "BILL" MCCOOL PROMOTIONAL CARD. Born July 14, 1944, the son of Carl F. and Deloris McCool of Lawrenceburg, William H. McCool, better known as Bill or Billy, reached great heights in the world of baseball. Bill McCool started his professional baseball career in 1963, playing class-D ball in Tampa, Florida. He jumped to class Triple-A ball in the same year, playing at San Diego. In 1964, he moved up to the major leagues. His rookie year was spent with the Cincinnati Reds as a relief pitcher. At the end of the season, Bill was named National League Rookie Pitcher of the Year. During the 1966 season, Bill was selected to the National League All-Star squad. He continued with the Reds until the 1969 season, when he was traded to the San Diego Padres. (Real Photo postcard by an unidentified photographer.)

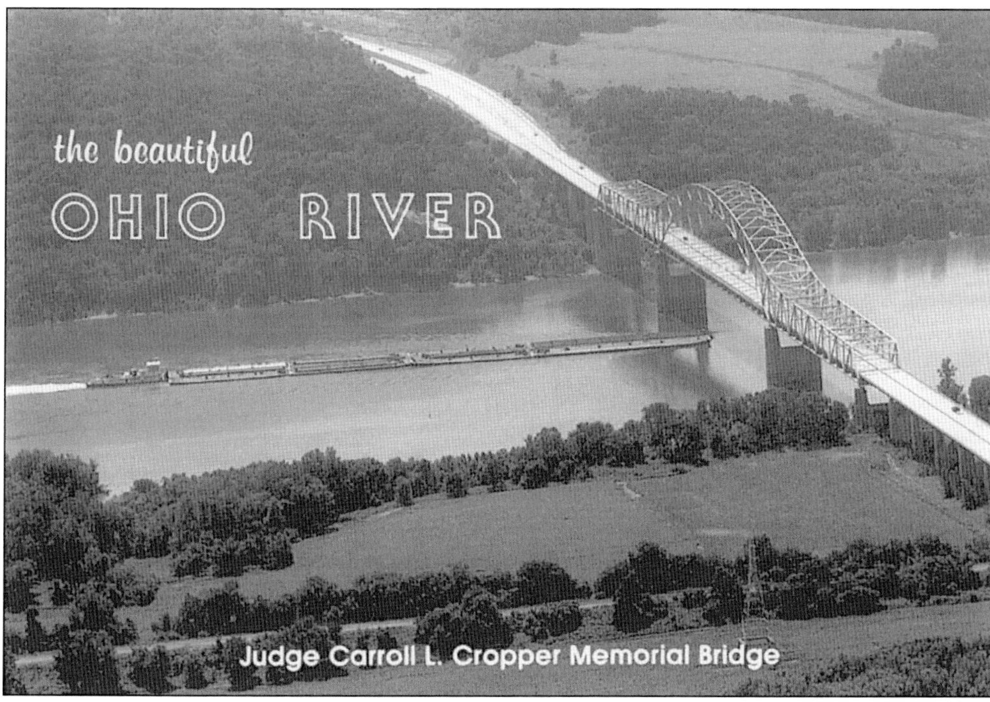

JUDGE CARROLL L. CROPPER MEMORIAL BRIDGE. On December 6, 1977, a dedication ceremony featuring remarks from the governors of three states opened the bridge pictured here. It was built at a total cost of $172,791,391. It was the first tri-state outer belt freeway in the country. Southeast Indiana has not been the same since it opened. (Photograph by Milt Masing, published by Tri-State Visuals.)

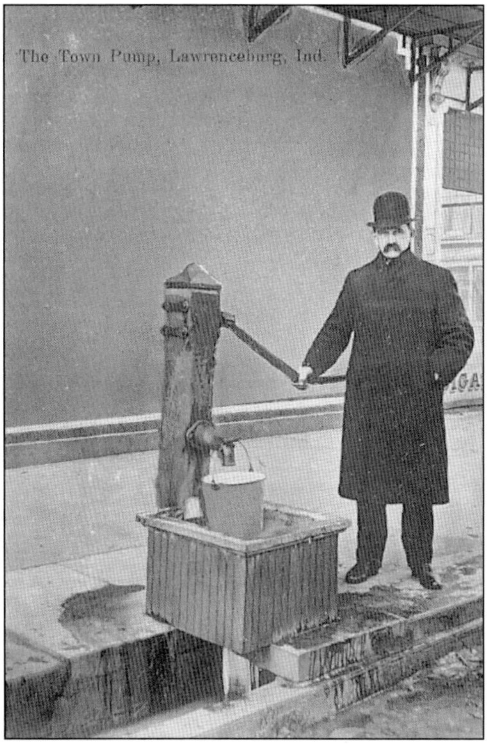

THE TOWN PUMP. There were actually several town pumps in the City of Lawrenceburg. Early city maps show that there was a town pump on almost every other block in the old and new parts of the city. Many, if not all, of the pumps were manufactured at the A.D. Cook Company. According to some sources, the individual that is posing at the pump for this picture is none other than the owner of Kraemer Art Company—the company that produced not only this card, but also many of the best-quality cards made in the country. (Produced by Kraemer Art Co., Cincinnati, Ohio.)

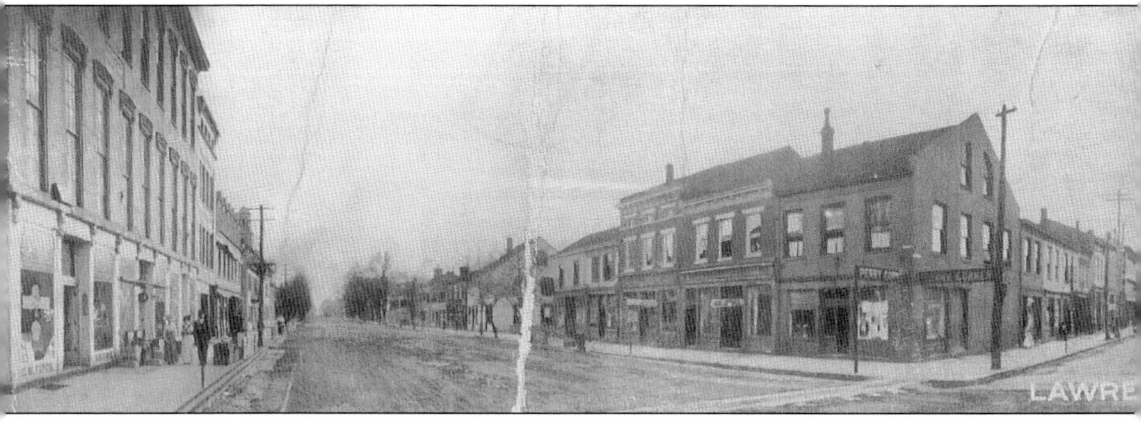

STREET PANORAMA, WALNUT AND HIGH STREETS. The left portion of this 3.75" by 20.5" mailing card shows West High Street from its intersection with Walnut Street. On the extreme left is the I.O.O.F. building, with Parry Corner opposite. As the viewer looks to the center of the picture, Walnut Street can be seen looking to the north.

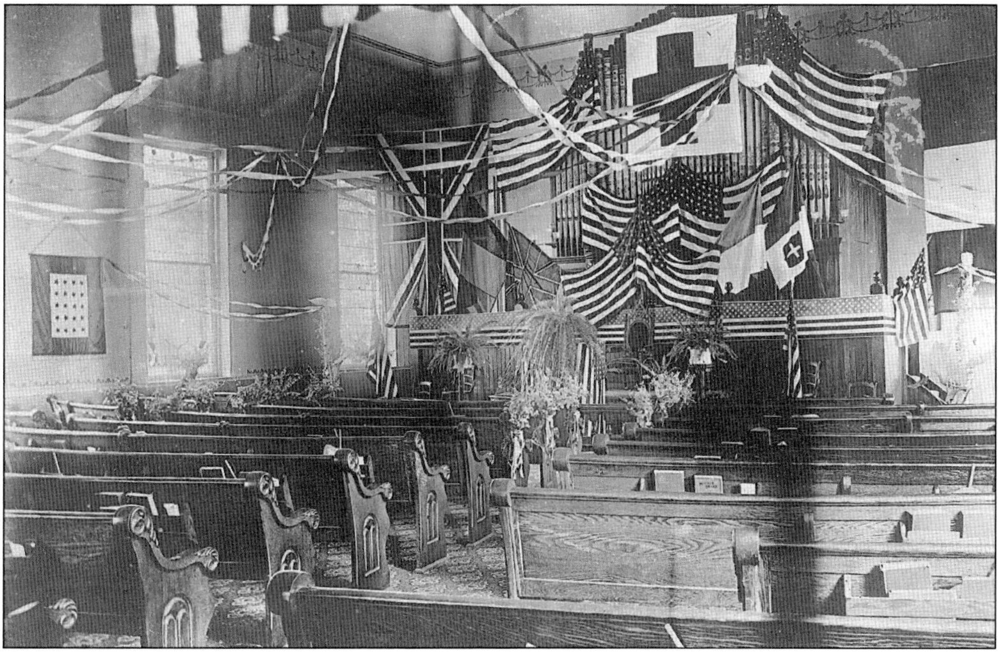

UNIDENTIFIED CHURCH INTERIOR. This card is not definitely identified as Lawrenceburg, but it was postmarked in Lawrenceburg in 1918. It shows the interior of a church decorated in a patriotic manner for the war effort. (Real photo postcard by an unidentified photographer.)

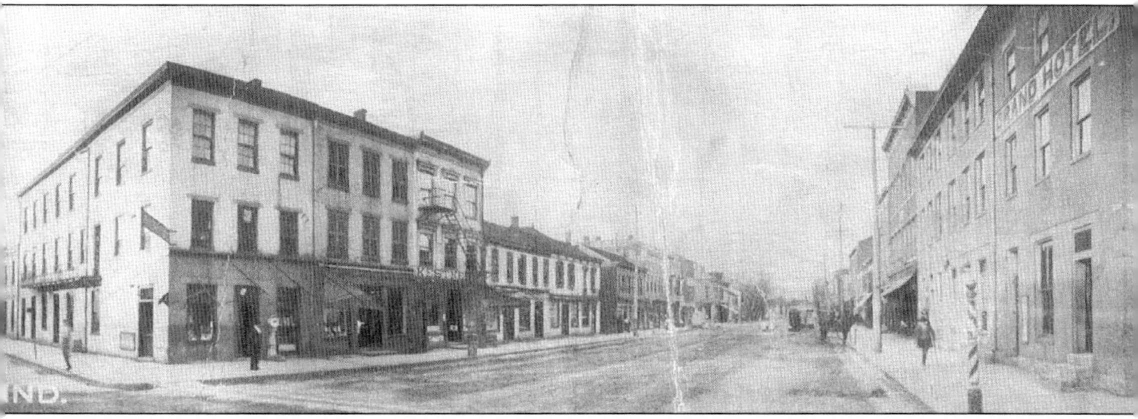

STREET PANORAMA, WALNUT AND HIGH STREETS, NEWTOWN. East High Street is seen on the right side of the picture, with the Grand Hotel in the extreme foreground. When constructed as the Jesse Hunt House Hotel, this building was the first three-story, brick building in the State of Indiana. (Unidentified printer and publisher.)

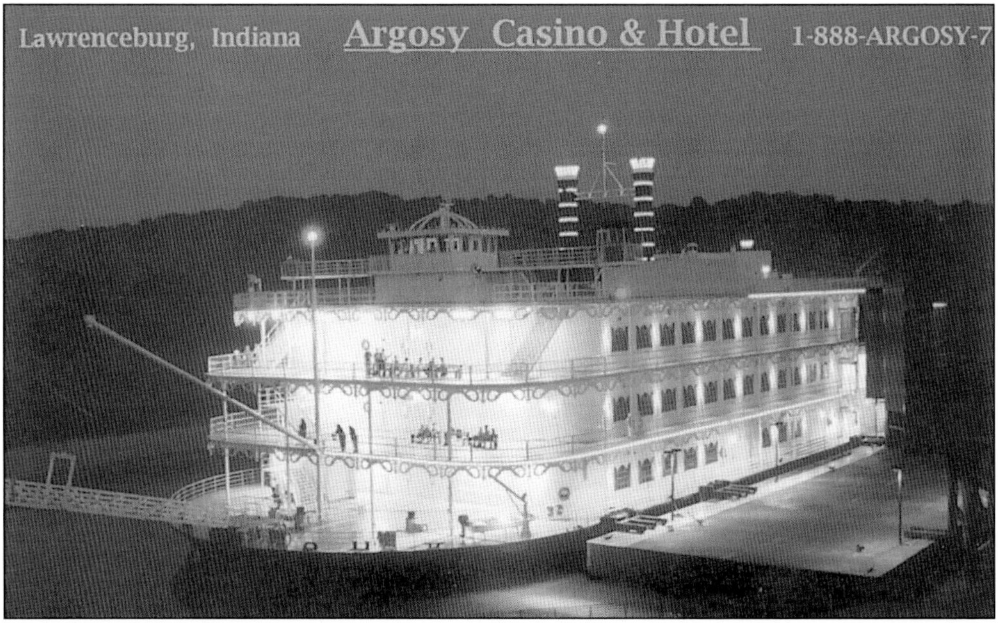

ARGOSY CASINO AND HOTEL. When first put into operation in Lawrenceburg in 1997, this boat was promoted as the largest riverboat casino in the country. It has 78,000 feet of gaming space, 1,734 machines, and 104 gaming tables. It has a capacity of 4,000 people. (Photograph by Milt Masing, published by Tri-State Visuals.)

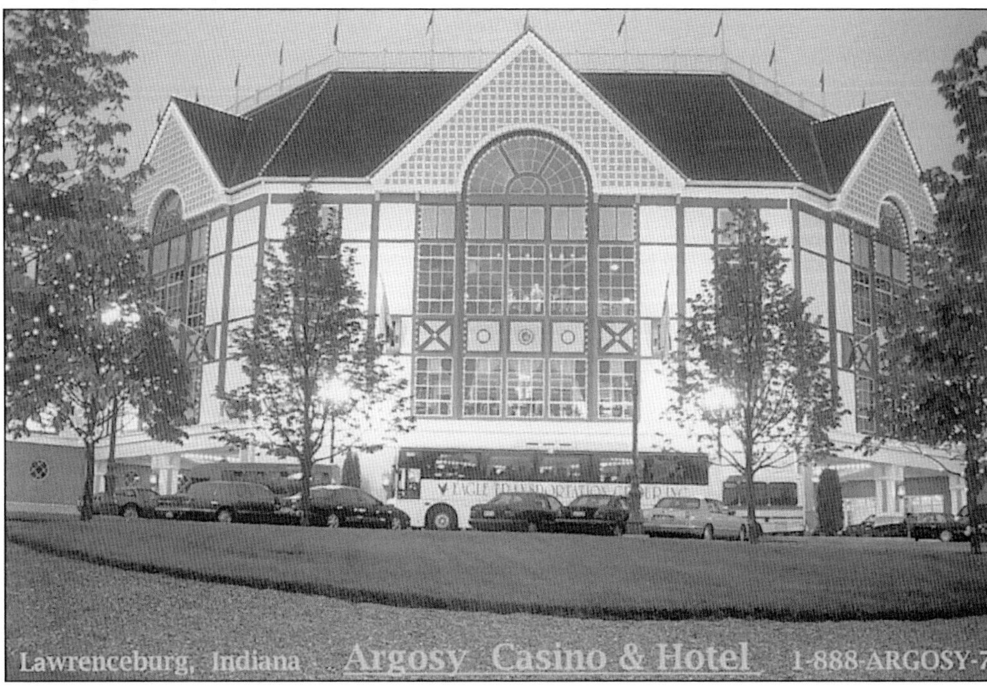

ARGOSY CASINO AND HOTEL. The Argosy Entertainment Pavilion is pictured in this continental-size postcard view. Architectural work for the resort was done by American Consulting Engineers, Inc. and Ratio Architects, both of Indianapolis. The building was completed in 1998. (Photograph by Milt Masing, published by Tri-State Visuals.)

Five

MOORES HILL

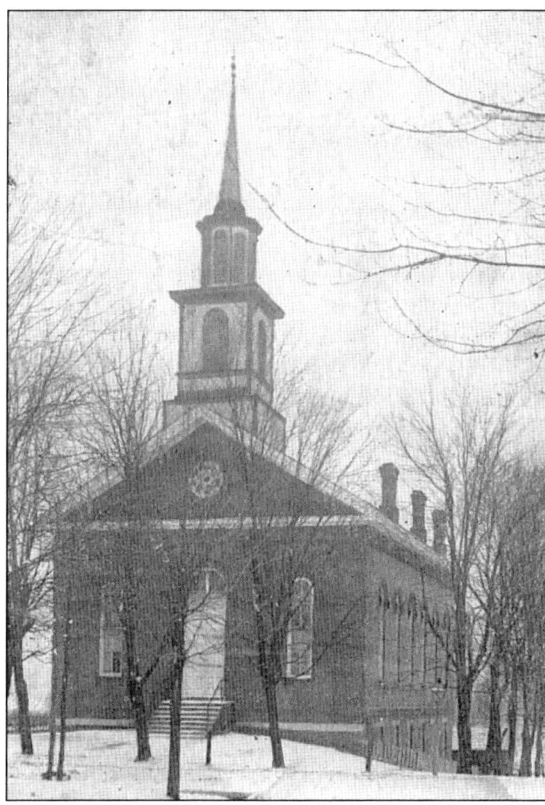

METHODIST EPISCOPAL CHURCH. The Moores Hill Methodist Church building, pictured above, was constructed in 1870–71 at a cost of about $15,000. It is largely Italianate in architectural style. The early beginnings of the Methodists in Moores Hill can be traced back to 1818, when a class was organized at the cabin house of Moses Musgrove. The first worship house built by the group was constructed in 1829. It was followed by another in 1839 that served the congregation until the 1871 structure above was completed. (Produced by Hustler Printing Co., Moores Hill, Indiana, for H.F. Zierer.)

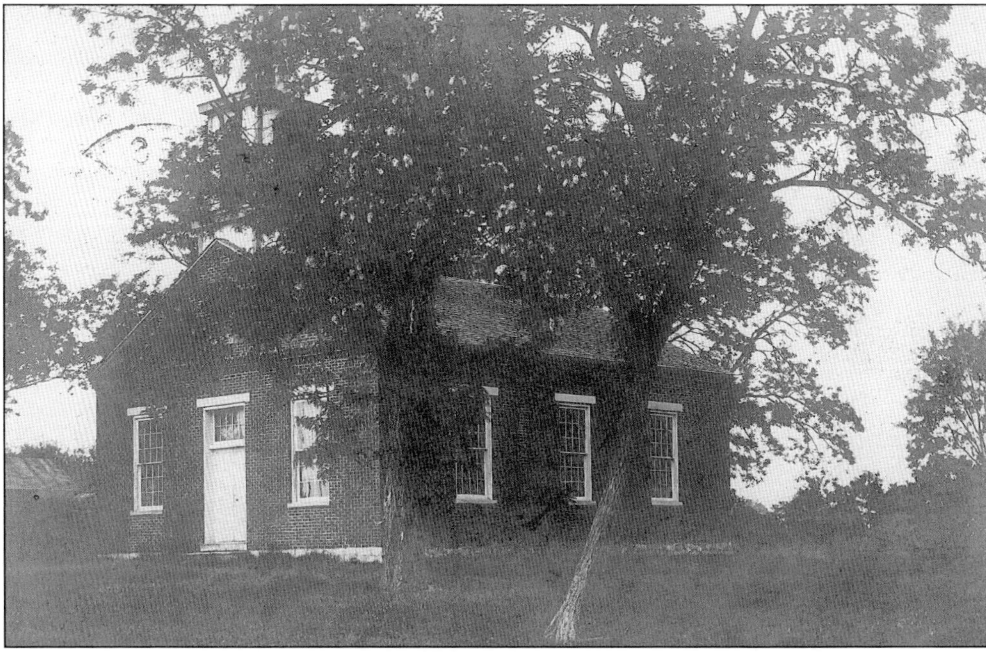

First Baptist Church. On South Broadway Street, at the corner of College Street, is located the Moores Hill First Baptist Church. The building is a small, box-like structure with Gothic Revival detailing. It was completed in 1866 on land belonging to Mr. Justus. (Real photo postcard by an unidentified photographer.)

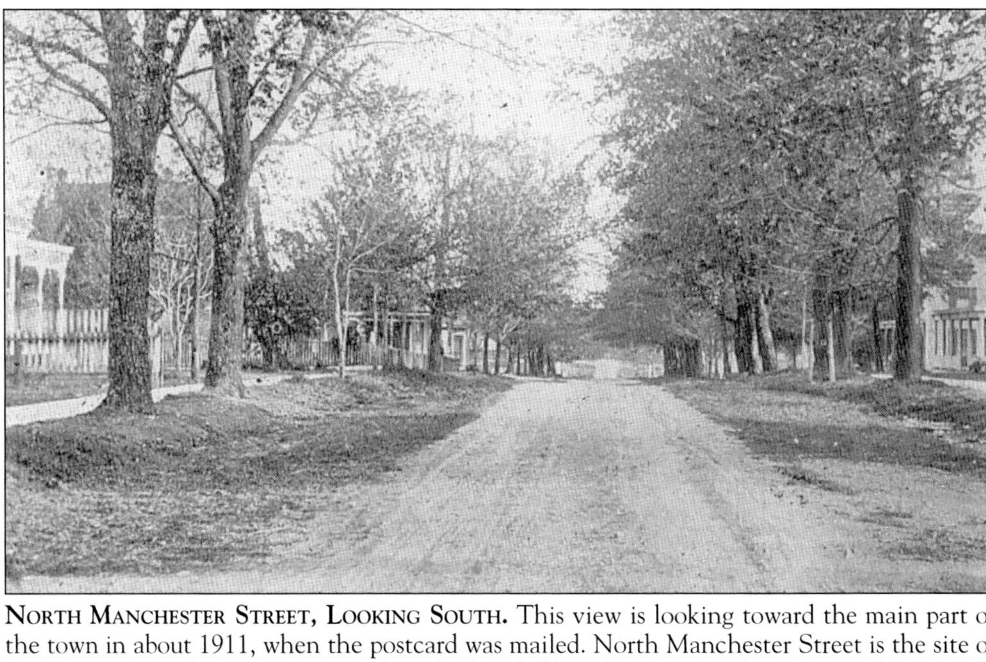

North Manchester Street, Looking South. This view is looking toward the main part of the town in about 1911, when the postcard was mailed. North Manchester Street is the site of many prominent homes constructed in the last half of the nineteenth century. The town of Moores Hill was platted in 1839 by Adam Moore and Andrew Stevens. (Unidentified printer and publisher.)

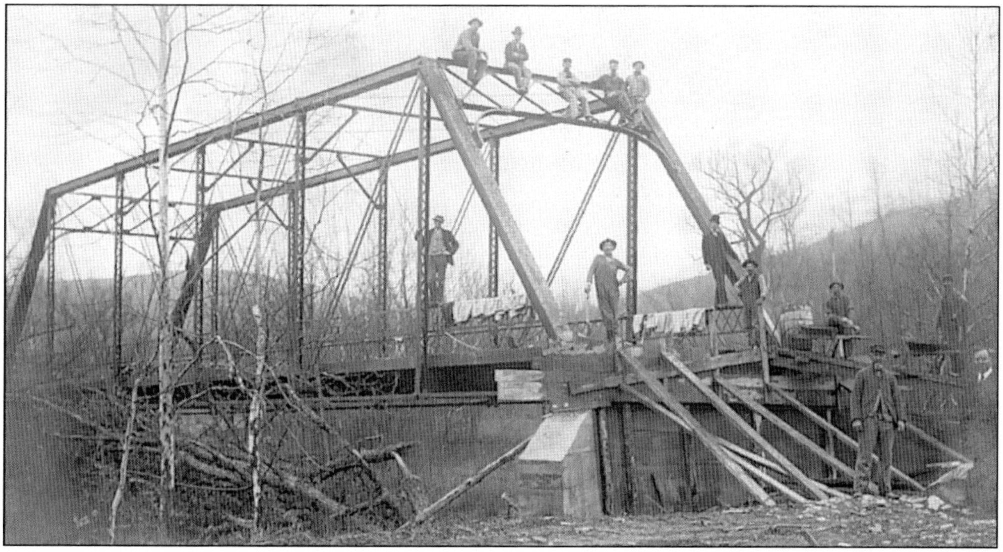

BRIDGE CONSTRUCTION SITE. This photo postcard of a construction site near Moores Hill was mailed in 1909 by the gentleman holding the wheelbarrow. The location of the bridge is not mentioned in the message, but a likely guess would be at the bottom of the Broadway Street hill, near the site of the old depot. (Real photo postcard by an unidentified publisher.)

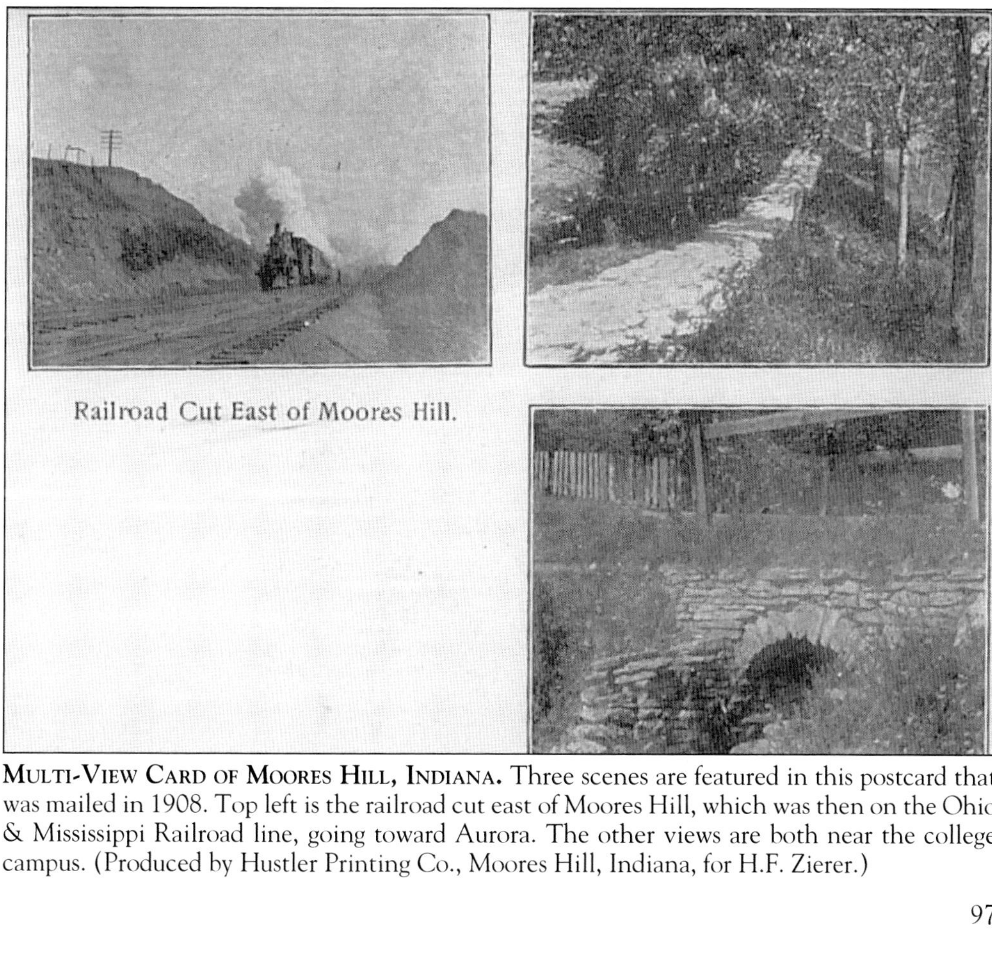

MULTI-VIEW CARD OF MOORES HILL, INDIANA. Three scenes are featured in this postcard that was mailed in 1908. Top left is the railroad cut east of Moores Hill, which was then on the Ohio & Mississippi Railroad line, going toward Aurora. The other views are both near the college campus. (Produced by Hustler Printing Co., Moores Hill, Indiana, for H.F. Zierer.)

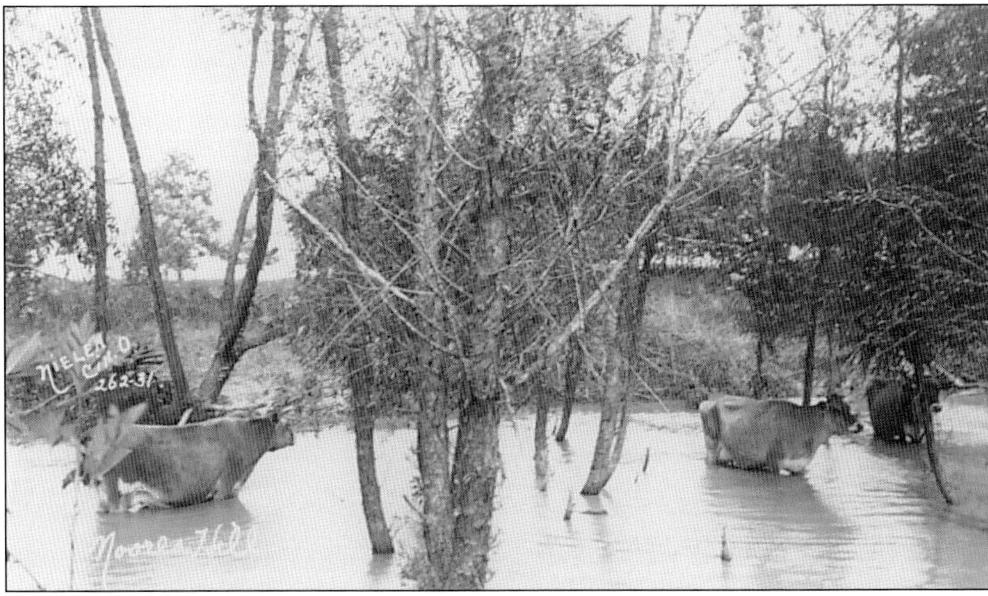

"Cool Cows." Not many people would think to print a postcard of cows submerged up to their utters in water, but in the "golden age" of postcards, printing costs were low and communication options few. Actually, during that period of time, few topics were considered inappropriate. (Real photo postcard, produced by Nieler, Cincinnati, Ohio.)

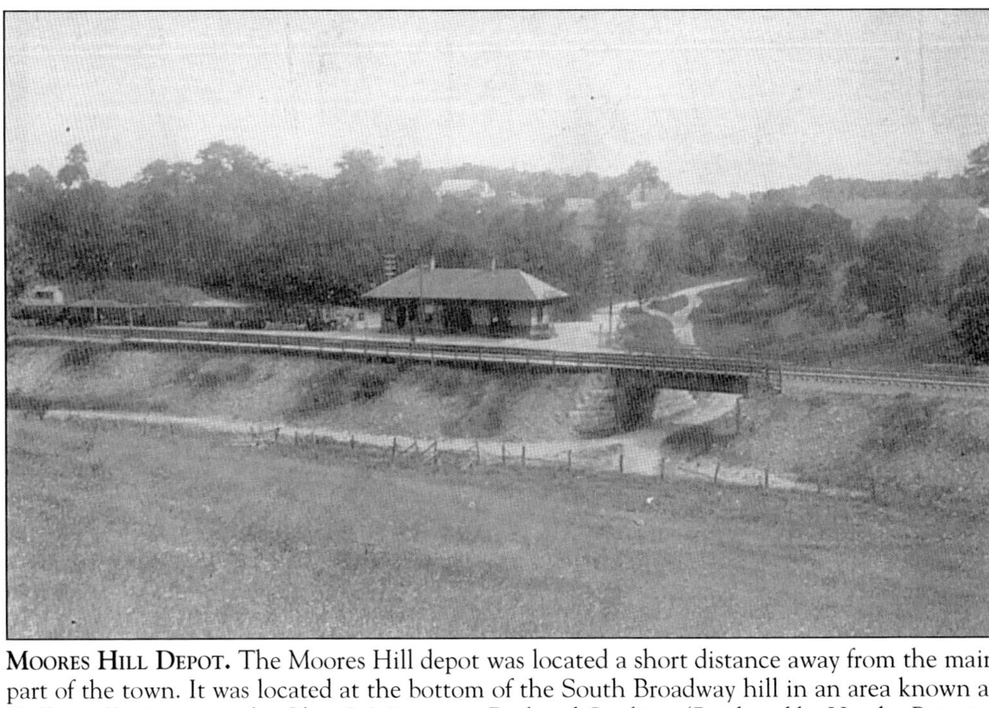

Moores Hill Depot. The Moores Hill depot was located a short distance away from the main part of the town. It was located at the bottom of the South Broadway hill in an area known as Collegeville. It was on the Ohio & Mississippi Railroad Co. line. (Produced by Hustler Printing Co., Moores Hill, Indiana, for H.F. Zierer.)

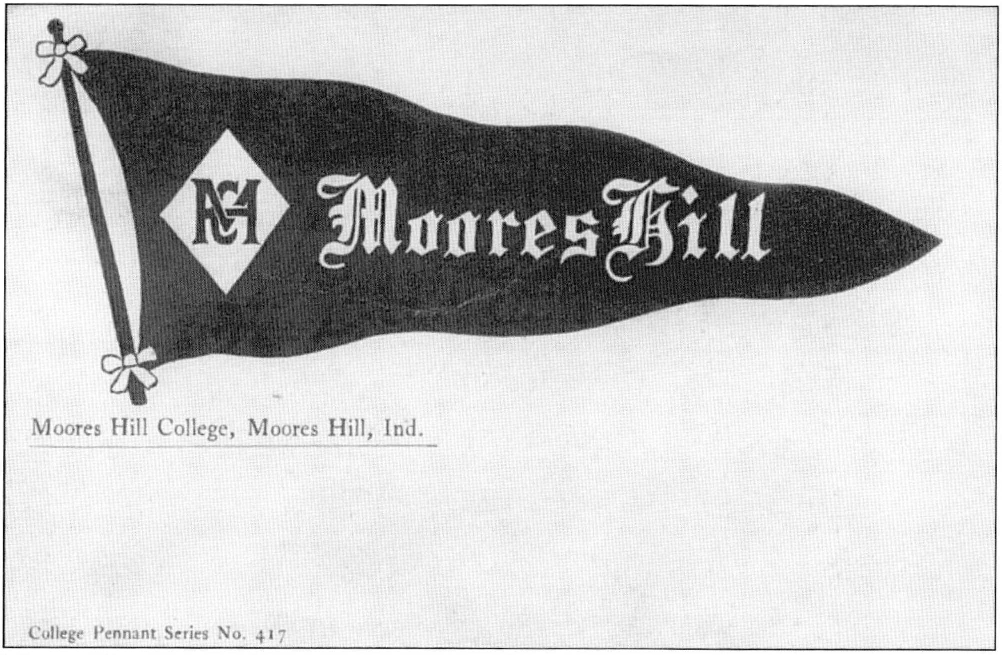

MOORES HILL COLLEGE PENNANT. This postcard was published as one of a series of several that featured colleges around the country. This particular series was published from 1906 through 1908. (Produced by W.E. Ewart, Birmingham, Alabama.)

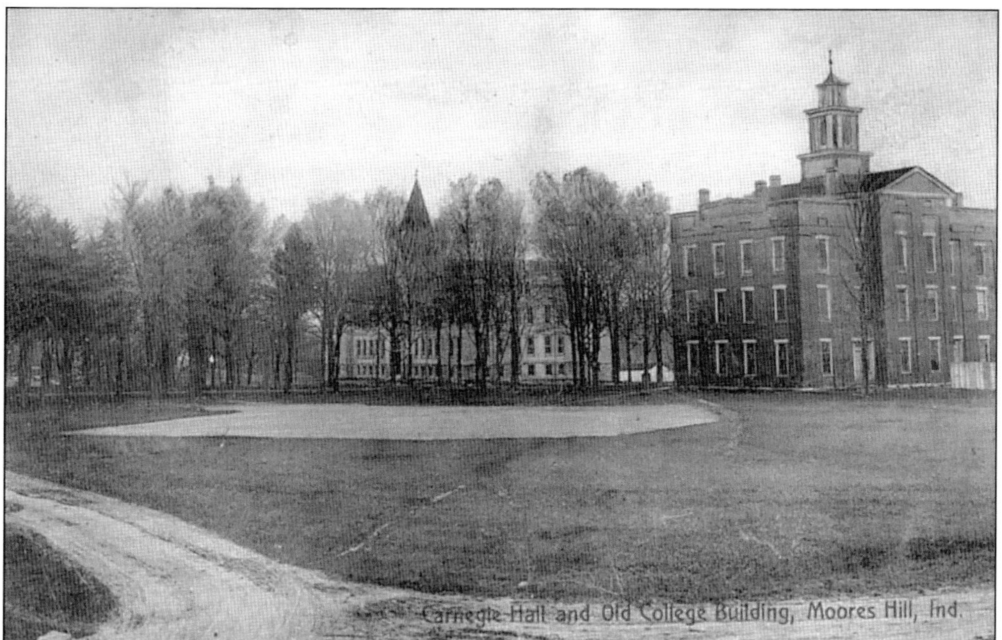

CARNEGIE HALL AND OLD COLLEGE BUILDING. The two buildings featured in this view were both standing for only seven years from 1908–1915. The back of the card bears a 1909 postmark, so the card was made a short time after Carnegie Hall was completed. (Produced by Kraemer Art Co., Cincinnati and Berlin, Germany.)

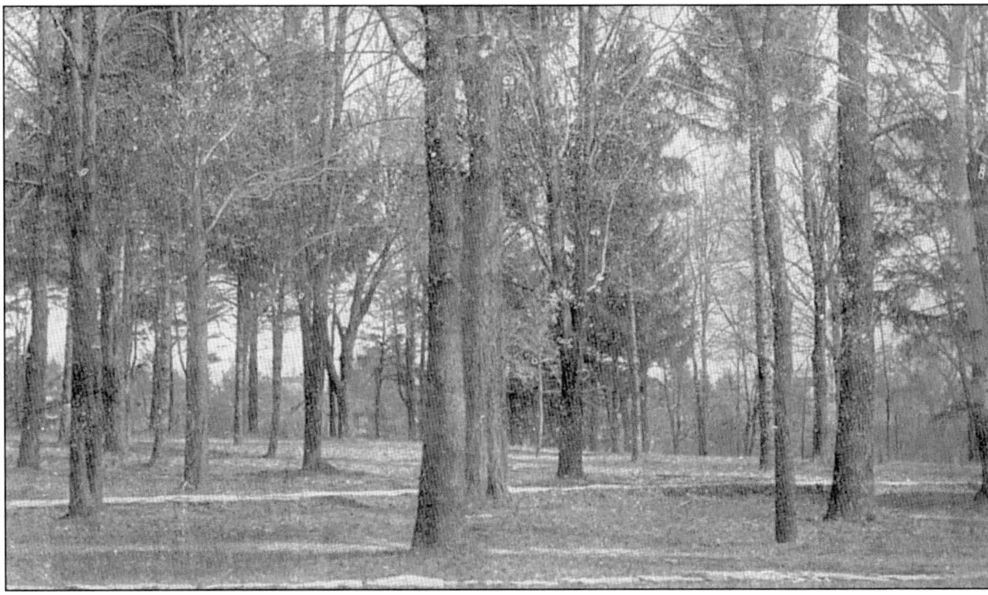

MOORES HILL COLLEGE CAMPUS. Moores Hill College was founded in 1854 as the Moores Hill Male and Female Collegiate Institute. It kept this name until 1887, when the name was changed to Moores Hill College. In 1915, a major fire destroyed the early building, and in 1919 the college became Evansville College. In 1967, Evansville College became the University of Evansville. (Unidentified printer and publisher.)

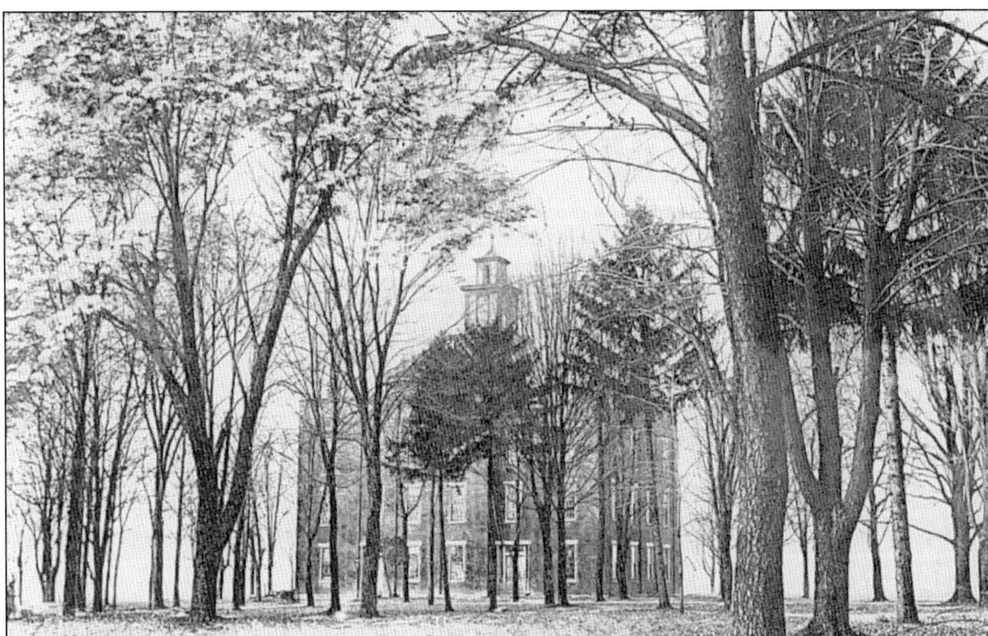

MOORE HALL. Moore Hall, constructed in 1854–1856, was the first building to be constructed on the campus of The Moores Hill Male and Female Collegiate Institute. The bell in the cupola first rang on September 9, 1856. On November 4, 1915, the building was destroyed by fire. (Produced by T.A. Jennings, Moores Hill, Indiana, printed in Germany.)

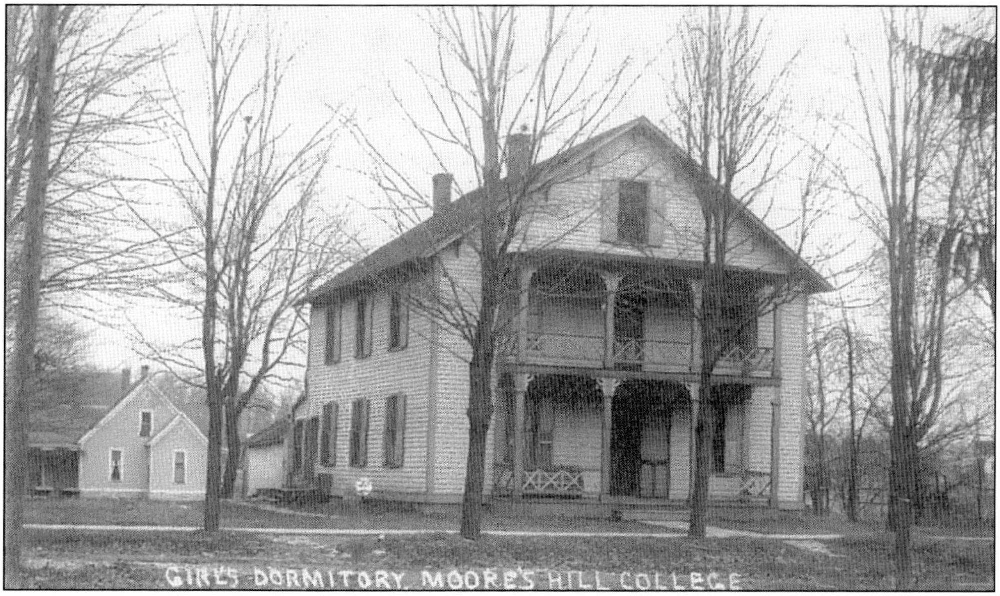

GIRLS' DORMITORY, MOORES HILL COLLEGE. This two-story frame building was constructed in 1898 as a dormitory for female students at the college. A year after its completion, the college constructed a 40' by 70' gymnasium and named it after Will F. Stevens. (Real photo postcard by an unidentified photographer.)

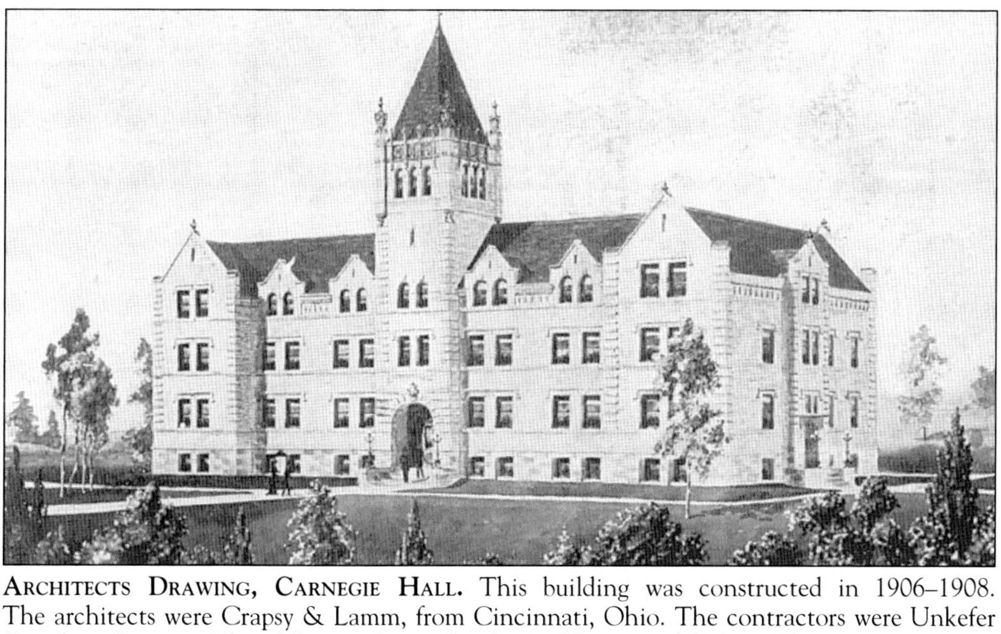

ARCHITECTS DRAWING, CARNEGIE HALL. This building was constructed in 1906–1908. The architects were Crapsy & Lamm, from Cincinnati, Ohio. The contractors were Unkefer Co., from Dayton, Ohio. The total cost for the building was $50,000. The cornerstone was laid June 12, 1907, and the dedication ceremony was June 18, 1908. (Unidentified printer and publisher.)

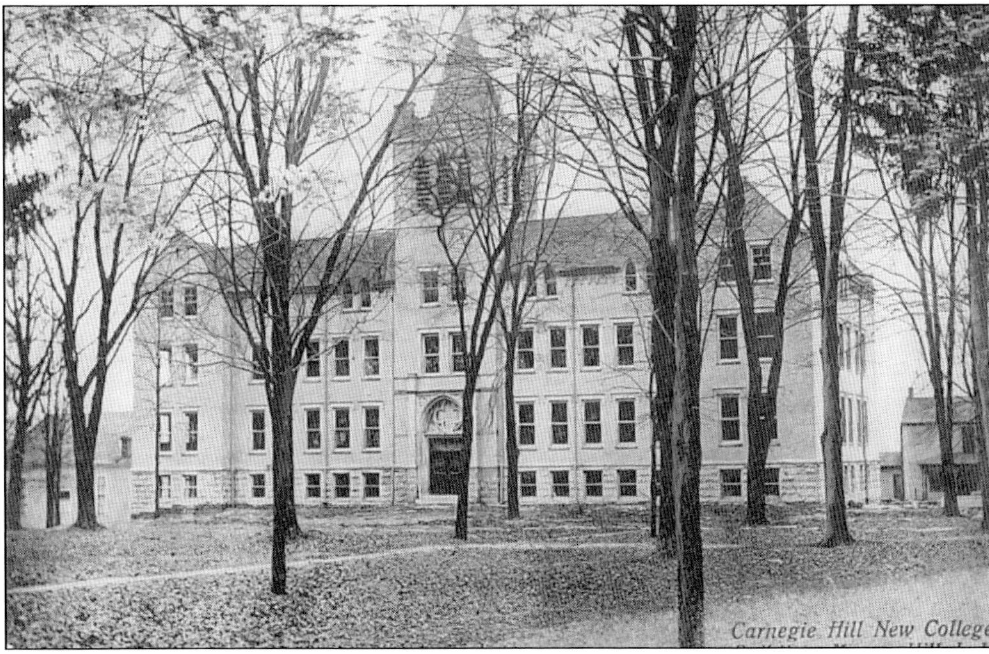

Carnegie Hall, Moores Hill College. After the college was moved to Evansville, Carnegie Hall became a public school. It was used for several decades for all of the grades—elementary through high school. After school reorganization took place in the south part of the county, a new elementary school building was constructed, and the building was donated to the town for use as a library/museum. (Produced by T.A. Jennings, Moores Hill, Indiana, printed in Germany.)

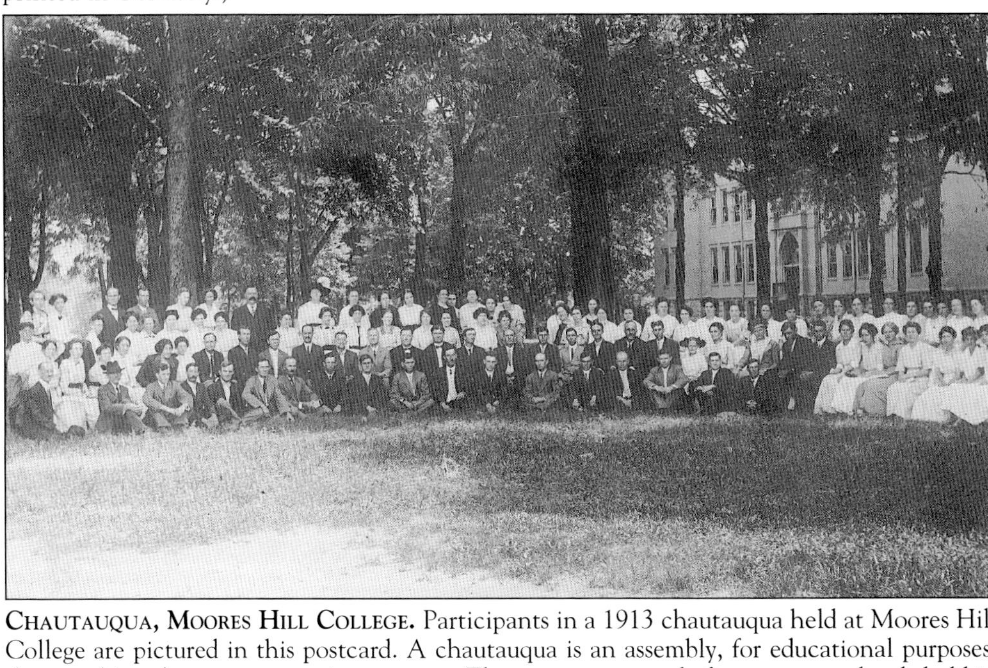

Chautauqua, Moores Hill College. Participants in a 1913 chautauqua held at Moores Hill College are pictured in this postcard. A chautauqua is an assembly, for educational purposes, that combines lectures, entertainment, etc. They were patterned after summer schools held in Chautauqua, New York. (Real photo postcard by an unidentified photographer.)

WINTER MULTI-VIEW POSTCARD, MOORES HILL, INDIANA. The top view of this postcard looks as if it could be used as a generic postcard. Except for the hilly terrain, it could be almost anywhere in the north or middle part of the country. The bottom view shows the tower of Moore Hall off in the distance. The photograph was probably taken from the tower of the Methodist Church on Main Street. The card was postmarked in 1907, making it one of the first divided-back postcards produced for the town. (Produced by Hustler Printing Co., Moores Hill, Indiana, for H.F. Zierer.)

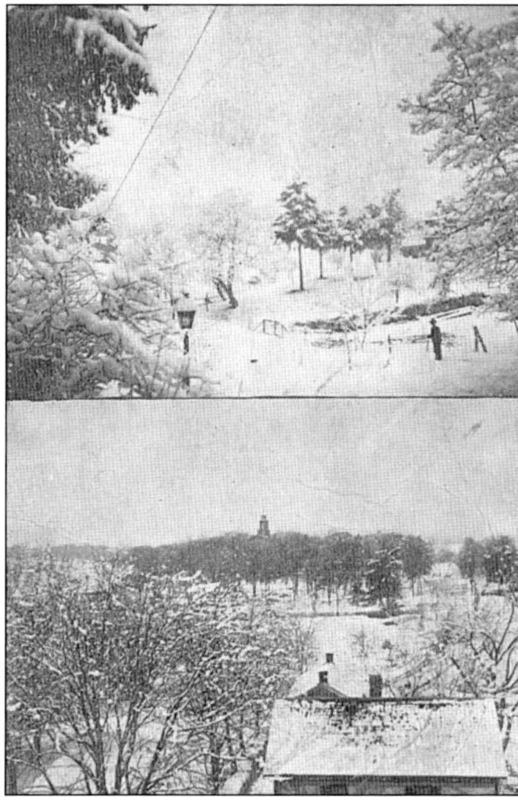

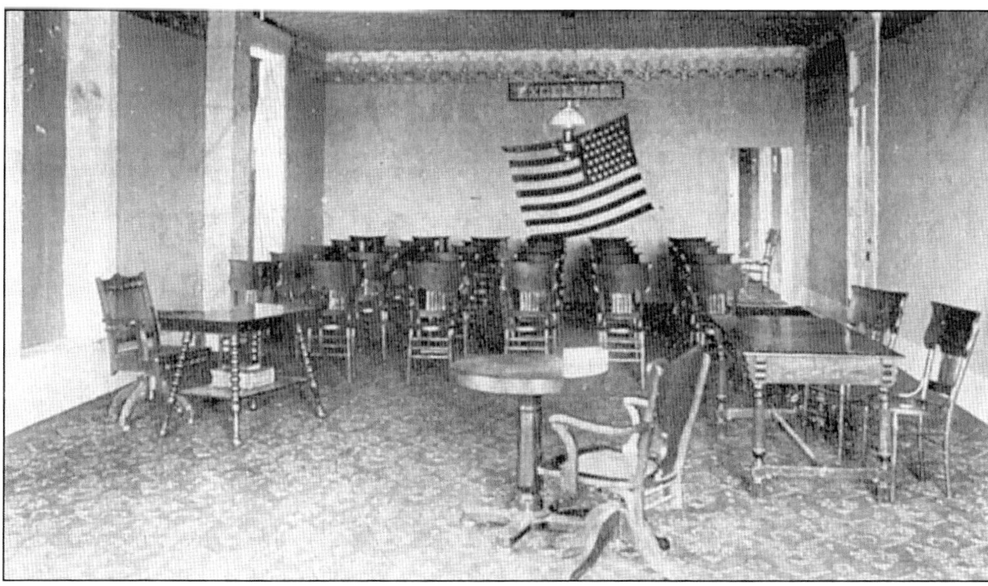

THE PHILONEIKEAN HALL, MOORES HILL COLLEGE. Private mailing card was a term required by law in a May 19, 1898 act of Congress to qualify for the one-cent rate. This view shows a room used by the Philoneikean Society, one of four literary societies at the college. Organized in 1856, when the school first started, this society was for males only. (Unidentified publisher.)

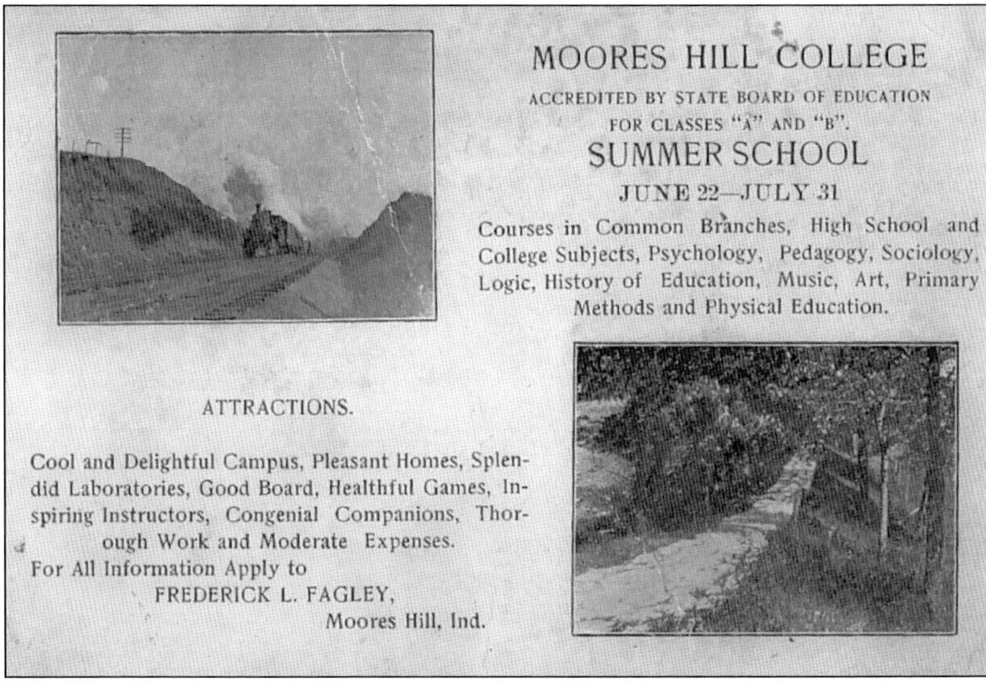

MOORES HILL COLLEGE

ACCREDITED BY STATE BOARD OF EDUCATION FOR CLASSES "A" AND "B".

SUMMER SCHOOL

JUNE 22—JULY 31

Courses in Common Branches, High School and College Subjects, Psychology, Pedagogy, Sociology, Logic, History of Education, Music, Art, Primary Methods and Physical Education.

ATTRACTIONS.

Cool and Delightful Campus, Pleasant Homes, Splendid Laboratories, Good Board, Healthful Games, Inspiring Instructors, Congenial Companions, Thorough Work and Moderate Expenses.

For All Information Apply to
FREDERICK L. FAGLEY,
Moores Hill, Ind.

Promotional Postcard, Moores Hill College. Frederick L. Fagley was an alumnus of Moores Hill College with the class of 1905. After graduation from the school, he became a teacher in the Education Department at the college. (Unidentified printer and publisher.)

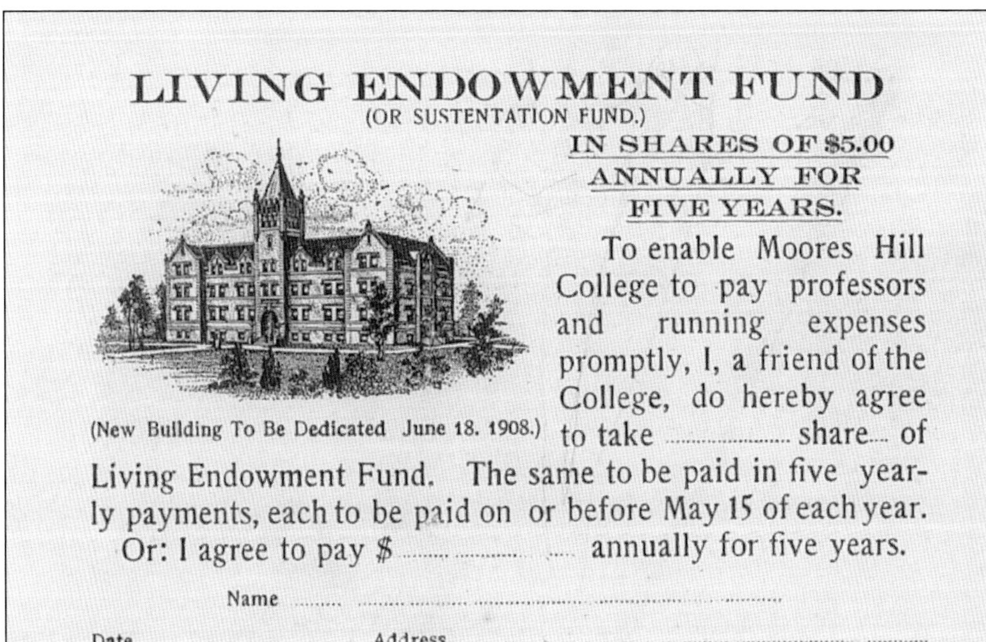

LIVING ENDOWMENT FUND
(OR SUSTENTATION FUND.)

IN SHARES OF $5.00 ANNUALLY FOR FIVE YEARS.

(New Building To Be Dedicated June 18. 1908.)

To enable Moores Hill College to pay professors and running expenses promptly, I, a friend of the College, do hereby agree to take .... share... of Living Endowment Fund. The same to be paid in five yearly payments, each to be paid on or before May 15 of each year.

Or: I agree to pay $ .... annually for five years.

Name ....

Date .... Address ....

Promotional Postcard, Moores Hill College. Financial concerns at Moores Hill College were a nagging problem. This card was used *c.* 1907 or 1908 to allow individuals to participate in a living endowment fund. (Unidentified printer and publisher.)

Six

The Small Villages

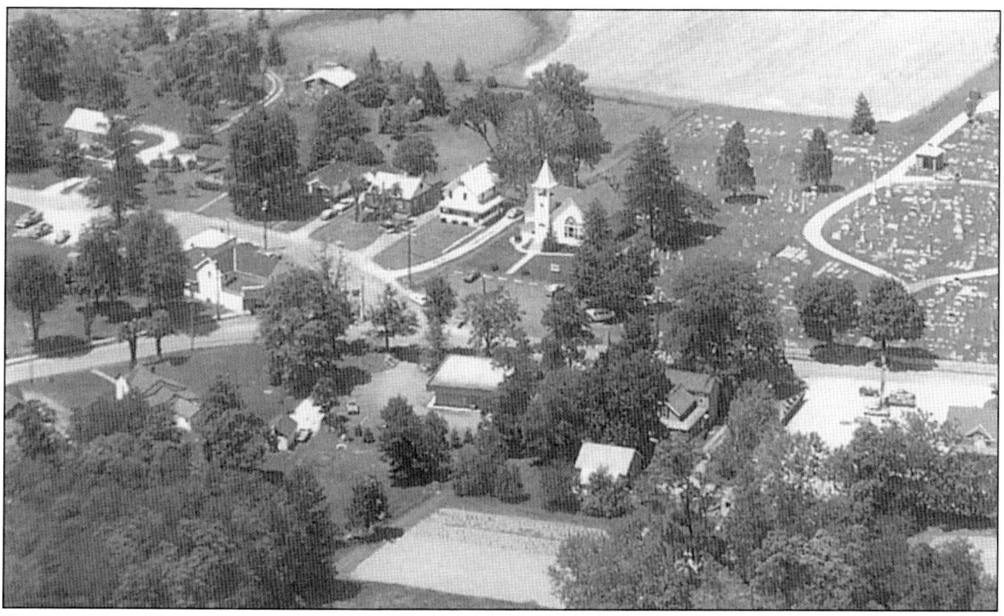

Aerial View, Bright, Indiana. In 1987, this photograph was shot from a small Cessna airplane rented from the Harrison, Ohio airport. It shows, at that time, a still small and quaint Village of Bright. In the decade since this picture was taken, many changes have taken place in the area pictured. Bright is now one of the fastest growing communities in Dearborn County, and in the State of Indiana. (Photograph by Milt Masing, published by Tri-State Visuals.)

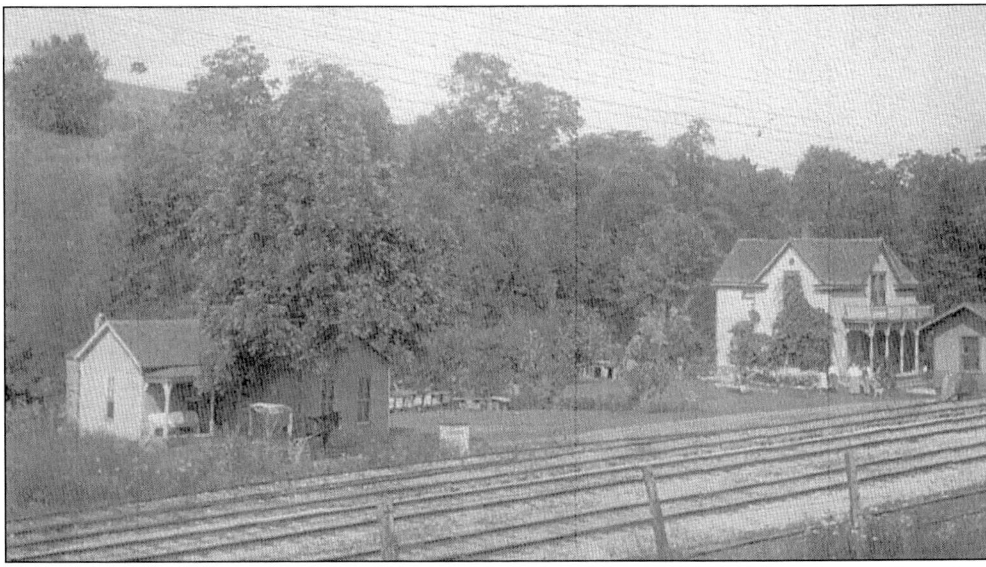

Cold Springs, Indiana. Cold Springs is a small railroad town located in Sparta Township, about mid-way between Dillsboro and Moores Hill. When the railroad line was owned by the Ohio & Mississippi Railroad Company, Cold Springs had a depot. It also had a store with a post office, a shoemaker shop, a church, and a few scattered houses. (Real photo postcard by an unidentified photographer.)

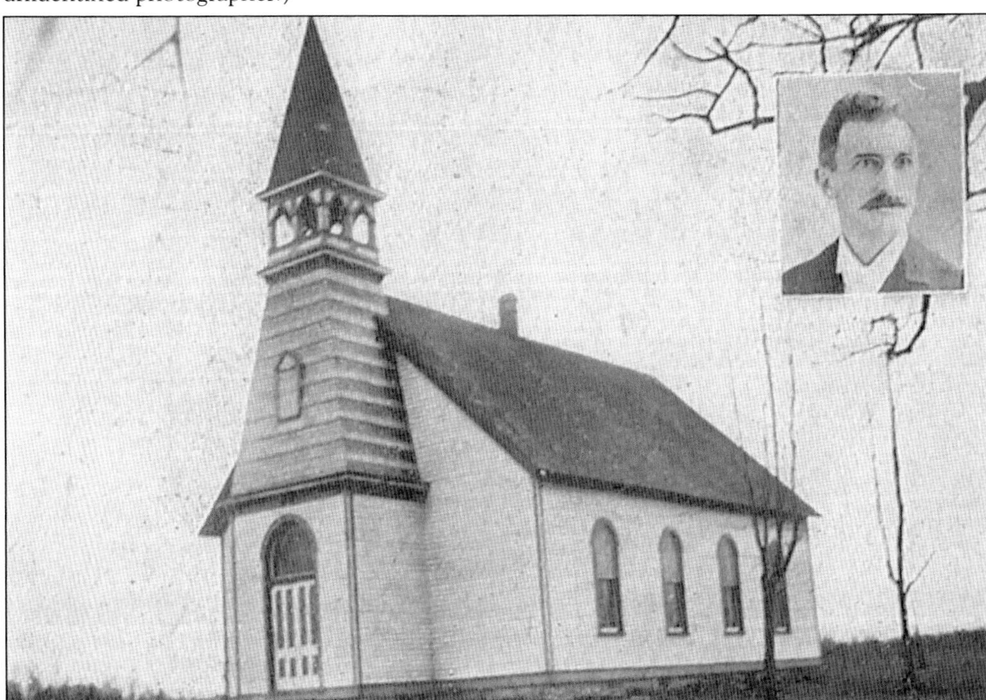

Cold Springs, Indiana Presbyterian Church. When the above postcard was mailed in 1915, the one church in Cold Springs was a Presbyterian Church. The 1875 and 1899 atlases of Dearborn County, however, indicate that the church in Cold Springs was a Lutheran church. The church is now gone, but a small cemetery remains. (Unidentified publisher.)

ST. JOHN'S CATHOLIC CHURCH, KELSO (DOVER), INDIANA. In order to avoid confusion with another town in the southwest part of Indiana with the same name, the town of Dover, in Dearborn County, used the name of the township in which it is located as the name of its post office. The post office name also appears on most of the postcards that depict the town. St. John's, the second oldest Roman Catholic Church in Indiana, was established in 1824. The church pictured here is the fourth church to be used by St. John's. It was dedicated on October 19, 1879, at a cost of $14,000. It is Romanesque Revival in architectural styling. (Unidentified printer and publisher.)

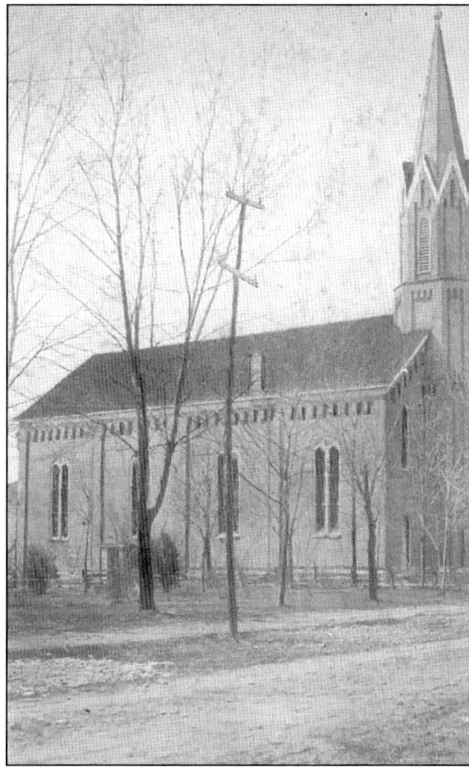

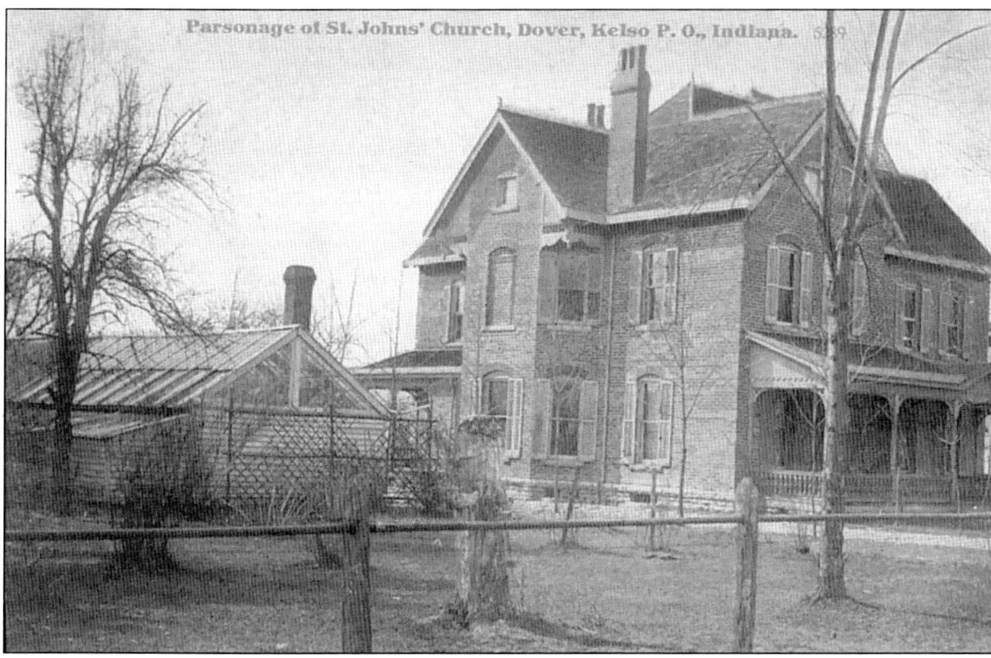

PARSONAGE OF ST. JOHN'S CHURCH, DOVER, KELSO POST OFFICE, INDIANA. The first settler in the township in 1814 was John Kelso. The township is currently named in his honor. In the early history of the community of Dover, the village was known as McKenzie Cross Roads. Henry McKenzie was the first merchant in the village. (Unidentified printer and publisher.)

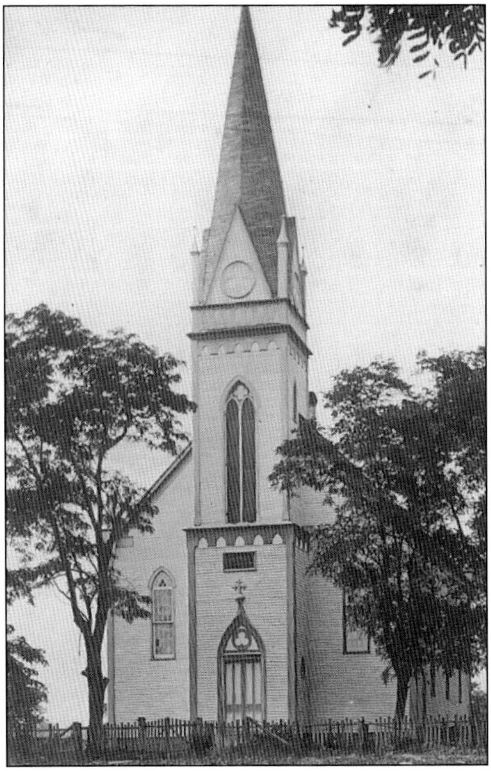

ST. JOHN'S LUTHERAN CHURCH, FARMERS RETREAT, INDIANA. In 1867, the Gothic Revival-style church pictured to the left was completed at a cost of $3,600. The contractor for the church was Julius R. Zernack of Olean, Indiana. Construction on the building was started on October 18, 1866, and required 282 days for completion. A new parsonage was built at the same time as the church building. The Reverend Theo Wichmann was pastor of the church at the time of its completion. In 1888, the congregation constructed a school building adjacent to the church. It was also done in the Gothic style of architecture. A new school was again constructed by the congregation, adjacent to the church, and completed in 1950. Johnson, McKenney & Schenck, of Columbus, Indiana, were the architects. The church complex is still used by the Lutherans of Farmers Retreat even today. And, the building is probably in better condition than ever before. (Real photo postcard by an unidentified photographer.)

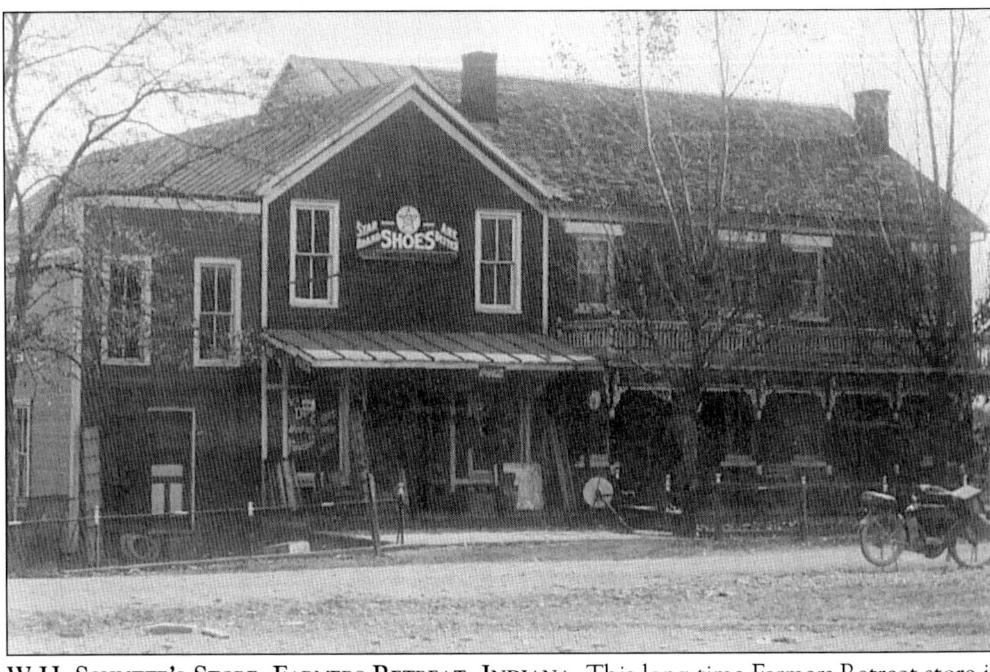

W.H. SCHUTTE'S STORE, FARMERS RETREAT, INDIANA. This long-time Farmers Retreat store is still in business today—although doing a different kind of business. Farmers Retreat, formerly known as Opptown, is located in Caesar Creek Township in the very southwest corner of Dearborn County. (Real photo postcard by an unidentified photographer.)

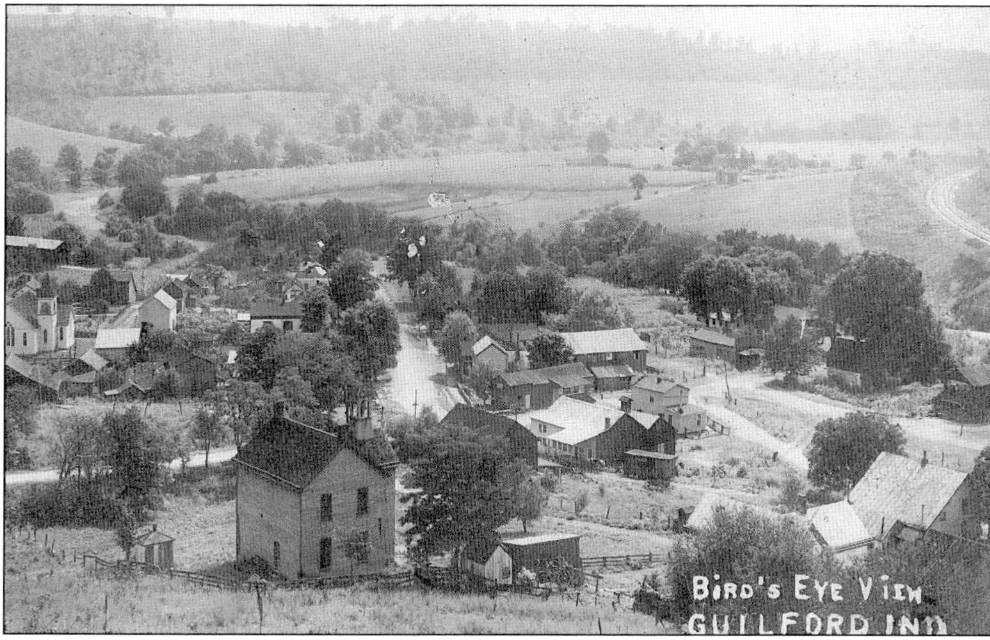

BIRD'S-EYE VIEW, GUILFORD, INDIANA. The Village of Guilford is located at the forks of Tanners Creek in a valley surrounded by hills. Both the creek and the hills help to create the picturesque view illustrated in the above postcard. The town was laid out by three members of the Campbell family on May 29, 1850. (Real photo postcard, published by B.F. Janszen, Newport, Kentucky.)

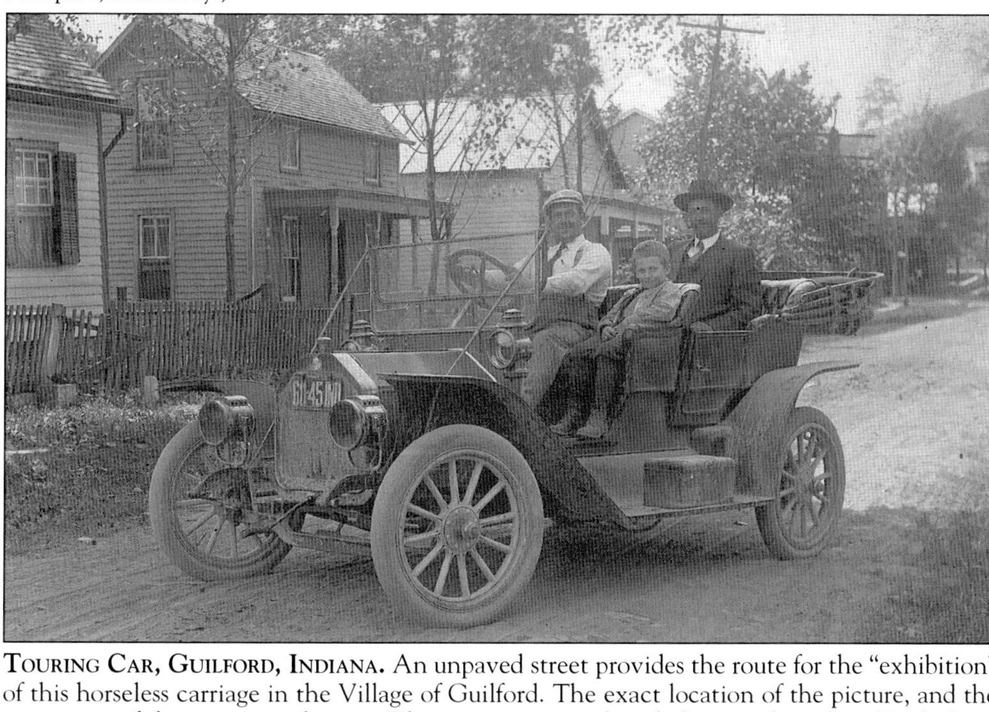

TOURING CAR, GUILFORD, INDIANA. An unpaved street provides the route for the "exhibition" of this horseless carriage in the Village of Guilford. The exact location of the picture, and the exact type of the car, are unknown. There is no postmark to help provide a clue. (Real photo postcard by an unidentified photographer.)

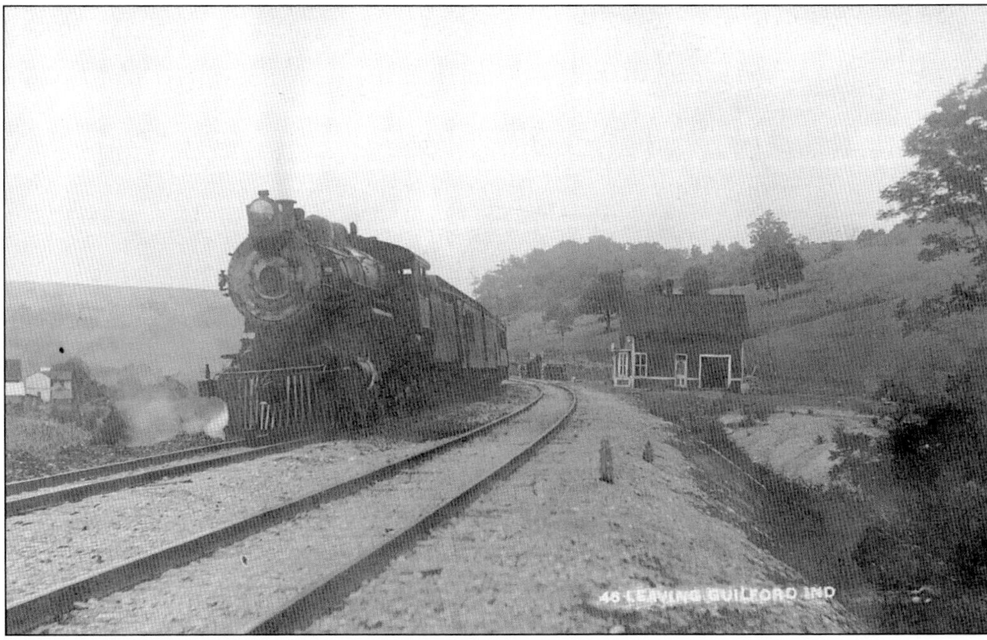

TRAIN 46, LEAVING GUILFORD, INDIANA. A May 1909 postmark on the back of this postcard indicates that this train departure was probably photographed in either 1908 or 1909. The railroad line pictured is the "Big Four Line," more accurately known as the Cincinnati, Indianapolis, St. Louis, and Chicago line. (Real photo postcard, published by B.F. Janszen, Newport, Kentucky.)

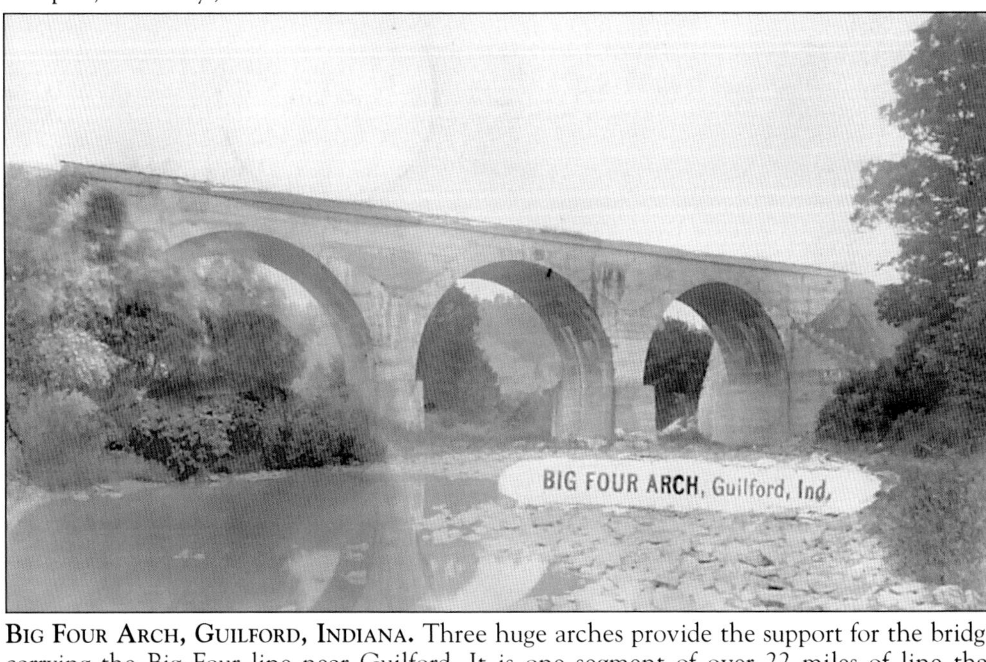

BIG FOUR ARCH, GUILFORD, INDIANA. Three huge arches provide the support for the bridge carrying the Big Four line near Guilford. It is one segment of over 22 miles of line that the company owned in Dearborn County. The postmark on the back of this card, like the one at the top of the page, reads 1909. (Real photo postcard, published by B.F. Janszen, Newport, Kentucky.)

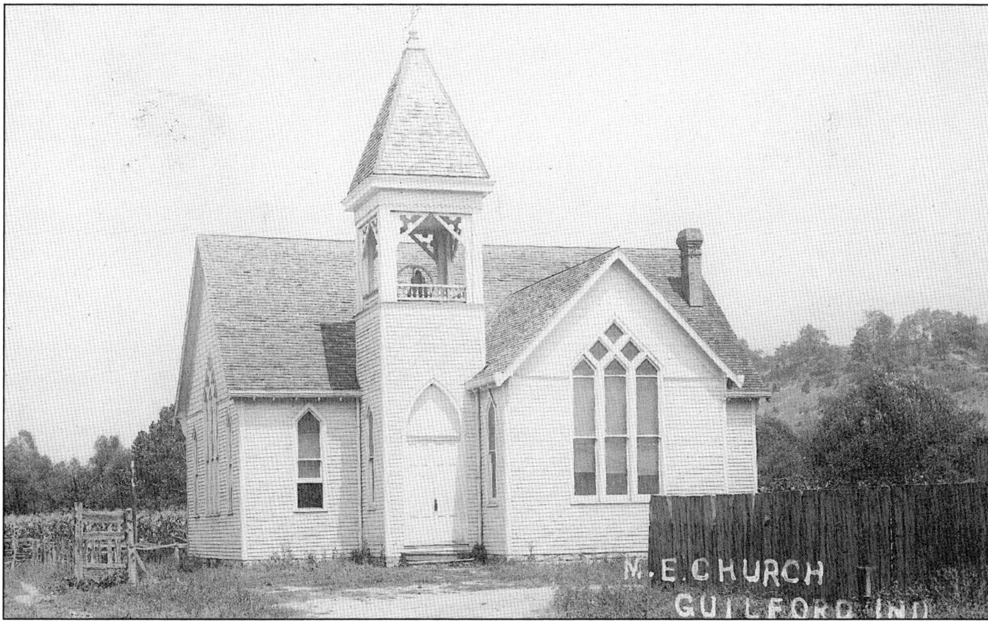

M.E. CHURCH, GUILFORD, INDIANA. The Guilford Methodist Episcopal Church was one of three churches that united on November 30, 1980, to form the Tanner Valley United Methodist Church. Other churches included in the merger were the Homestead Methodist Church and the Mt. Pleasant Methodist Church. (Real photo postcard, published by B.F. Janszen, Newport, Kentucky.)

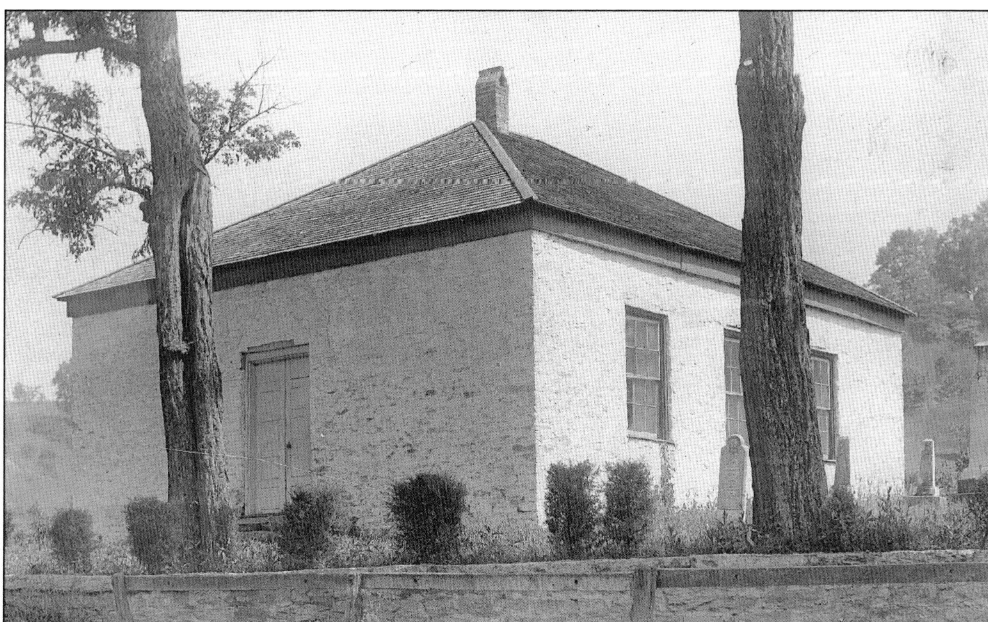

EAST FORK CHAPEL, GUILFORD, INDIANA. Nestled near the east bank of the East Fork of Tanners Creek, this chapel dates to the earliest time of the county. It was constructed in 1821, from stones found in the nearby creek. The original use of the chapel was as a Methodist church. (Real photo postcard, published by B.F. Janszen, Newport, Kentucky.)

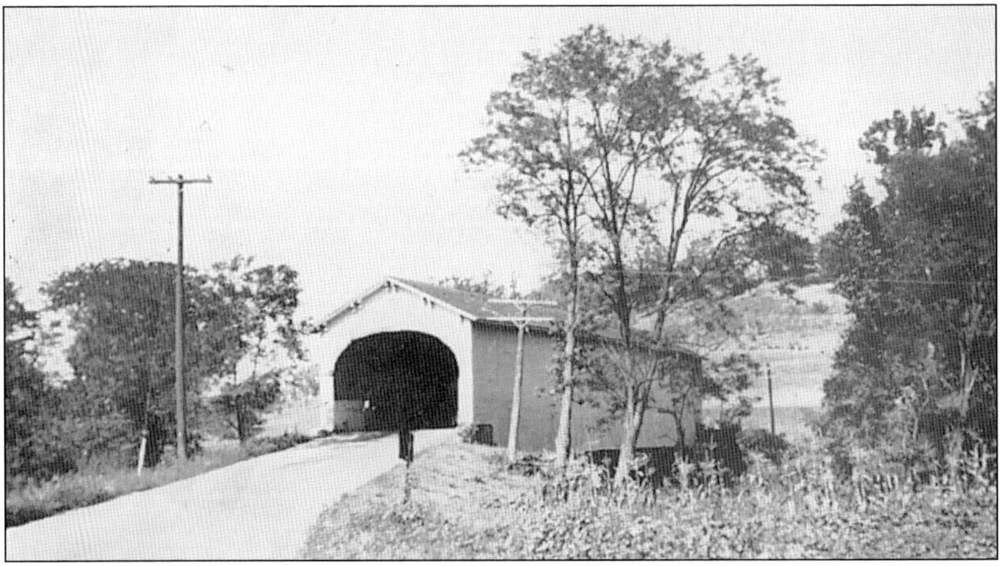

GUILFORD BRIDGE, GUILFORD, INDIANA. A.M. Kennedy & Sons completed this bridge in 1879, over the East Fork of Tanners Creek, near the Village of Guilford. When threatened with demolition in 1960, the structure was moved to become part of a county park. In the early 1990s, that bridge was destroyed by fire. It was rebuilt in the late 1990s. (Produced by Bryan E. Ketcham, Lockland, Ohio.)

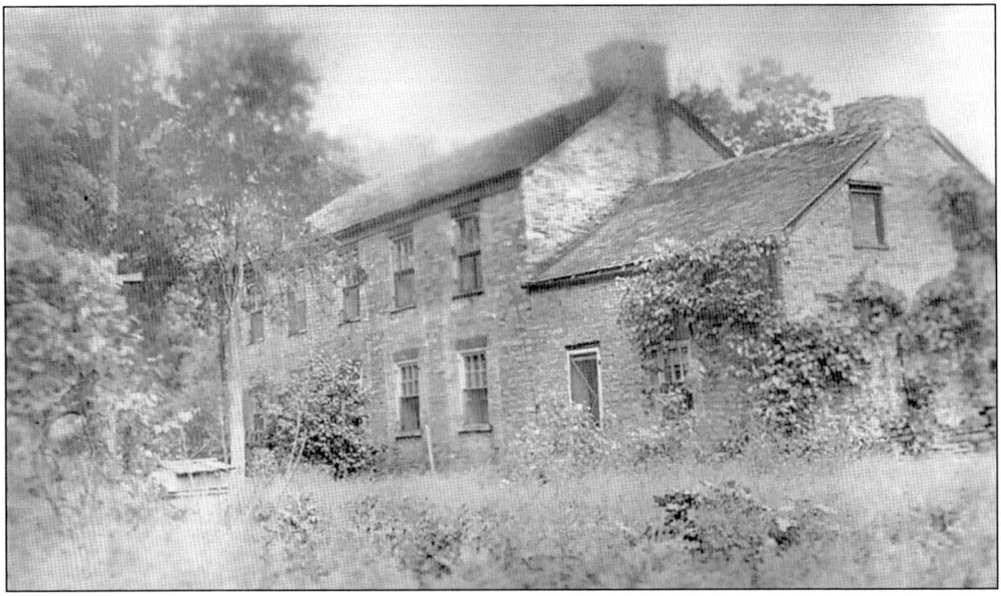

EWBANK HOMESTEAD, NEAR GUILFORD, INDIANA. John Ewbank Sr. built a log cabin on the site of this house in 1811. In 1829, he replaced it with this house constructed of stones. The stone house had a brick oven in the kitchen that was used both to heat the walls and prepare the food. The house is still owned today by a descendent of the builder. (Real photo postcard, photograph by E.K. Ewbank.)

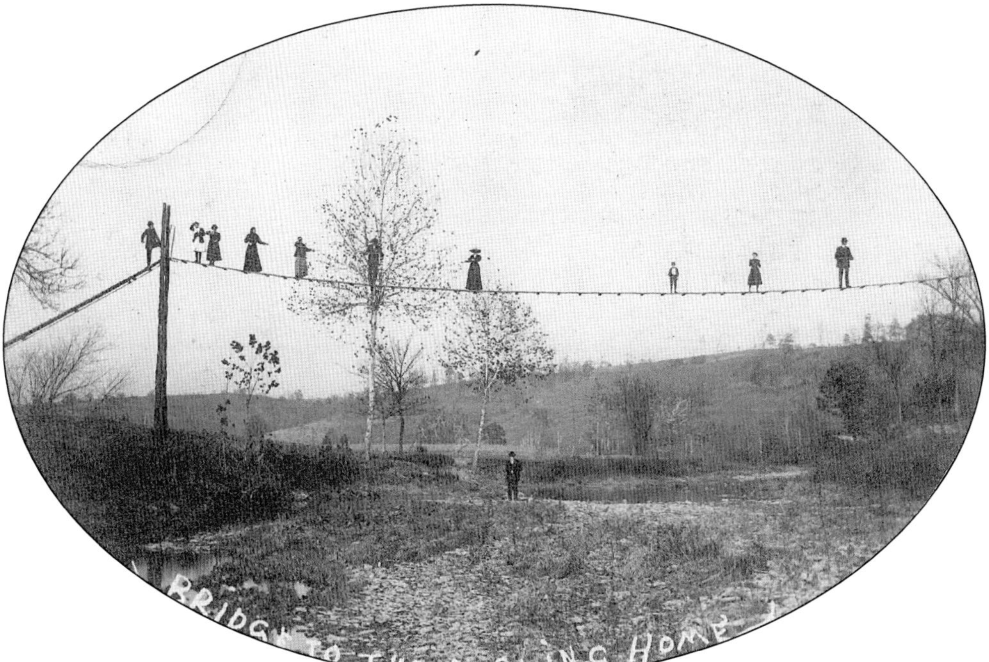

DARLING HOMESTEAD, NEAR KENNEDY, INDIANA. The Darling families of Dearborn County lived in York Township, near the village formerly known as Kennedy. Today the village is called Bonnell. Suspension bridges, like the one pictured here, were commonly used in the county to span the many creeks that were frequently subjected to flash floods. The height of this bridge suggests that it probably spanned Tanner's Creek, the largest creek in the area. (Real photo postcard by an unidentified photographer.)

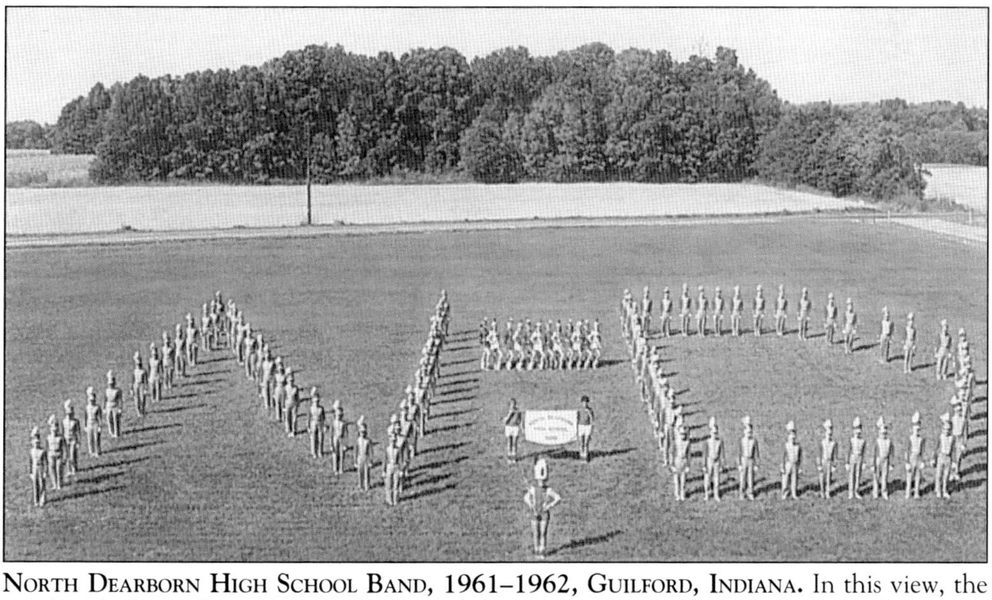

NORTH DEARBORN HIGH SCHOOL BAND, 1961–1962, GUILFORD, INDIANA. In this view, the one hundred members of the marching band are pictured on the front lawn of the school. Charles Green was the band director, and Stephen Gabbard the principal. (Produced by Dexter Press, West Nyack, New York, for Osborne Photographic Laboratories, Cincinnati, Ohio.)

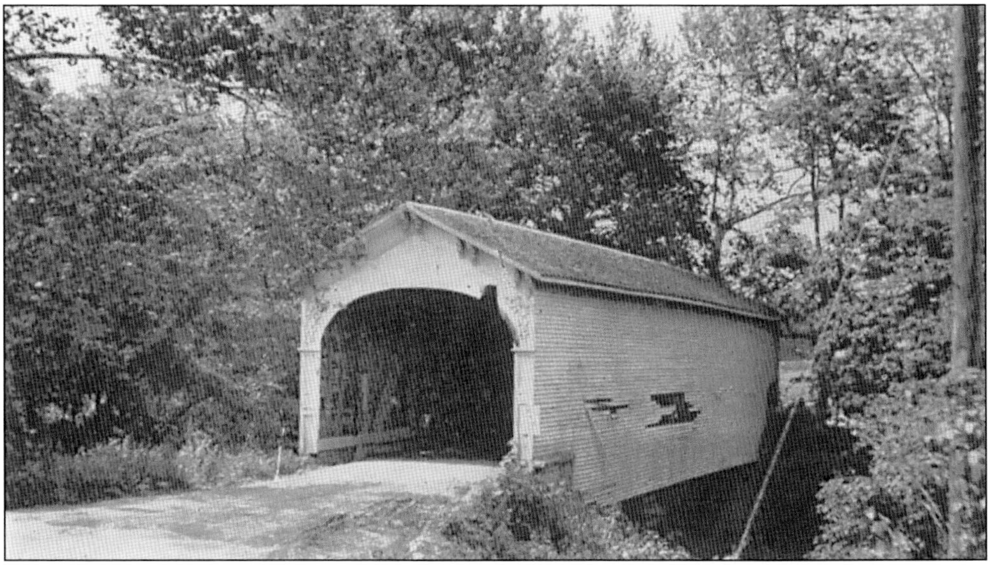

Logan Creek Bridge, near West Harrison, Indiana. Covered bridges were rather commonplace in the early history of the eastern part of the United States. The bridge pictured here was located between the villages of Logan and West Harrison, near the Whitewater River. (Produced by Bryan E. Ketcham, Lockland, Ohio.)

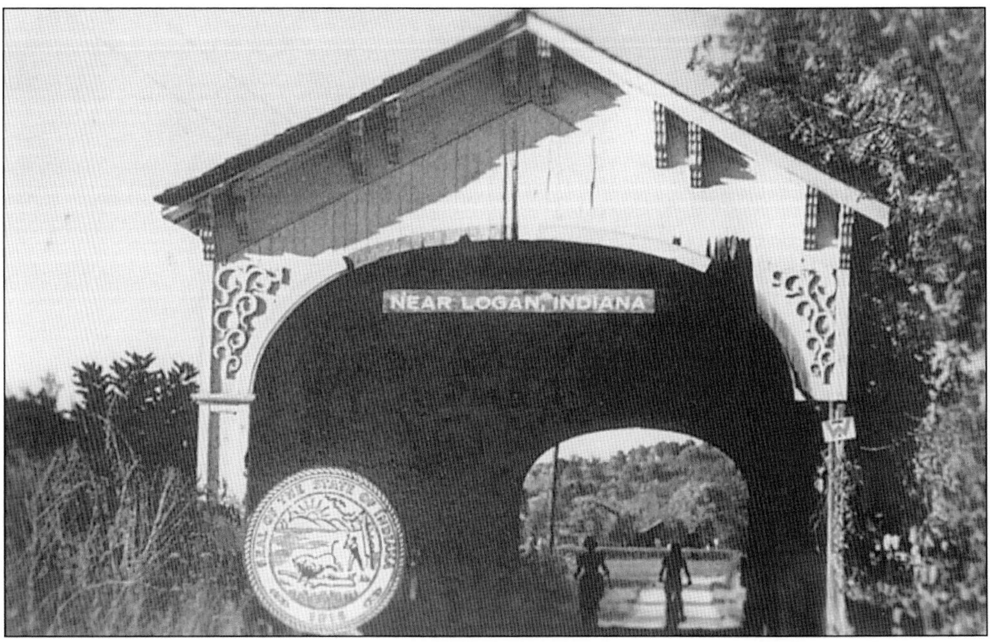

Covered Bridge, near Logan, Indiana. Built in 1874 by A.M. Kennedy & Sons, this single-span bridge spanned Logan Creek, near the village of Logan Cross Roads. The bridge was 94-feet long, 15.5-feet wide, 13-feet tall, and had cut stone abutments and a shingle roof. (Real photo postcard by an unidentified photographer.)

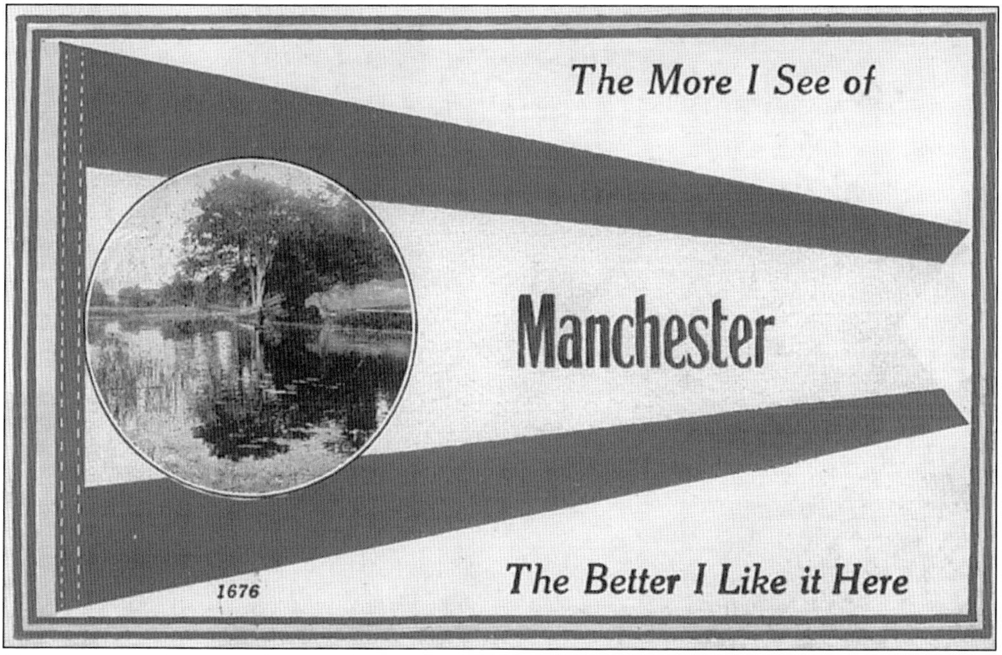

MANCHESTER, INDIANA, GENERIC POSTCARD. The early history of the community of Manchester has the village divided into four distinct settlements: Upper Manchester or Muletown, Middle Manchester, Lower Manchester or Plummertown, and Wright's Corner. Initial settlement in the area was in 1809. (Unidentified printer and publisher.)

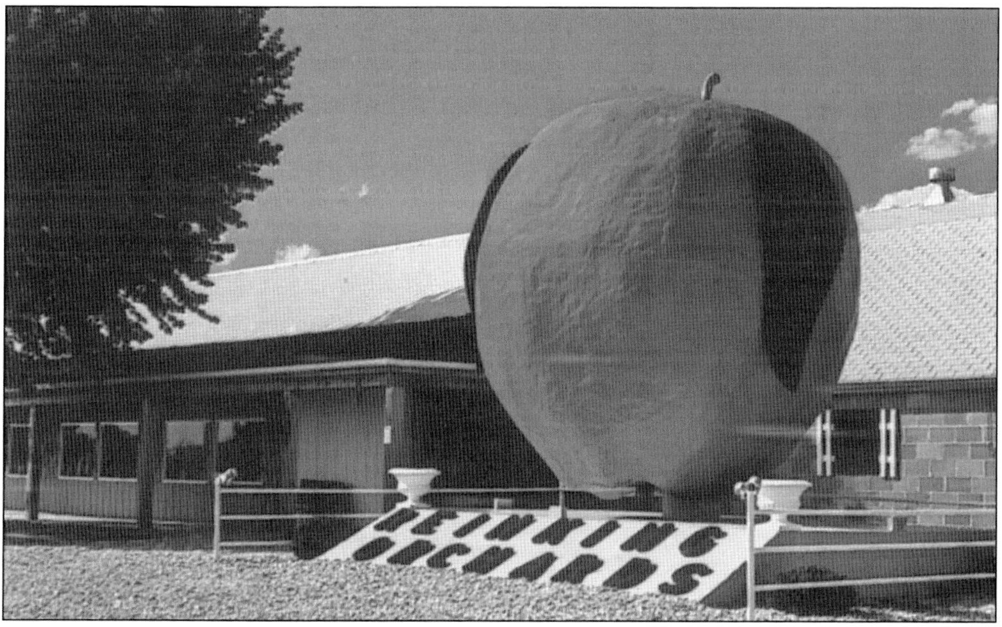

REINKING ORCHARDS, HOME OF THE FAMOUS BIG APPLE. This standard-sized chrome postcard was produced in the 1960s to promote the Reinking Orchards. The orchards, located on State Road #48, are between Manchester and Lawrenceburg. The orchards sold fresh apples, peaches, and other homegrown country produce in season. The orchard remains today, but ownership has changed. (Produced by International Graphics Inc., Hollywood, Florida.)

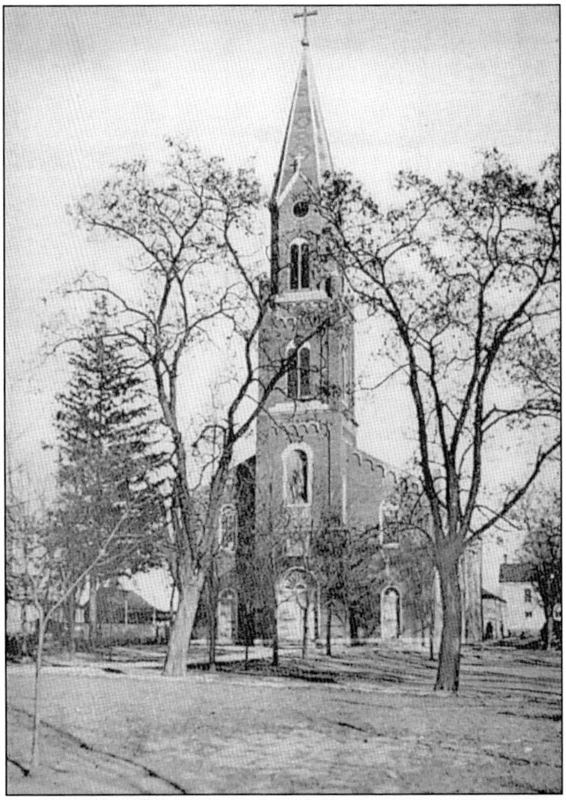

St. Paul's Church, New Alsace, Indiana. The first church built on this site was constructed of logs and completed in 1834. In 1836, because of the encouragement of Bishop Brute, the 150 members of the St. Paul parish, under the direction of Father Ferneding, began the construction of a new brick church. On July 8, 1838, the church was blessed by the bishop. In 1868–1870, from plans drawn by architects Alard & Kloster of Cincinnati, Ohio, the building was expanded and enlarged. The additions made at this time included a tower, remodeled front, alter, and a fresco-decorated sanctuary. St. Paul's Catholic Church is located on North Dearborn Road in the Village of New Alsace. (Produced by Kraemer Art Co., Cincinnati and Berlin, Germany.)

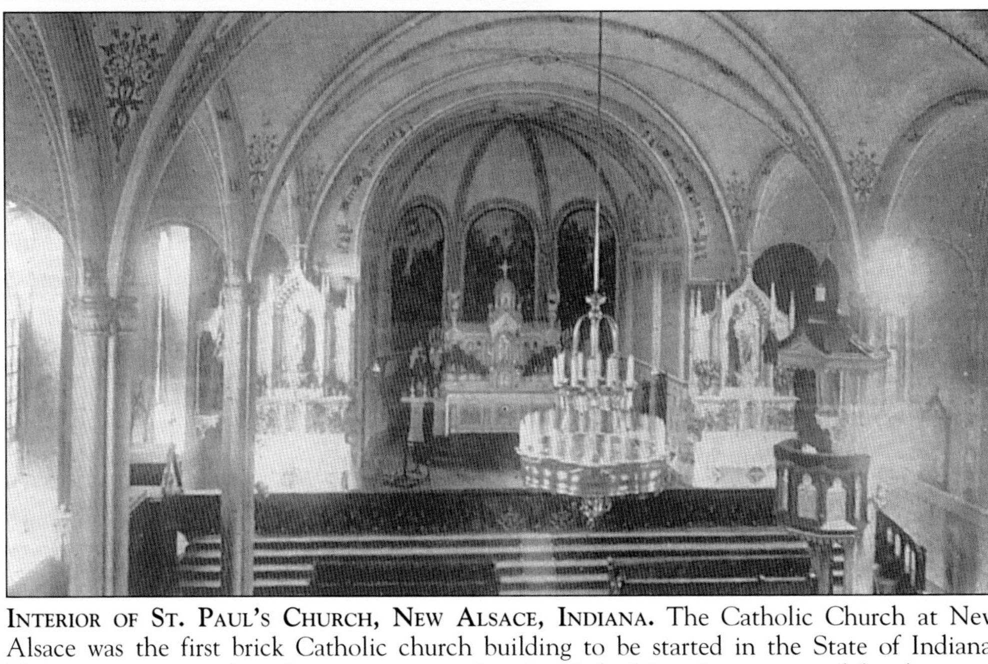

Interior of St. Paul's Church, New Alsace, Indiana. The Catholic Church at New Alsace was the first brick Catholic church building to be started in the State of Indiana. The town was started at the same time as the church building. It was named for the many settlers to the area that were from the Alsace-Lorraine region between Germany and France. (Unidentified printer and publisher.)

Main Street, St. Leon, Indiana. Large in area, but small in numbers. This description has often been used to describe the village of St. Leon. How the village acquired its name is not completely known. One story claims that the name is a misnomer. When the community applied for a post office, the name St. Joseph was already assigned in Indiana, so the name of St. Leo was given as the name and was then incorrectly read. When the post office application was approved, the name was registered by the postal authorities as St. Leon, and the name stuck. Since the year 1842, the dominant influence on this community has been St. Joseph's Catholic Church. Since Interstate Highway #74 was built through the northern part of the county, St. Leon has been the subject of considerable growth, with even more growth likely to occur in the future. (Real photo postcard, mounted on a generic postcard, produced by an unidentified printer and publisher.)

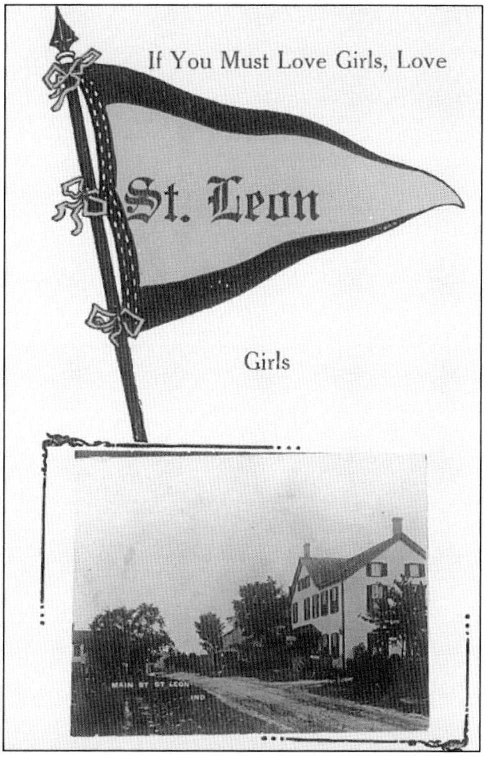

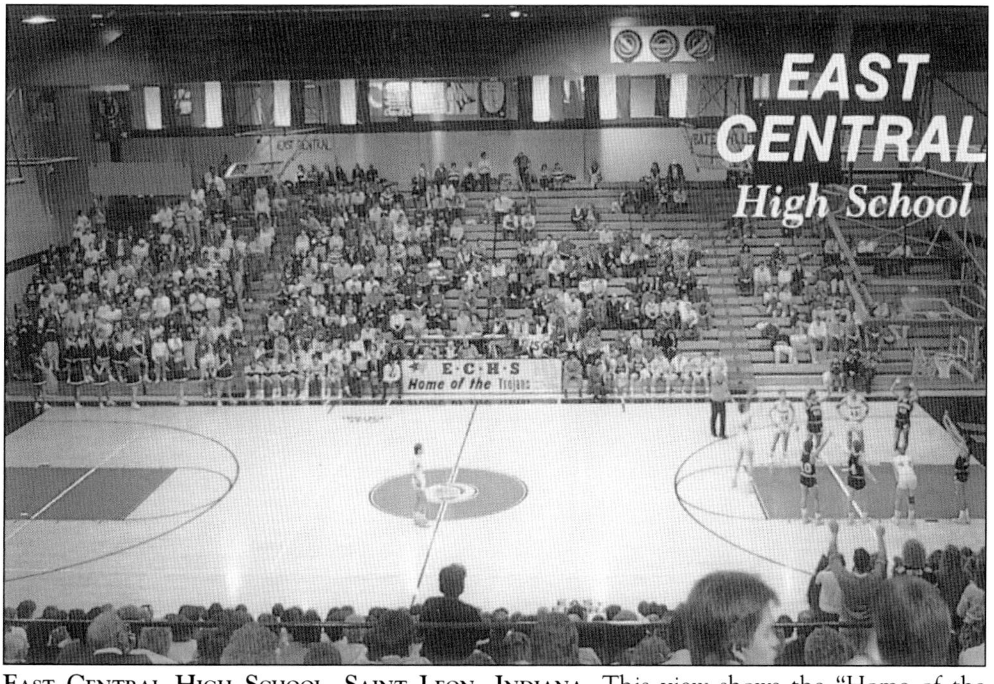

East Central High School, Saint Leon, Indiana. This view shows the "Home of the Trojans" during the 1988 boys basketball sectional. The East Central gymnasium pictured on this postcard is part of a three-million-dollar facility that was constructed in 1973–1974. (Photograph by Milt Masing, published by Tri-State Visuals.)

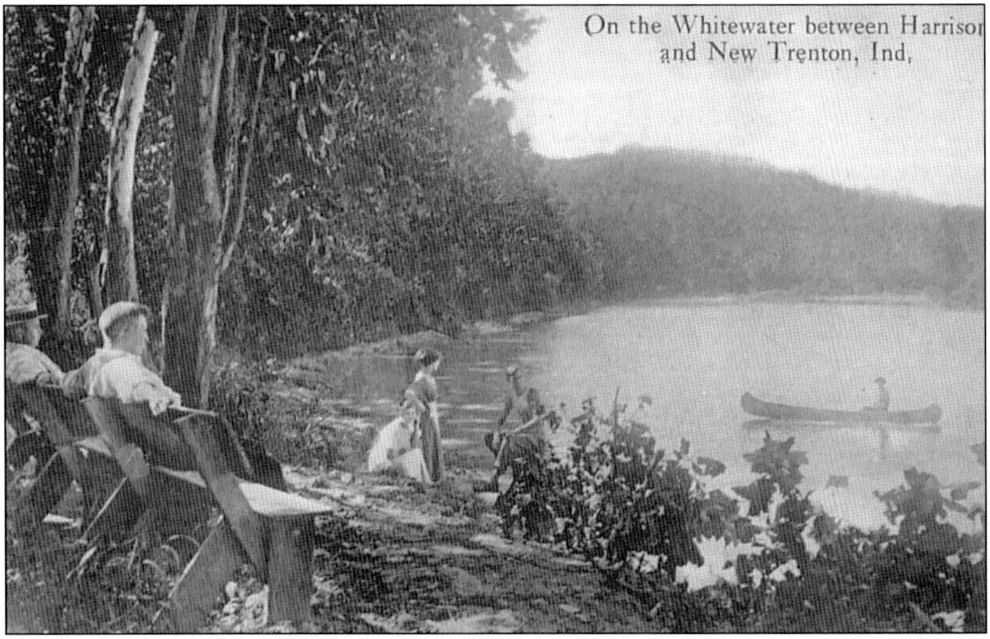

ON THE WHITEWATER, BETWEEN HARRISON AND NEW TRENTON, INDIANA. The exact location of this tranquil scene is undeterminable. However, maps of the area show the Whitewater River between New Trenton and Harrison as being mostly in Harrison and Logan Townships, Dearborn County. (Produced by Kraemer Art Co., Cincinnati and Berlin.)

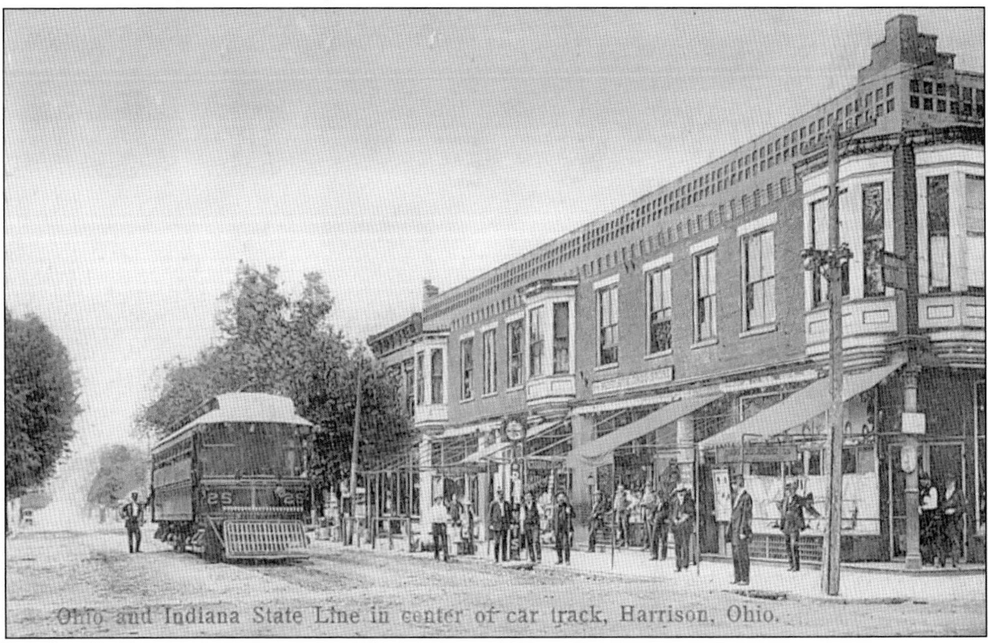

OHIO AND INDIANA STATE LINE, IN CENTER OF CAR TRACK, HARRISON, OHIO. Main Street is the dividing line between Indiana and Ohio, and also West Harrison, Indiana and Harrison, Ohio. The communities were founded in 1813. West Harrison was laid out by John Allen and Peter Hannan. This view is looking toward the Indiana side of the street, from the Ohio side. (Produced by Kraemer Art Co., Cincinnati and Berlin, Germany.)

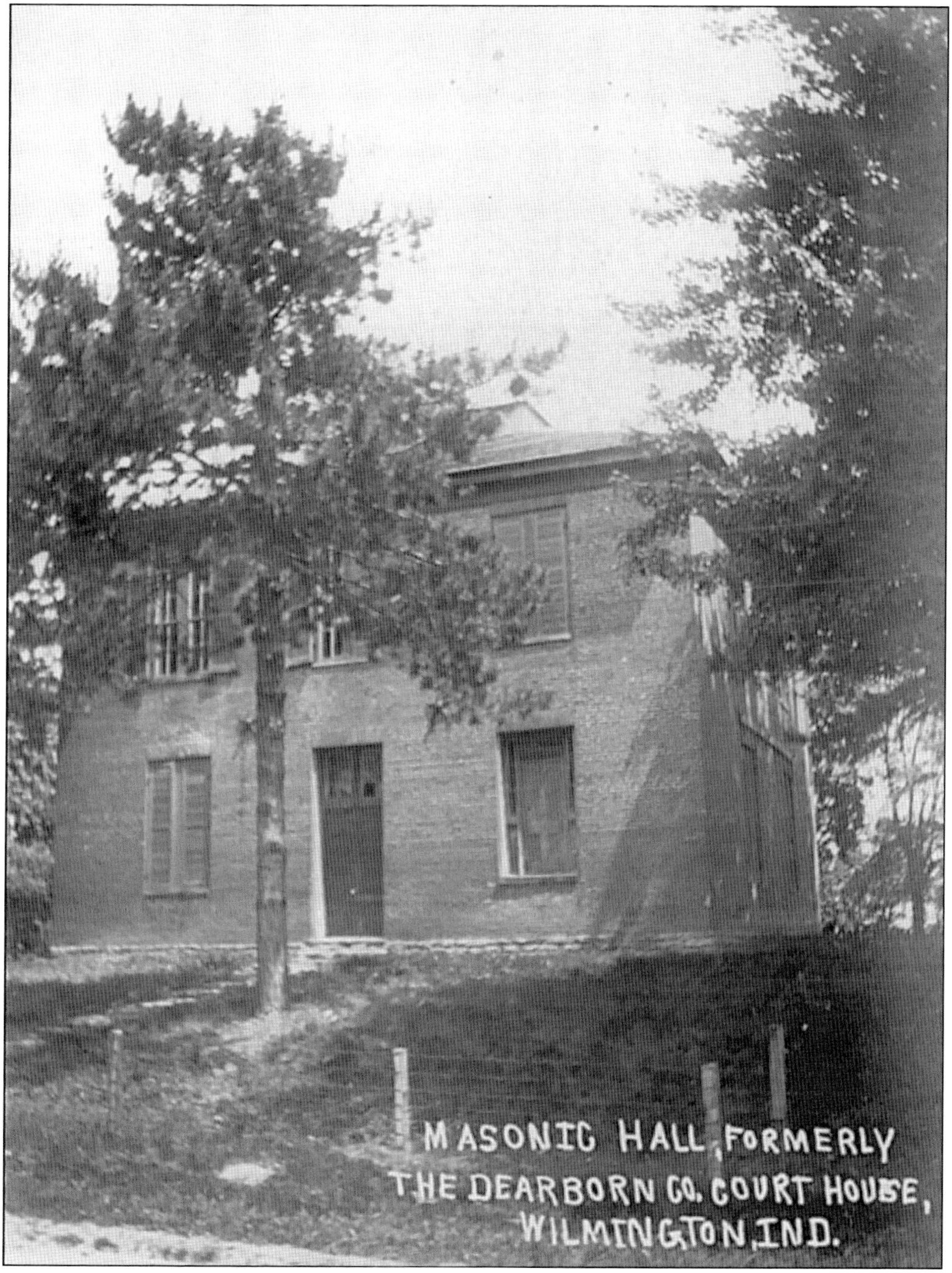

MASONIC HALL, FORMERLY THE DEARBORN COUNTY COURTHOUSE, WILMINGTON, INDIANA. Dearborn County has constructed four buildings for use as a courthouse. The building pictured above was the third building constructed. It was completed in 1834, on the corner of Ripley and New Streets, at a cost of $4,000. From 1836 to 1844, the building was used as a courthouse. In 1844, the county seat was moved back to Lawrenceburg. By the time that the 1875 Atlas of Dearborn County was published, the building was put to use as a Masonic Hall. (Real photo postcard by an unidentified photographer.)

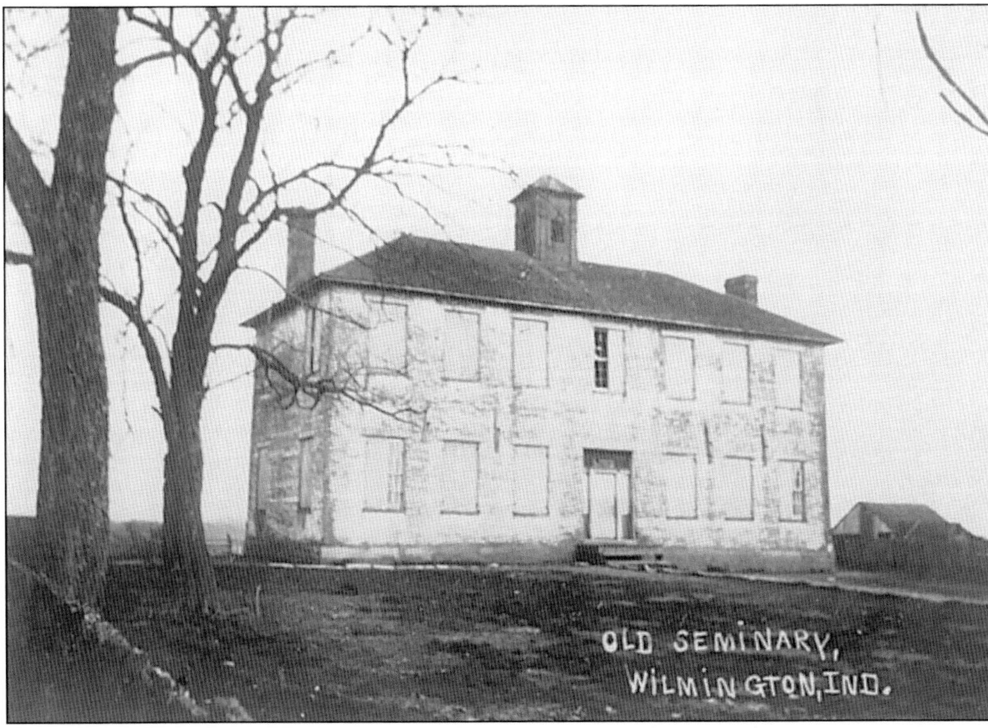

OLD SEMINARY, WILMINGTON, INDIANA. The Dearborn County Commissioners ordered the construction of the county seminary in 1833. The two-story building measured 64' by 28'. In 1854, the building was sold by the county to a private company for use as an academy. (Real photo postcard by an unidentified photographer.)

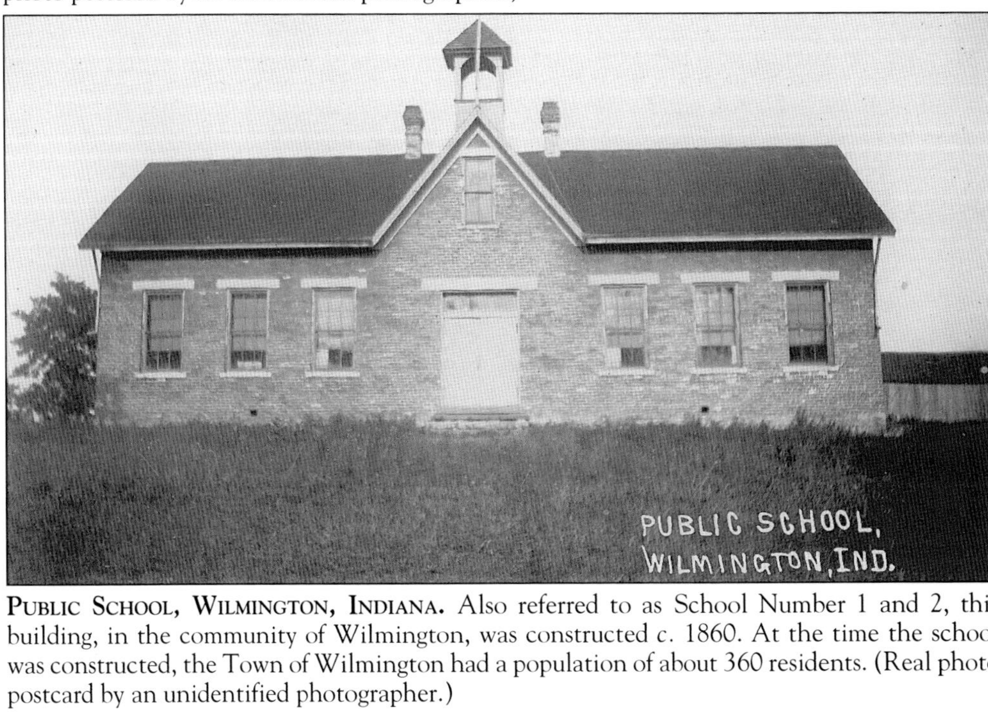

PUBLIC SCHOOL, WILMINGTON, INDIANA. Also referred to as School Number 1 and 2, this building, in the community of Wilmington, was constructed *c.* 1860. At the time the school was constructed, the Town of Wilmington had a population of about 360 residents. (Real photo postcard by an unidentified photographer.)

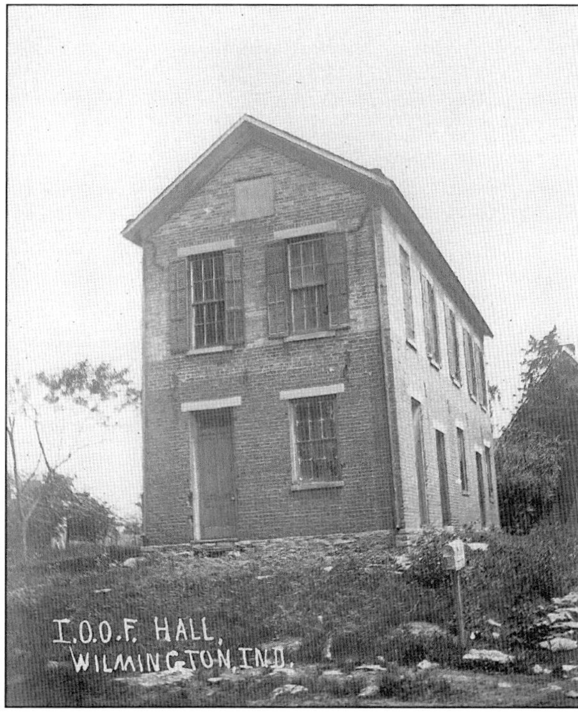

I.O.O.F. Hall, Wilmington, Indiana. Federal-style architecture is represented in this *c.* 1840 landmark that once housed the Odd Fellows Hall in Wilmington. The building was also used at one time as the Wilmington Inn. When the author visited this building in 1990 to take photographs, the structure was in very poor condition. It appeared as if the building would crumble the next time a storm passed. But now, nine years later, the building still stands and still looks as if it is ready to crumble. If this building and the adjacent old courthouse were to be restored and utilized, a very quaint park-like setting could be created. Unfortunately, the few attempts that have been made in this direction have all failed. (Real photo postcard by an unidentified photographer.)

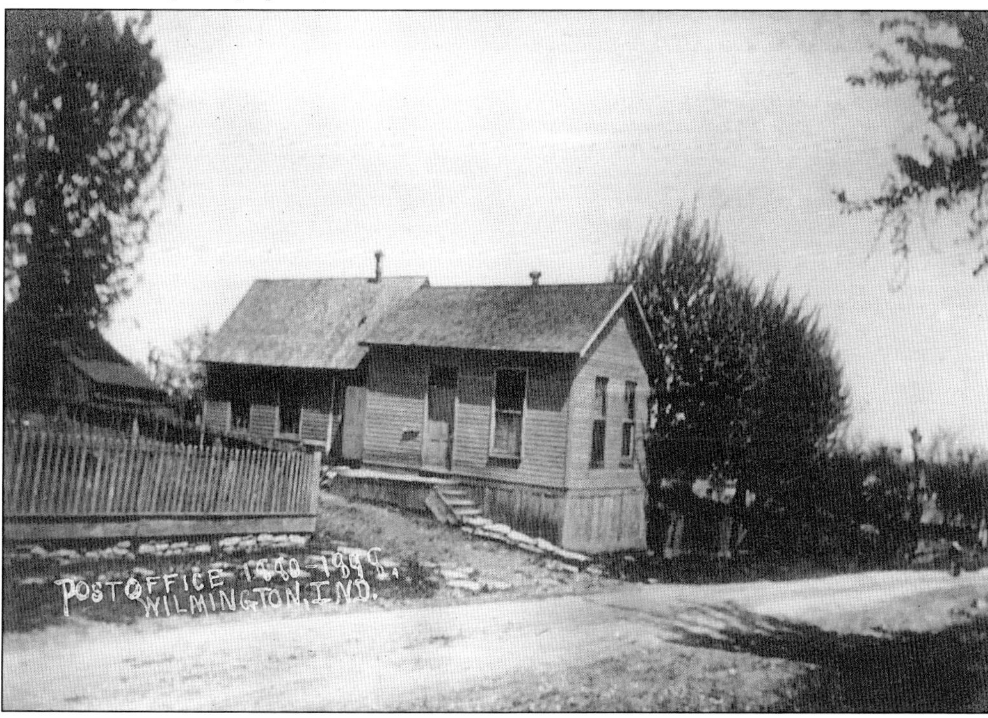

Post Office, 1880–1898, Wilmington, Indiana. The exact location of this structure that once housed the Wilmington Post Office is unknown. County atlases published in 1875 and 1899 provide no assistance in locating the building. (Real photo postcard by an unidentified photographer.)

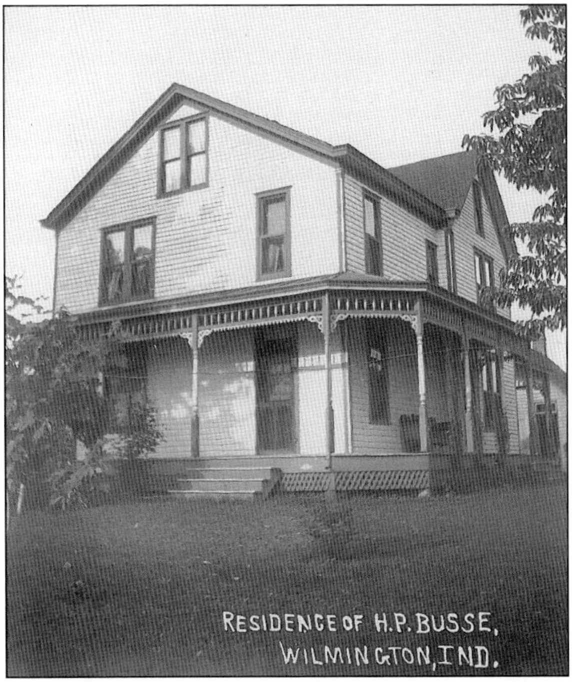

RESIDENCE OF H.P. BUSSE, WILMINGTON, INDIANA. Henry P. Busse owned a considerable tract of land to the southeast of Wilmington, opposite Main Street (now called Probst Road) and the cemetery. The house pictured here is very typical of carpenter-built houses of the late nineteenth century. Henry P. Busse was born June 27, 1856, the son of Henry Christian Busse and Angelica Gesell, both natives of Germany. In 1879, Henry P. Busse was united in marriage with Louise Oehlmann. Mr. and Mrs. Busse had six children: Irene, Frederick, Henry, Bertha, Lydia, and Christian. (Real photo postcard by an unidentified photographer.)

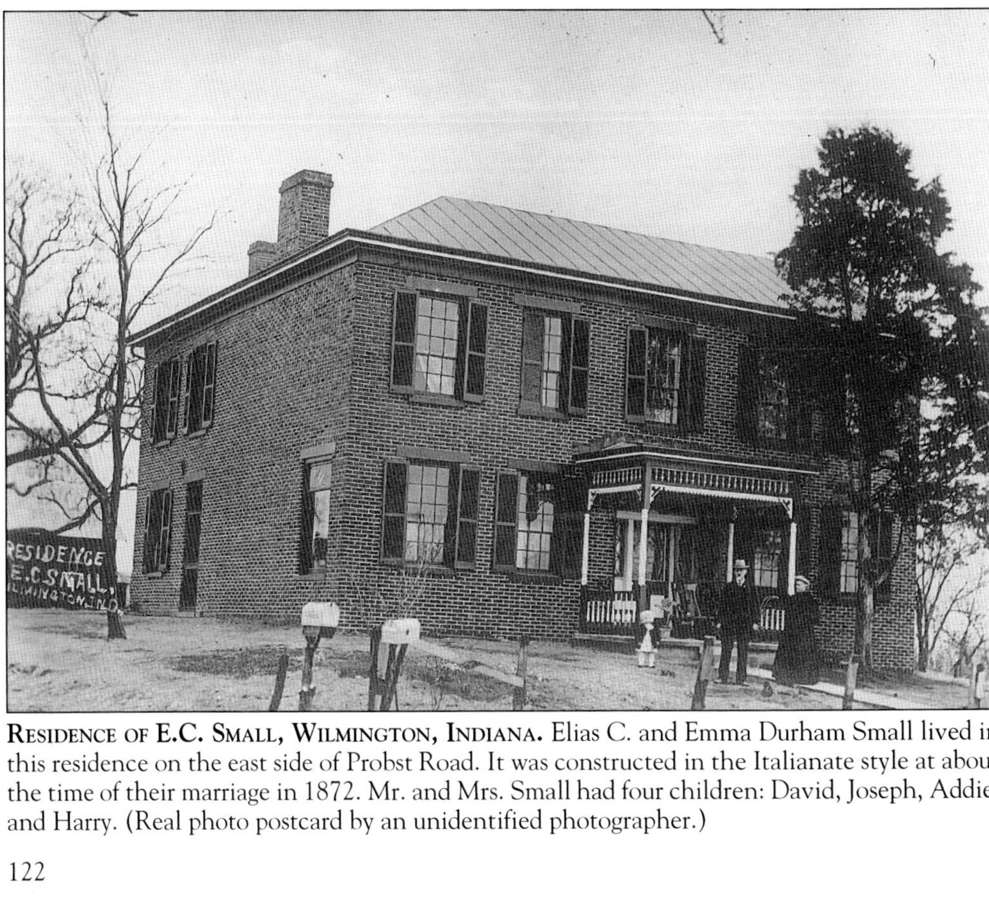

RESIDENCE OF E.C. SMALL, WILMINGTON, INDIANA. Elias C. and Emma Durham Small lived in this residence on the east side of Probst Road. It was constructed in the Italianate style at about the time of their marriage in 1872. Mr. and Mrs. Small had four children: David, Joseph, Addie, and Harry. (Real photo postcard by an unidentified photographer.)

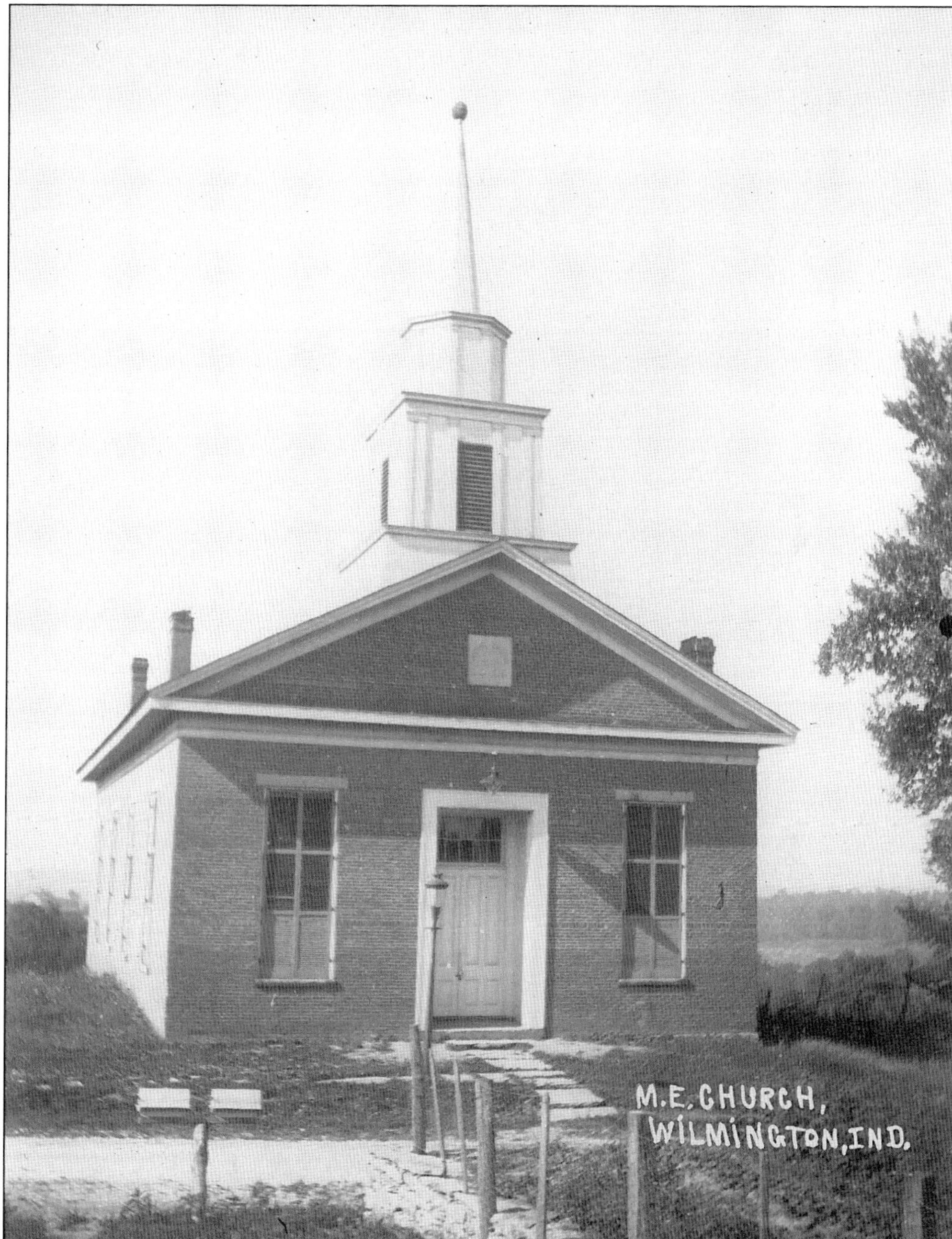

M.E. CHURCH, WILMINGTON, INDIANA. The Town of Wilmington was laid out in the years 1815 and 1816 by William C. Chamberlain, Adam Flake, Robert Moore, and William Bainum. After the seat of justice was moved back to Lawrenceburg, the Town of Wilmington continued to grow for some time. In the 1860s, the Village of Wilmington continued to experience prosperous times, with the construction of several large buildings. One of the buildings constructed during this decade was the Wilmington Methodist Episcopal Church, completed in 1865. This Greek Revival church building has been in continuous use ever since. (Real photo postcard by an unidentified photographer.)

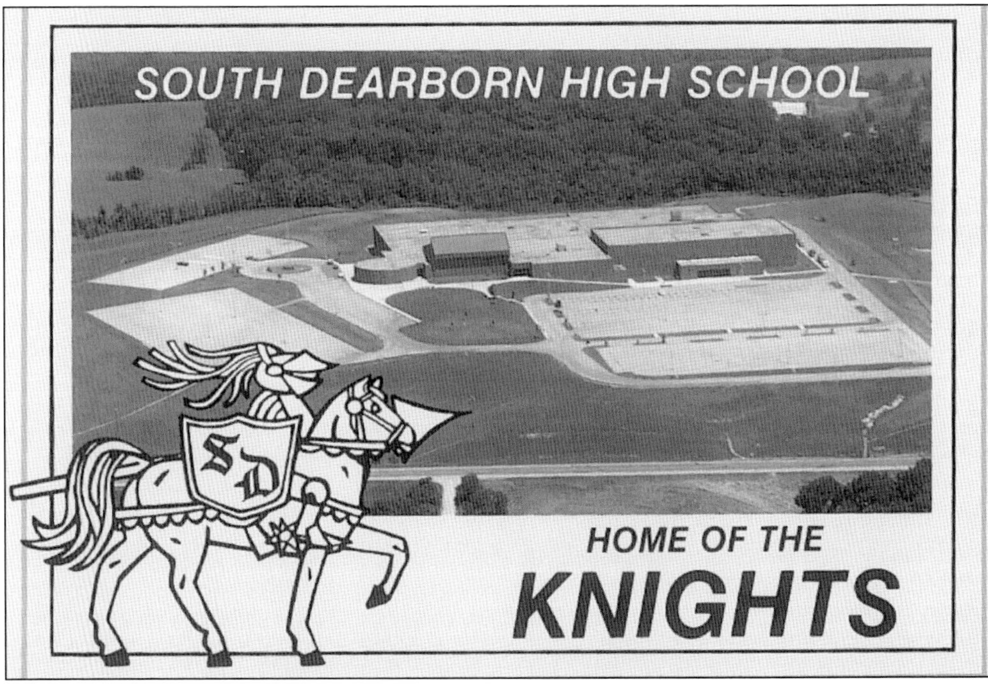

South Dearborn High School, Home of the Knights. Red, white, and blue, the school colors, are featured in the borders and art work on the front of this continental-sized postcard published in 1987. The award-winning plan for the school building was produced by the Indianapolis architectural firm of James Associates. The building was opened in time for the 1978–79 school year. (Photograph by Milt Masing, published by Tri-State Visuals.)

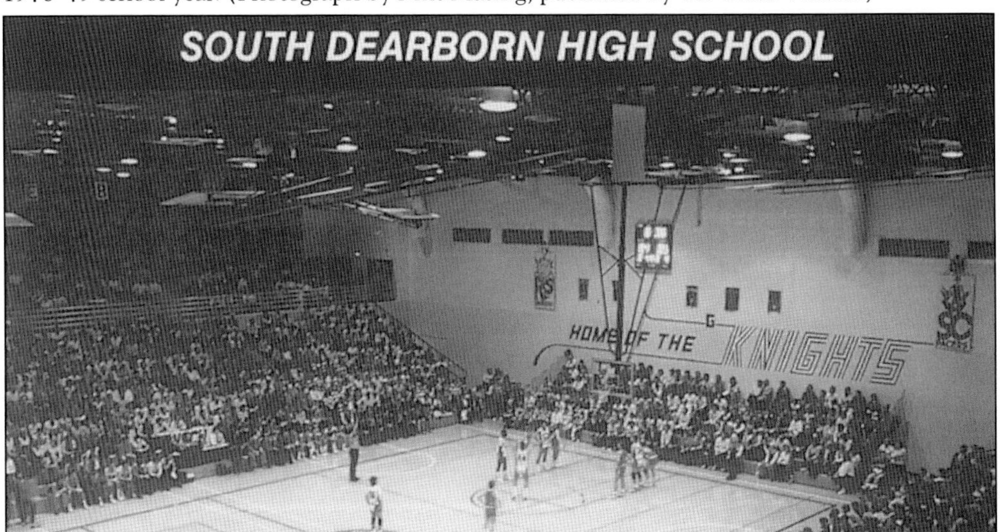

South Dearborn High School. High school sectionals in Indiana produce many memorable experiences. In this 1987 sectional game at South Dearborn, the host "Knights" are in action in the opening game of the tournament. A portion of these cards were altered on the back for use by Bill Slayback, athletic director at the time. (Photograph by Milt Masing, published by Tri-State Visuals.)

INDEX

INDIVIDUALS, ARCHITECTURAL FIRMS, AND BUSINESSES

A. D. Cook Tube Works 65
Alard & Kloster 116
Allen, John 118
American Consultanting Engineers, Inc. 94
American Express Co. 16
American Steel & Pump Co. 65
Anchor Glass Company 64
Anderson Bus Line 20
Arends & Arends 58
Argosy Resort 85, 94
Aurora State Bank 22
Aurora Steam Laundry 24
Aurora Traction Company 20
Bailey Grocery Company 19
Bailey, J.W. 46
Bainum, William 123
Bardes Forge & Foundry Co. 65
Bartholome House Hotel 71
Batesville Lumber and Verneer Company 85
Beecher, Rev. Henry Ward 81
Berner, Chub 52
Bertsch, F. William 58 89
Bielby, Mayor 72
Blue, T. D. 47
Boll & Taylor 66
Booster, Jesse J. 47
B.&O.S.W. R.R. 42
Braunagel, Maggie 25,
Michael 25
Bronfman, Mr. 83
Brookie, True L. 82
Brown, Everett I. Company 76
Brown, Sandra 6
Brute, Bishop 116
Bulthaup, Henry 47
Bushorn Hotel 44
Bushorn, Gertrude 44
, J. W. 44
Busse, Angelica Gesell 122
, Bertha 122
, Christian 122
, Frederick 122
, Henry 122
, Henry Christian 122
, Henry P. 122
, Irene 122
, Louise Oehlmann 122
Byron Jackson Pump Company 65
Campbell family 109
Carnegie, Andrew 82
Central Hotel 89
Chamberlain, William C. 123
Chambers & Stevens Company 37
Cincinnati, Indianapolis, St. Louis, & Chicago R.R. 110
C.L.&A. Company 20, 69
Cochran Chair Company 23
Coney Island 17
Cook, A.D. Company 85, 92
Cook Well Pump Works 65
Cook, August D. 65, 66

Cosby Barbershop 38
Cottage Hotel 38
Crapsy & Lamm 101
Crescent Brewing Company 32
Cropper, Judge Carroll L. 91
Currin, Jerome M. 6
Darling families 113
Davidson, Charles B. 79
Davis, E. H. 22
Dearborn Country Club 36
Dearborn Mills 39
Diamond Brathurst Inc. 64
Dillsboro First National Bank 43, 45, 47
Dillsboro Health Resort 54
Dillsboro Sanitarium 53
Dillsboro State Bank 47
Downey, George E. 34
Driver, Hal 31
Drury, Mark 6
Shirley 6
Victor M. 83
Dunn, Isaac 69
Eads, James Buchanan 69
Evansville College 100
Ewbank, John Sr. 110
Fagley, Frederick 104
Farrar, Carol 18
Charles 18
Jane 18
Ferneding, Father 116
First National Bank 22, 33
Firstar Bank 89
Fisher, Martin 56
Fisse, J. H. 47
Fitch Brothers Funeral Home and Livery Stable 88
Fitch, C.W. Drug Store 87
Fitch, Joseph H. 88
Joseph T. 88
Theodore H. 88
Thomas 88
Flake, Adam 123
Fleming, J.W. Store 47
Franz, John 23
Gabbard, Stephen 113
Gaff, Thomas W. 32 35
Gambles Store 37
Garber & Woodward 36
Garnier, J.B. Brewery 86
Garnier, John B. 86
Gillett, Rev. S. T. 79
Gordon, Eddie 6
Grand Hotel 70, 93
Grand Theater 10, 37
Graver Hotel 43
Gray, W. J. 47
Green, Charles 113
Greendale Distilling Co. 61
Grove, Benjamin 55
Hamline, Leonidas L. 79
Hannaford & Hannaford 66
Hannan, Peter 118
Hansen, W. Erb 76
Hayes, Ezra G. 66
Helms Drug Company 49
Henkle, Karl P. 77
Herzberg, Reverend E. 51
Hess, Margaret 47
Hill, A & Sons 17
Holman, Jesse L. 29
Hornberger, John F. 88
Horr, Philip 22
Howe, H. T. 22
Huffman, Earl 33
Hunt House Hotel 70, 93
Indiana Michigan Electric Power Company 87
Interdesign Group 82
James Associates 124
James & Meyer Buggy Factory 85
James Walsh & Co., Inc. 62
Johnson, McKenney & Schenck 108
Johnston, R.L. Store 37
Jones, Jesse 40
Joseph E. Seagram & Sons, Inc. 83, 86
Justus, Mr. 96
Kamman, F.W. 47
Kelso, John 107
Kennedy, A.M. & Sons 112, 114
Kerr, Bill 6
Kiefer. Carl J., Inc. 64
King, H.M. 27
Klausing, H. F. 16
Klein, Father 26
Knickerbocker, Bishop 79
Kriete, Louis 15
Kuhlmeier, J.H. & Son 38
Kuhlmeier, Cliff 6
Frank 38
John H. 38
Kyle, George H. 90
Lakeview Tourist Court 48
Lawrenceburg Ferry Company 74
Lawrenceburg Roller Mills 84
Leive, Herman 23

Lischkge's Boat Harbor 18
Lyric Theater 2
Marlman, Henry Jr 47
Martin, Frank 6
Masing, Milton 4
  Sharon 6
Mathias, Ethel 48
  Hubert 48
Maxwell, Susan L. 6
McCool, Carl F. 91
  Deloris 91
  William H. 91
McDonald Brother 15
McGuire, Shook, Compton, Richey, and Associates 77
McHenry Bus Line 20
McHenry, Chris 6
  Timothy 20
McKenzie, Henry 107
Miller, Dr. A.G. 53
Monk's Boat Club 18
Moore, Robert 123
Moores Hill College 100, 101, 102, 103, 104
Moores Hill Male and Female Institute 100
Musgrove, Moses 95
Nees Hotel 71
Niebrugge Livery Stable 52
Niebrugge, Charles F. 52
Niemeyer, George 49
Oberting, Victor 86
O'Brien, Cornelius 65
Ohio & Mississippi R.R. Company 97, 106
Ohio Valley Coffin Company 84
Ohlmanseik, William 47
Old Quaker Co. 63
Orr, Lt. Governor Robert 83
O'Shaughnessy Brothers 62
Owen, F.W. Company 77
Patterson, Rev. David 6
Peoples National Bank 71, 89
Pierson Hollowell Company 85
Ragen Hotel 89
Ratio Architects 94
Reinking Orchard 115
Riedinger, Louis (Ludwig) 78
Rogers, Isaiah 35
Roots, G.Y. Flour Mills 84
Ross, Dellas 6 54
Rossville Distilling Co. 61, 86
Royer Wheel Co. 23
Rullman, Henry H. 39
Rupel Development Corp. 59
Schenley Distillers, Inc 63, 64
Schmutte, Frederick 23
  Harry 22
Schricker, Gov. Henry F. 57
Schulte, Edward J. 76
Scovel, Rev. Sylvester 81
Schutte, W.H. Store 108
Shutts, Frank B. 22
Simon, Louis A. 19, 83
Simpson, Rev. Dr. 79
Slayback, Bill 124
Small, Adie 122
  David 122
  Elias C. 122
  Emma Durham 122
  Harry 122
  Joseph 122
Smith, Adeline 6, 44
  Alan 6
  Harry 48
  Hugh F. 56
Smittie's Band 57
Spaeth, H. P. 22
Squibb, George 66
  Nathaniel 66
  William P. 66
Standard Vehichle Company 85
Star Flour Mill 39
Stedman, Nathan 34
Stedman Foundry & Machine 36
Steigerwald, David L. 6
  Mary Ann 6
Stephens, Rev. 26
Stevens, Will F. 101
Stoll Filling Station 60
Stratton, Mary A. 29
Sutton, Carroll 6
  Dr. George 34
  Georgiana E. 36
  Dr. Harley H. 34
  Susan Folbre 34
Taft, William Howard 16
Thatcher Glass Company 64
Tinsley, William 40
Ullrich's Drug Store 39
Ullrich, John 39
United Community Bank 69
Unkeeper Company 101
University of Evansville 100
Vance, Capt. Samuel C. 67
Viet Hotel 43
Vinup, Henry 47

Walker, W.W. 24
Weber, W.V. 22
Webster, Mildred 6,
Robert 6
Wichmann, Rev. Theo 108
Wilson, Clarence B. 22
Wood, Enoch G. 79
Woods, John R. 47,
John W. 47
W.P. Squib Distillery 63
Wright J.C. & Son 36
Wymond, family 36
Zernack, Julius R. 108

Publishers, Printers, and Photographers

Art Mfg. Co. 88
Auburn Post Card Mfg. Co. 65
69 82 85
Bethlehem Lutheran Church 59
Cline, W. M. Co. 18, 19 54
Curt Teich & Co. 11,, 15, 29, 36, 54, 64, 77
Detmer, Tom 35
Dexter Press 76, 77, 86, 90
Dillsboro Health Resort 54
Drake Studio 12, 24, 33, 38
Ewart, W.E. 99
Ewbank, E.W. 112
FasFoto, Inc. 57, 58, 76, 77, 90
Henry, Dan 73
Holler, Dolph 2, 8, 10, 23, 26, 27, 33, 34, 39
Hoover-Watson Printing Co. 21, 46
Hustler Printing Co. 95, 97, 98, 103
Indianapolis Post Card Co. 2, 75
International Graphics 115
Jackson's Dry Goods Store 2, 75
Janszen, B.F. 109, 110, 111
Jennings, T.A. 100, 102
Ketcham, Byron E. 112, 114
Ketter Co., The 39
Kraemer Art Company 2, 8, 10, 17, 20, 21, 23, 26, 27, 29, 33, 34, 35, 36, 37, 39, 40, 55, 56, 61, 62, 65, 66, 68, 70, 71, 72, 74, 75, 76, 78, 79, 80, 81, 84, 85, 89, 90, 92, 99, 116, 118
Krider, William 48, 67, 86
Lane Studio 72
Lee, E.M. 81
Masing, Milt 11, 25, 71, 82, 91, 94, 105, 117, 124
Mathias, Mr and Mrs. 48
Mattingly, Robert J. 39
Nieler 98
Osborne Photographic Lab's 113
Real Estate Book, The 59
Schenley Distillers, Inc. 64
Shannon, Frank 54
Standard Packaging Co. 35
Triplett, G.A. 46
Tri-State Visuals 11, 25, 67, 71, 82, 91, 94, 105, 117, 124
Wayne Paper Box & Printing 18
Whitney, M.O. 10, 29, 60, 63, 73
Whitney's Studio 73, 83
Wilson & Son Photography . 32
Young & Carl 53
Zierer, H.F. 95, 97, 98, 103